Ain't Got No Home

AIN'T GOT NO HOME

America's Great Migrations
and the Making of an Interracial Left

ERIN ROYSTON BATTAT

The University of North Carolina Press Chapel Hill

This book was published with the assistance of the Fred W. Morrison Fund for Southern Studies of the University of North Carolina Press.

Set in Quadraat and Amatic by codeMantra.
Manufactured in the United States of America.

The paper in this book meets the guidelines for permanence and durability of the Committee on Production Guidelines for Book Longevity of the Council on Library Resources.

The University of North Carolina Press has been a member of the Green Press Initiative since 2003.

Library of Congress
Cataloging-in-Publication Data
Battat, Erin Royston.
Ain't got no home : America's great migrations and the making of an interracial left / Erin Royston Battat.
pages cm
Includes bibliographical references and index.
ISBN 978-1-4696-1402-1 (paperback)
ISBN 978-1-4696-1403-8 (ebook)
1. Migration, Internal—United States—History—20th century. 2. Migration, Internal—Political aspects—United States—History—20th century. 3. Migration, Internal, in literature. 4. American literature—20th century—History and criticism. 5. Literature and society—United States—History—20th century. 6. Populism—United States—History—20th century. 7. Right and left (Political science)—United States—History—20th century. I. Title.
HB1965.B38 2014
304.80973—dc23
2013035598

18 17 16 15 14   5 4 3 2 1

THIS BOOK WAS DIGITALLY PRINTED.

For James

CONTENTS

ILLUSTRATIONS

ACKNOWLEDGMENTS

It is my great pleasure to thank the many colleagues, friends, family members, and institutions that helped me to research and write this book. I owe a tremendous debt to John Stauffer, who trained me in interdisciplinary scholarship, sparked my interest in protest literature, and guided the project through its early stages. John unfailingly expressed his faith in me as a scholar, and his encouragement sustained me through the most difficult stretches. Werner Sollors challenged me to think expansively about migration narratives—to make connections between internal migrants and various immigrant groups and migration mythologies. Werner not only offered keen insights on the manuscript but has also been a steadfast mentor. When I encounter difficult career decisions, his wise counsel puts the ground under my feet. Evelyn Brooks Higginbotham's support kept me going at crucial moments. I discovered my passion for American Studies as an undergraduate at Georgetown University, and I thank my excellent professors there, especially Hugh Cloke, Elizabeth McKeown, Lucy Maddox, Alison Hilton, and Peter Cole.

The History of American Civilization program at Harvard University provided a warm, invigorating intellectual community for a young scholar. Christine McFadden was our compass as we navigated the unfamiliar waters of graduate school. I thank my fellow students for their friendship and feedback, particularly Peter Becker, George Blaustein, Lauren Brandt, Sarah Carter, Marti Frank, Mark Hanna, Brian Hochman, Hua Hsu, Jamie Jones, Judy Kertész, Sonia Lee, and Yael Schacher. Sara Schwebel read several drafts, and her sharp comments pushed me to clarify the argument, tighten the structure, and polish the prose. In sharing her immense gifts as a writer, Sara has made this a better book. Most of all, her friendship sustained me through the process. I am deeply grateful to Noam Maggor, who has pushed my thinking about the relationship between race and populism, and whose friendship I treasure.

I was also privileged to be a part of Harvard's History and Literature program. Being assigned an office with Eoin Cannon was a fantastic stroke of good luck, for sharing this space gave us the opportunity to discuss our books, collaborate on teaching, trade parenting adventures, and become friends. I thank also my students, particularly Aviva Gilbert, Ofole Mgbako, Rikka Strong, Miyoko Pettit, and D. Patrick Knoth, who helped me to think about migration narratives in new ways. Finally, it is difficult to find the words to express my gratitude to Jeanne Follansbee. Jeanne read almost every chapter of this book, generously sharing her knowledge of 1930s radical literature and her insights into the relationship between historical forces and literary forms. I have turned to her for advice on writing, on teaching, and on my career, and I am deeply grateful for her mentorship.

My work has also greatly benefited from several writing groups and from scholars in my field. I thank Ally Field, Laura Murphy, Jeanne Follansbee, Amy Spellacy, Anne Verplanck, Jen Hirt, and Robin Veder for their careful, critical readings. My colleagues in Werner Sollors's *Doktorandenkolloquium* gave formative comments on early drafts of several chapters, as did Susan Shillinglaw, Michael Meyer, and Michael Kazin. Douglas Wixson, Julia Mickenberg, Lawrence Rodgers, and Joanne Dearcopp generously shared what they knew about Sanora Babb. Thanks to the Haverford and Bryn Mawr College Faculty Working Group in American Studies for their feedback on Chapter 5.

My colleagues in Humanities and American Studies at Penn State Harrisburg provided vital support as this project neared completion. School director Kathryn Robinson approved research support and protected my time as a junior faculty member. Patricia Johnson and Matthew Wilson shared my interest in women writers and African American literature. With Simon Bronner at the helm, the American Studies program kept me afloat; thanks to Michael Barton, Anthony Buccitelli, John Haddad, Anne Verplanck, David Witwer, and especially Charles Kupfer, who gave me helpful feedback on Chapter 5. I benefited also from many discussions of race and migration with my American Studies graduate students. My research assistants, Peter Bryan and John Price, did some careful digging and helped me get the manuscript into shape. Many thanks to librarian Heidi Abbey for her invaluable assistance, to Shivaani Selvaraj for her enthusiasm about the history of interracial organizing, and to Penn State's Commission for Women for the opportunities to share my work.

This book would not be possible without funding from several organizations. The Du Bois Institute for African and African American Research provided a generous fellowship, beautiful office space, and a stimulating intellectual community. Epifanio San Juan and I had exciting discussions about Sanora Babb and Carlos Bulosan, while Mark Solomon expanded my thinking about Marxism and race. Hana Ali provided excellent research assistance. I owe a special debt of gratitude to Henry Louis Gates Jr. for his enthusiastic support of this project and of my career. Thanks also to Vera Grant, Donald Yacavone, the DBI staff, and my cohort of fellows from 2009. This project was also generously supported by the American Association of University Women, the Harvard University Graduate Society, the Charles Warren Center, and the Harvard University Graduate Council.

The editors and staff at the University of North Carolina Press have guided me expertly through the publication process. Thanks to Sian Hunter for expressing initial interest in the manuscript, to editor Mark Simpson-Vos for his leadership, and to Caitlyn Bell-Butterfield for fielding my many questions. Barbara Foley and an anonymous reviewer read my manuscript with incredible attention to detail and high critical standards. Their constructive reports guided my revision process and allowed me to achieve my interdisciplinary aims.

Words cannot express my gratitude to my family for their unfailing support, love, and good humor. My parents, David and Eunice Royston, cultivated my love of reading and intellectual debate. My family keeps me tied to the earth when the pressures of academia threaten to send me into orbit; thanks to John and Regan Royston and their children Virginia and Charlotte; Sheila and Peter Murphy and their children Patrick, Kevin, and Maeve; and David and Neile Royston and their children Camryn and Lachlan. I am grateful to my wonderful parents-in-law, Joseph and Brenda Battat, for their encouragement, personal insights on academia, and many hours of babysitting! My children, Sebastian and Kiernan, brought immeasurable joy to my life as I wrote this book.

I am deeply grateful for the love and support of my husband, James. His steadiness gave this project a foundation; his love gave it wings. I dedicate this book to him.

ABBREVIATIONS AND ACRONYMS

AFL	American Federation of Labor
CIO	Congress of Industrial Organizations
CP	Communist Party
FSA	Farm Security Administration
ILD	International Labor Defense
IWW	Industrial Workers of the World
NAACP	National Association for the Advancement of Colored People
OWI	Office of War Information
SSCAC	South Side Community Art Center
UCAPAWA	United Cannery, Agricultural, Packing, and Allied Workers of America
WPA	Works Progress Administration

Ain't Got No Home

INTRODUCTION

In May 1940, while on his honeymoon in Mexico, Richard Wright joined left-wing documentary filmmaker Herbert Kline and his screenwriter, the famous novelist John Steinbeck, in boozy planning sessions for the film *The Forgotten Village*. Both writers were basking in the glow of literary success. Steinbeck had recently won the Pulitzer Prize for *The Grapes of Wrath*; Wright's *Native Son* had just leaped ahead of *Grapes* to reach the number one slot on the *New York Times* best-seller list.[1] The poverty and injustice they witnessed during the Great Depression outraged Steinbeck and Wright. They wrote novels that put a human face on this suffering, identified capitalism as a root cause, and looked to Marxism for a revolutionary solution. Wright identified with Steinbeck as a fellow member of what he called "the latest literary generation" that was united by "its great political preoccupation."[2] Even so, during their visit in Mexico, the two authors fought bitterly over the political implications of their art. Steinbeck accused Wright of having tunnel vision, of viewing the whole world solely through the problems of black men.[3]

For many scholars, this quarrel between Wright and Steinbeck is emblematic of the fraught relationship between African Americans and the Old Left. Steinbeck's accusation subordinated race to class. It implied that Bigger Thomas's experience of segregation and alienation was a problem particular to black men rather than a central issue in Left-labor politics. To make matters worse, Steinbeck's charge was hypocritical. One could argue that he viewed the whole world through the problems of white families. When Ma Joad famously proclaims, "We're the people, we go on," in one of the most memorable scenes in *The Grapes of Wrath*, she presumably speaks for the poor and downtrodden everywhere. Steinbeck's assumption of default whiteness has prompted cultural critic Michael Denning to characterize the novel as "racial populism that heroized the plain people."[4] In light of this quarrel, it is perhaps not surprising that many African Americans felt that the white Left did not give enough priority to civil rights. Black radicals like Wright were particularly critical of the Communist Party's (CP)

Popular Front policy, which emphasized interracial unity, sometimes at the expense of black political aims. The relationship between African Americans and the Left was undoubtedly vexed. However, as we shall see in the following pages, to take conflicts like Steinbeck and Wright's showdown in Mexico as typical obscures the vitality and lasting impact of the black-red alliance.

Ain't Got No Home claims that writers and artists turned to the theme of migration to bolster the alliance between African Americans and the Popular Front. Depicting migrants as emblems of "the people," the writers and artists I study participated in the populist fervor of the late 1930s, but they continued to advance an anticapitalist and antiracist agenda. My comparative analysis of migration narratives revises the scholarly perception of populism and antiracism as antithetical.[5] Close readings of novels, photography, radical journalism, and other cultural texts uncover how black and white writers experimented with new literary forms that recast the relationship between African American and southern white workers and testified to the possibility of class-based interracial alliances. Yet they also grappled with conflicts between black and white workers that arose out of migration—conflicts that prompted political journeys even after the geographic destination was reached. Through these stories of conflict, writers highlighted the formidable obstacles to integration, particularly in the realms of housing and family life. These migration narratives, then, both resist Jim Crow and warn of its spread to the North and West.

I shift the focus away from towering figures like Steinbeck and Wright, shedding light on lesser-known writers and artists whose work speaks to the uneasy melding of class- and race-based politics from the onset of the Popular Front in 1935 until the start of the Cold War in the late 1940s.[6] For example, radical dust bowl writer Sanora Babb translated the oppositional politics of southwestern populism to the multiracial context of California's industrial agriculture. Similarly, I show how African American writer William Attaway was influenced by both Steinbeck and Wright, producing a creative tension between populism and race in his work. Moreover, I examine the works of African American women on the Left—such as Elizabeth Catlett, Marita Bonner, and Ann Petry—which offer a multidimensional critique of capitalism that extends well into the 1940s.[7] These and other migration novels, stories, photographs, and works of visual art insist that black and white migrants had shared interests as workers, while casting a critical eye on the points at which these interests diverge within a racialized class system. Thus, these narratives shed light on the aesthetic dimension to what scholars call the "long civil rights movement"—the struggle for economic and racial justice rooted in the labor struggles and Left politics of the 1930s and '40s.[8] Two decades before the landmark civil rights legislation of the 1950s and '60s, these radical writers envisioned a broad social movement forged from the bottom up.

Anticommunist sentiment, which simmered during the late 1930s and escalated during the Cold War, may explain the tenacity of the view that African Americans made a wrong turn when they went Left. In 1949 Wright published a disavowal of his communist past in the essay "I Tried to Be a Communist," collected in Richard Crossman's *The God That Failed*. Most famously, Ralph Ellison's *Invisible Man*, published at the height of the McCarthy era in 1952, depicted the CP as a self-serving organization that used black pawns for its own political ends. These retrospective accounts have shaped scholars' understanding of the interracial Left. During the Cold War and long afterward, scholars argued that the CP had a "stultifying influence" on black writers.[9] Likewise, more recent studies of African American literature downplay black writers' creative engagement with the Left in the 1930s and '40s, instead charting racial lineages and valorizing the aesthetics of black nationalist politics in African American literature.[10] Yet dramatic renunciations like Wright's and Ellison's should not be taken at face value. Instead, they must be considered in the context of postwar anticommunism and the vicious purges of the McCarthy era. Ellison emerged as an anticommunist spokesman after the U.S. government charged Paul Robeson and W. E. B. Du Bois with sedition, deported C. L. R. James and Claudia Jones, and interrogated Langston Hughes.[11] As critic Barbara Foley argues, Ellison did not make a decisive break from the Left but, rather, went through a drawn-out divorce that indicates how deeply ingrained was his Marxist worldview.[12] In the last two decades, scholars such as Foley, Cary Nelson, Michael Denning, James Smethurst, Bill Mullen, Alan Wald, William Maxwell, Stacy Morgan, and Anthony Dawahare have rejected the idea that the CP stymied African American literature, exposing this view as a vestige of Cold War anticommunism.[13] Instead, they analyze the creative ways black writers negotiated the competing, yet overlapping, ideologies of Marxism and black nationalism.

In the context of the migration narrative, I argue, writers explored this project of building an interracial, anticapitalist movement. Alan Wald contends that interracial alliances are vague in African American literature because they were "not part of the day-to-day life experiences of ordinary African Americans in the segregated United States; and daily existence offers the raw materials of any sustained, rich, multifaceted, and fully textured work in the realist vein."[14] The very fact that interracial working-class solidarity was so difficult to achieve, in terms of both political practice and literary representation, is precisely why so many leftist writers turned to the migration narrative to articulate their reform visions. As we shall see in the following chapters, some radical writers imagined mixed-race utopias among freight-hopping hoboes, while others used migration and interracial exchange to set up their protagonists' conversion to class consciousness.

My work places cultural texts in a broader context of Depression-era migration and itinerancy and looks at how radical writers imagined this geographic movement as a vehicle for social change. During the 1930s, unemployment and homelessness forced millions of people onto the roads and rails. By 1933 the capitalist economy was on the brink of collapse. Rural Americans, already in the throes of depression in the 1920s, saw farm prices drop further and markets shrink. According to historian Robert S. McElvaine, the Great Depression of the 1930s hit harder than previous depressions because most people lived in urban areas by 1929 and could not grow their own food.[15] Droughts devastated the land and machines replaced human labor; a way of life seemed to be coming to an end. As Dorothea Lange and Paul Taylor reported in their photo-book American Exodus, "Plantations of the Delta are coming under the machine. The sharecropper system is collapsing at its advance, and croppers are being cut from the land."[16] But the industries that had absorbed millions of black and white migrants in the 1920s now turned them away.[17] In a one-day survey conducted in 1932, social scientist Nels Anderson, who had ridden the rails himself as a boy, found 1.5 million people without shelter. In Chicago, homeless shelters served 20,000 men in a single day, which is as many as they helped annually in the 1920s.[18] Many men left their families out of shame or in the hopes that they would fare better without them. According to a social worker in a southern mill town, if men "get laid off, and can't get another job, they seem to think the best thing for them to do is to leave town, because then the charities will have to take care of their families."[19] Although men were more likely to strike out on their own, leaving their families to move in with extended kin or seek charity, women and children also hit the roads and rails in the 1930s. Women constituted a scant 1 to 3 percent of the itinerant population hitching rides on freight trains, but itinerant migrant workers and homeless families commonly traveled together by car.[20] Most famously, more than 300,000 people, often traveling in family groups, migrated from the southwestern states of Oklahoma, Arkansas, Missouri, and Texas to California between 1935 and 1940. This "dust bowl migration" became an emblem of the Depression at the time and continues in the present-day public memory of the era. Songwriter Woody Guthrie voiced the lament of the displaced sharecropper in a song that inspired the title of this book: "Rich man took my home and he drove me from my door / And I ain't got no home in this world anymore."[21]

This economic collapse caused unimaginable suffering for the world's most vulnerable peoples, yet it gave radicals hope that a revolutionary over-throw of capitalism was at hand. When the stock market crashed in 1929, it produced the conditions necessary for Left politics to take hold in the United States after a decade of conservatism. Revolutionary protest swept the country in 1933 when the economy hit rock bottom. A staggering 1.5 million workers participated in 1,800 strikes in 1934, from migratory workers in California's fields to general strikes that shut down entire cities in Toledo, Minneapolis, and San Francisco.[22] Enjoying significant influence in the United States for the first time, the Communist Party forged an alliance of labor and civil rights, providing training for black leaders, holding inte-grated union meetings and social events, and attracting black recruits to the trade union movement.[23] Energized by this insurgency, radical writers and artists produced a flurry of "little magazines," theater and poetry groups, and art exhibitions in the hopes of producing a genuine revolutionary work-ers' culture. As Left critic Edmund Wilson later recalled, "To the writers and artists of my generation, who had grown up in the Big Business era and had always resented its barbarism, its crowding-out of everything they cared about, these years were not depressing but stimulating. One couldn't help being exhilarated at the sudden, unexpected collapse of that stupid, gigantic fraud. It gave us a new sense of power to find ourselves still carrying on, while the bankers, for a change, were taking a beating."[24]

Political developments in both the New Deal administration and the CP caused Left-labor politics and culture to shift toward the center after 1935, making strict accountings of which writers were officially members of the CP of limited value. What bound together this wide constellation of left-leaning artists and activists was a fervent belief that ordinary people could transform social relations. In passing the National Labor Relations Act, particularly section 7(a), which guaranteed the rights of most workers to organize, the government mediated between employers and labor, thus staving off the more radical labor protests of the previous year. In 1936 and 1937, there was another strike wave that made significant gains for work-ers, but this time it was led by federally protected unions affiliated with the

Congress of Industrial Organizations (CIO). The CIO's model of interracial unionism challenged segregation and suggested that the labor movement could encompass larger social goals. Meanwhile, the CP shifted from its radical Third Period (1928–35), in which it declared all liberal organizations enemies in the class war, to its Popular Front policy, which viewed liberals as allies against the looming threat of fascism. In his seminal work *The Cultural Front*, Michael Denning decentered the CP in his analysis of Popular Front culture, reconceiving it as a loose network of left-leaning individuals and organizations that agitated against capitalism, racism, colonialism, and fascism. This new paradigm countered a long-standing view that the Left literary and cultural scene of the 1930s was an aberration in the dominant trajectory of modernism and mass culture and that dismissed Popular Front writers and artists as dupes awaiting orders from Moscow. Yet Denning's more diffuse notion of the "age of the CIO" tends to marginalize the Communist-led Left. In the pages that follow, I argue that Marxist theory and communist organizations were central to the literary and artistic developments of the period, whether or not these cultural producers were card-carrying Communists. With a few exceptions, the texts in this study were written by middle-class writers with varying degrees of Left commitments who aimed to give voice to the hoboes, migratory workers, and rural migrants of the Great Depression.[25]

During the Depression era, the Communist Party reached "unprecedented heights" of popularity among African Americans, according to historian Mark Solomon.[26] The U.S. Communist Party was the only white-led organization that prioritized racial issues in both theory and practice, cultivated African American leaders, encouraged social equality between the races, and worked tirelessly to rout "white chauvinism" from its ranks.[27] Across the nation, the CP took direct action to improve conditions in black neighborhoods. In Harlem, for example, the hub of the black-Left alliance, the CP organized the Harlem Tenants' League, which organized rent strikes, street protests, and unemployment campaigns that addressed the most pressing daily needs of the urban poor.[28] The CP formed Unemployed Councils that demanded unemployment insurance, cash and work relief, and government jobs at union wages. According to Solomon, the Unemployed Councils recognized that African Americans bore the brunt of the Depression and called for racial unity among the jobless and equal access to relief.[29] Activists publicly displayed their interracial solidarity in the streets. On 6 March 1930, millions of demonstrators demanding unemployment insurance stirred up a media frenzy over "the unusual spectacle of several white girls walking with colored men during the 'picketing.'"[30] Due to its work on the ground for advancing African American civil and economic rights, the CP attracted a significant number of black members and sympathizers for the first time. After 1935 the newly formed CIO committed itself to organizing African Americans and women on an industrywide basis. These workers had been excluded from the conservative American Federation of Labor (AFL), which organized skilled workers according to their particular crafts. The CIO's Left-led unions battled Jim Crow in meetings, workplace facilities, and hiring and promotion practices in order to cultivate a unified workforce.

Radical and left-leaning organizations also nurtured black writers, who in turn helped to shape Marxist theory and aesthetics.[31] The CP sponsored John Reed Clubs with the explicit agenda to promote "cultural activity among the Negro masses."[32] The Chicago John Reed Club launched Richard Wright's career. "I was meeting men and women whom I would know for decades to come," he wrote in his autobiography, "who were to form the first sustained relationships in my life."[33] Radical literary magazines such as the *New Masses*, *Daily Worker*, the *Workers Monthly*, and *Left Front* provided publishing outlets for fledgling black writers and became models for African American leftist magazines such as *Challenge*.[34] New Deal cultural programs such as the Federal Writers' Project also brought African American writers into Left political and artistic circles, providing financial support, social networks, publishing outlets, and a forum for exhibiting and discussing their work. According to African American poet Margaret Walker, "The long isolation of the Negro artist ended with the advent of the Works Progress Administration (WPA) projects, where there was a mingling or racial mixing, and a great deal of exchange between black and white writers, artists, actors, dancers, and other theater people."[35]

Yet writers, artists, and intellectuals struggled to define their role in this revolutionary movement. Debates raged in the radical press over the relationship between art and activism and the definition of proletarian literature. In 1931 the Workers' Cultural Federation declared "Art Is a Weapon!" in the *New Masses*, insisting on the power of language to effect social change.[36] Refusing to separate "art" from "life," radical artists described themselves as "culture workers," declaring allegiance with the working class and raising art and theory to the level of action.[37] However, for many writers and artists, the political work of literature seemed to pale in comparison with the direct action of organizers in the streets, factories, and fields. Many of the writers and artists in this study combined their literary and political endeavors, often at great risk to life and limb: William Attaway worked as a labor organizer, Sanora Babb helped migratory workers access relief and shelter, Tillie Olsen was jailed in San Francisco during a general strike, Elizabeth Catlett taught at Harlem's Marxist George Washington Carver School—the list goes on.

Moreover, Marxist writers and critics were troubled by the bourgeois origins of literary culture and the middle-class status (and sensibilities) of most professional authors and their audiences. Was the goal of literature to foment revolutionary consciousness among workers or to enlist middle-class allies? The literary organ of the CP, the *New Masses*, combined these aims. It provided a crucial publishing outlet for working-class writers and enjoyed a robust working-class readership, but it appealed mainly to middle-class intellectuals and published and reviewed their work. Distressed by the cultural gap between most literary artists and the working class, Marxist critics fiercely debated the definition of "proletarian literature"—was it written *by* workers (authorship), *for* workers (audience), *about* workers (subject matter)? Was it aligned with workers' political interests (perspective)? By 1935, Marxist critics generally agreed with Edwin Seaver that what mattered was the "class loyalty of the author," meaning a Marxist perspective.[38] Although this inclusive definition made room for middle-class novelists in the proletarian movement, the essential problem remained: The writers and artists who were so fervently committed to economic and racial justice struggled to reach working-class readers. Writers such as Tillie Olsen, Sanora Babb, and William Attaway saw their art as a political weapon, yet they sought (and often failed) to reach a wider audience through mainstream publishing houses. They had to compete with a burgeoning mass culture for the attention of ordinary readers, and the commercial success of proletarian novels was limited. While my analysis of book reviews, author interviews, and newspaper accounts explores how critics at the time responded to these images and stories, I have chosen to focus on cultural producers rather than the reception of these texts and images by ordinary readers. I have used newspaper articles and book reviews to find traces of the perspectives of average readers, but this kind of reception history is difficult, as few left records of their aesthetic experiences.[39] Nevertheless, literature and art provide unique insights into social movements, revealing the contours and limits of their visions for change. These writers and artists on the Left imagined ways to dismantle hierarchies of class and race using the framework of the migration narrative. Radical women fought for gender equality as well, folding an incipient feminism into their literature and art to advance a sweeping social revolution.

The migration narrative flourished in the mid- to late 1930s due, in part, to the national obsession with regional diversity and the search for an "American character." Scholars, writers, folklorists, and photographers ventured into the fields and factories to collect the voices and images of "the people." These cultural producers participated in what Susan Hegeman calls the "spatial re-articulation of culture" that understood difference in geographic terms. This new concept of culture, pioneered by anthropologists Franz Boas and Ruth Benedict, allowed for a range of human experience without the hierarchical ordering implied in the concepts of "civilization" and "race."[40] Migration narratives—both internal and transnational—brought regional differences into broad relief, tying human difference to *place* rather than bloodlines or skin color. These texts built on the traditions of the frontier and exodus myths but produced an ideological shift away from Anglo-Saxon ascendancy toward a new national story of America as a "nation of immigrants."

Americans were hungry for stories of Depression-era quests. Beginning in 1935, the Farm Security Administration (FSA; called Rural Rehabilitation until 1937) sent a cadre of professional photographers out to the fields and highways to document rural poverty and the efforts of New Deal programs to alleviate it. Photographs of overloaded jalopies traversing America's roads and highways appeared in countless newspapers, magazines, photo-books, museum galleries, and even the halls of Grand Central Station. The popular FSA traveling exhibit on migrants was requested more than eighty times—more than any other theme.[41] Dorothea Lange and sociologist Paul Taylor arranged Lange's FSA photographs into a migration narrative in their photo-book *American Exodus*, which traced the routes of black and white sharecroppers to the North and West. Millions of Americans read John Steinbeck's *Grapes of Wrath* in 1939, and many more flocked to see the film version that premiered in 1940. Country and blues music gained national audiences in this radio age, and crooners of both races lamented the loneliness of the road and their longing for home to listeners from coast to coast. For instance, folk musicians Woody Guthrie and Huddie "Lead Belly" Ledbetter migrated from the South under very different circumstances, yet they wrote similar songs of homelessness and forged a lifelong friendship. Dozens of socially conscious writers, black and white, shared this popular fascination with migration, producing narratives that built on a long-standing American tradition but challenged its capitalist faith in progress and prosperity.[42]

My focus on the migration narrative engages one of the great debates about Depression-era culture: Are these populist texts "far more conservative than radical," as Warren Susman argues, or do they participate, in Michael Denning's words, in the "laboring of American culture"?[43] At issue in these debates are the implications of American populism for the politics of class and race in the United States. Does the American celebration of the "common man" obscure class divisions and racial conflicts, or does it provide the foundation for popular resistance to racial capitalism? The CP's shift from its radical Third Period to the Popular Front was controversial at the time and continues to be a subject of scholarly debate, particularly its impact on African Americans.[44] At the 1935 American Writers' Congress, theorist Kenneth Burke sparked controversy by suggesting they replace the term "worker" with "the people" as their revolutionary symbol. Unlike the more proletarian-inflected terms "worker" or "masses," the term "the people" is "closer to our folkways," argued Burke, and would thus enlist the middle class in the revolutionary struggle.[45] Marxist critic Joseph Freeman shot back that "the people" was a symbol of the bourgeois revolution that concealed class hierarchy, and others pointed out the obvious associations with Nazi rhetoric and "demagoguery of the most vicious sort."[46] These Marxist critics felt that populist rhetoric betrayed the class politics of the proletarian struggle. Many black radicals also became disenchanted with the CP during the Popular Front period because it shifted away from anticolonial politics committed to African American self-determination in favor of an ethic of "multiculturalism" that supported the project of U.S. nationalism. Nothing symbolizes the convergence of the Popular Front and U.S. nationalism more than the fact that black Communist Paul Robeson's song "Ballad for Americans," which celebrates the diversity of the American working class, was played at the Republican National Convention in 1940. But if the populist turn was so damaging to African American political and aesthetic goals, why did so many African American migration narratives embrace Popular Front aesthetics in the late 1930s and '40s, and why did so many white migration narratives engage questions of race? When writers and artists answered CP chairman Earl Browder's call to dig "into the treasures of our national traditions and cultural inheritance" to inspire a revolutionary consciousness, they produced images of displaced tenant farmers, self-sacrificing merchants, lonely hoboes, and migrant mothers—the populist heroes of migration narratives, black and white. African American migration narratives infused with Left commitments flourished after 1935, as did similar stories about white migrants. In my view, the populist turn precipitated a surge in narratives after 1935 that envisioned the migrant as a revolutionary symbol of "the people" and the harbinger of a more democratic society.

John Steinbeck's best-selling novel *The Grapes of Wrath* is perhaps the most popular and enduring example of the populist migration narrative. Its predominance in American memory overshadows, however, migration narratives that more explicitly engage with the intersections of class and race in the migration experience.[47] I have selected texts that recognize the multiethnic nature of Depression-era mobility. Sanora Babb's dust bowl novel *Whose Names Are Unknown*, William Attaway's Great Migration novel *Blood on the Forge*, and Chester Himes's novel of wartime migration *If He Hollers Let Him Go* anchor this study, as they depict black and white migration as intertwined, fraught with tension, and potentially transforming. I also examine various other cultural forms—hobo novellas, photographs and visual images of migrant mothers, and histories and ethnographies of migrant shipyard workers—that consider the impact of migration on race and gender relations. By placing texts like these within the framework of the migration narrative, I revise the critical tendency to categorize them as distinctly "proletarian" or "African American" phenomena.

Ain't Got No Home begins with the infamous Scottsboro case of 1933, in which nine black boys riding a freight train in Alabama were falsely accused of raping two white girls, summarily convicted by an all-white jury, and sentenced to death. When the Communist-led International Labor Defense (ILD) took over the young men's appeals, it convinced many African Americans that the CP was seriously committed to their social struggle. Radical journalists forged this black-Left alliance, I argue, by building on and revising the tradition of the hobo narrative. An imagined space free from social constraints, the boxcar provides a setting for illicit sex, gender-bending, and interracial camaraderie. Later in the 1930s, John Steinbeck and African American writer William Attaway translated this radical discourse to popular audiences through their sentimental tales of interracial hobo communities, *Of Mice and Men* (1937) and *Let Me Breathe Thunder* (1939). I show how Attaway self-consciously revises Steinbeck's *Of Mice and Men* to complicate the image of the hobo friendship that was so appealing to general readers. Attaway offers an image of an interracial hobo collective that is more radically egalitarian than Steinbeck's but also more unstable and, like Marx's *lumpenproletariat*, susceptible to reactionary swings. My analysis of Attaway's attempt to formulate a radical antiracist populism challenges the standard historiography that marks the unraveling of the black-Left alliance with the Popular Front.

Chapter 2 centers on Sanora Babb's dust bowl novel *Whose Names Are Unknown*, which was written in the late 1930s but remained itself "unknown" until it was belatedly published in 2004. Editors at Random House sang the manuscript's praises but revoked Babb's contract after the publication of *The Grapes of Wrath* in fear that the literary market could not sustain two books on the same subject. This fateful decision deprived readers of a unique perspective on the Depression era's best-known migration. Whereas Steinbeck's novel erases workers of color and expresses a conservative gender ideology, Babb narrates the dust bowl migration from a woman's point of view and imagines interracial alliances among white, Filipino, and African American workers. I argue that Babb uses a regionalist form to express the daily routines, sense of place, and populist politics of her dust bowl characters, which translates to gender-inclusive interracial unionism in the California context.

In contrast to Babb, William Attaway was more skeptical of the industrial union as a vehicle for civil rights and anticapitalist reform, as evident in his second novel, *Blood on the Forge* (1941). He set his Great Migration novel in 1919, a year of severe antileftist repression and deadly race riots. Whereas Babb's migrant characters join together in a union, Attaway's black and white migrants battle one another in a race war aided and abetted by mill owners and the police. Attaway takes on the insidious stereotype of the black strikebreaker, which stymied the CIO's interracial organizing efforts in the 1930s, and challenges the white Left to prioritize issues of segregation and racial discrimination. Most critics thus read *Blood on the Forge* as a kind of insider critique of the Left: sympathetic to Marxism yet concerned primarily with the seemingly insurmountable racial barriers to proletarian revolution. What critics underestimate, I argue, is the role of blues music, both in the novel's form and as a central theme, as a site of interracial exchange and as a catalyst for changes in consciousness. The novel's blues form replaces Marxist determinism with an understanding of African American migration—and interracial alliances—as open-ended and improvisational. Attaway's depiction of aesthetic experience as transformative—if not explicitly leftist in content—does not signal a rupture in the black-Left alliance but, rather, an attempt to broaden the definition of political art.

In Chapter 4 I claim that writers and artists from a broad racial and political spectrum used the image of the migrant mother to offer a gender-based critique of capitalist and racist oppression. The writers and artists I examine pushed beyond Dorothea Lange's iconic photograph known as "Migrant Mother" to send a more urgent call for change. For example, visual artist Elizabeth Catlett created powerful images of militant black mothers, while white writer Tillie Olsen used grotesque imagery of miscarriage and murderous mothers to offer a feminist critique of capitalism. Lange's iconic photograph is another example of a "long shadow" that obscures a more racially diverse and politically charged iconography of migrant motherhood.

Chapter 5 places African American writer Chester Himes's novel *If He Hollers Let Him Go* (1945) in the context of the crisis of unions and the fracturing of the Left in the 1940s. Himes depicts the conflicts between white Okies and African American migrants as they jockeyed for position in the California shipyards during World War II. When a white female Okie frames the black protagonist for rape, she transplants Jim Crow to California, using the force of the American legal system and the U.S. military to shore up her claims to white femininity. Himes highlights the stark contradictions between the democratic aims of the war and the treatment of people of color at home and abroad. While most critics read Himes's novel as an anticommunist polemic, I read it as a voice of black leftist internationalism that links capitalism, imperialism, and racial problems on the home front.

Ain't Got No Home transforms our understanding of the role of migration in the American imagination during this vital period of social reform and cultural introspection. It replaces the traditional view of black and white migration as separate streams feeding different political and aesthetic pools. These black and white migration narratives emerged from a shared context and responded creatively to the tensions between race and class within the American Left. This argument contests the faulty assumption that Marxism had nothing to offer the black freedom struggle, that the white working class was irrevocably racist and to blame for the postwar fall of the American Left, and that class-based and race-based revolutionary ideologies were always, and continue to be, irreconcilable. Taken together, this body of literature reveals the extent to which America's fundamental mythologies—myths that explain and impel social action—could be stretched to include, however tenuously, both black and white Americans.

CHAPTER 1 RACE, SEX, AND THE HOBO

On 25 March 1931, a group of black boys got into a fight with some white boys on a Memphis-bound freight train. When the police rounded up the black youths near Scottsboro, Alabama, they found a couple of white girls hiding on the train and coerced them into filing rape charges. Although Alabama's Governor Benjamin Meek Miller and the National Guard prevented a mass lynching, the outcome was just about the same: A white jury quickly convicted the boys, sentencing all but the youngest to death. The Communist-led ILD quickly took charge of the boys' appeals. The speed with which the ILD responded to the case, the intensity and reach of its mass protests and publicity campaigns, its top-notch defense team, and the vocal support of the mothers and families of the Scottsboro boys convinced many African Americans that the CP was a trustworthy ally dedicated to their particular needs as black people. As Ada Wright, mother of two of the boys, attested, "We know our friends when we see them and we're a goin' to stick to the League of Struggle for Negro Rights and the International Labor Defense Committee."[1] Black schoolchildren carried pickets; African American Girl Scouts attended rallies; college students raised money; and ordinary people took to the streets.[2] By 1935 the ranks of African Americans in the CP swelled from a few hundred to 2,500. The black membership of the ILD in Birmingham alone was 3,000, making it the largest Civil Rights organization in the city.[3]

Yet a closer inspection of the Scottsboro case reveals how complicated was the relationship between African Americans and the Communist Party in the 1930s. The CP championed the working-class and unemployed masses, but these were precisely the people who had terrorized the black boys on the train, falsely accused them of rape, and would have lynched them without the governor's intervention. Antilynching activists, on one hand, and labor defenders, on the other, relied on diametrically opposed conceptions of the populist masses and the law. Whereas the antilynching movement called for the rule of law to quell mob hysteria, labor defense stood up for workers against a prejudicial legal system.[4] These opposing views posed a challenge to the CP in attracting black members and sympathizers. While communists prophesied a future revolution led by an international proletariat, the most visible form of proletarian collective action in the South, according to some skeptical observers at the time, was the lynch mob. As African American editors I. Willis Cole of the *Louisville Leader* and William Kelley of the New York *Amsterdam News* pointed out, lynch mobs were driven by poor whites, while white advocates of black civil rights tended to be middle-class liberals.[5] This vexing issue of white working-class racism led W. E. B. Du Bois to conclude in the early 1930s that "throughout the history of the Negro in America, white labor has been the black man's enemy, his oppressor, his red murderer," and therefore "imported Marxism . . . does not at all fit the situation."[6] Writers and activists who wanted to build an interracial coalition out of the ferment over Scottsboro had to deal with the contradiction between the "masses" and the "mob."

According to James A. Miller, the ILD's success in the Scottsboro case depended on its ability to disrupt the white South's powerful rape-lynch myth by constructing a compelling counternarrative that debunked the stereotypes of the black rapist and the pure white victim.[7] Accordingly, commentators at the time and subsequent historians have placed the Scottsboro protests in the political and aesthetic tradition of antilynching. African Americans such as Ada Wright saw the protest as a "fight goin' on against lynchin'," and the ILD had been using the term "legal lynching" to describe the southern courts' liberal use of capital punishment for black males since at least 1929.[8] Yet the ILD also had to create an alternative to the *antilynch* narrative that counterposed respectable, often middle-class African Americans and the white rabble, for this characterization was at odds with its Marxist outlook. The most powerful rhetorical tool in this arsenal of the literary Left was, in my view, the hobo narrative.

Left-wing journalists drew upon different hobo "types" to depict the Scottsboro boys as vulnerable workers, to discredit their accusers as promiscuous tramps, and to imagine a counternarrative of masculine proletarian unity. While this strategy inverted the "rape-lynch triangle" of the black male rapist, white female victim, and white male avenger, it still relied on conservative sexual and gender ideologies. The proletarian hobo was reconfigured during the Popular Front period as a symbol of "the people" but remained constrained by notions of manhood that relied on sexual access to white women. In his widely read sentimental novella *Of Mice and Men* (1937), John Steinbeck popularized the radical hobo narrative by depicting an interracial community of transient workers that resembled a family more than a union. However, its racial inclusiveness depended on the exclusion and demonization of white women and the emasculation of black men. In response, fledgling African American writer William Attaway self-consciously revised Steinbeck's story in his novella *Let Me Breathe Thunder*, published two years later. Attaway draws upon this populist image of the masculine hobo family but explodes the tinderbox of race and sex that lingers in the background of Steinbeck's story. Tracing the hobo narrative from radical Scottsboro journalism to Steinbeck's popular version to Attaway's response reveals how Left interracialism contended with the tangled thicket of race, sexuality, and gender.

The hobo had its origins in the rapid industrialization following the Civil War, which both dislocated single men in the urban Northeast and demanded a mobile, seasonal, and temporary workforce in western agriculture and construction industries.[9] According to Marxist theory, capital created "an army of unemployed" as production became increasingly large in scale and mechanized.[10] Although hoboes may call to mind carefree irresponsibility to modern readers, commentators in the 1910s and 1920s distinguished them from other "vagrants" by their willingness to work. For example, Ben Reitman, a medical doctor who cultivated an avant-garde "hobohemian" subculture in Chicago, differentiated between "the hobos who work and wander, the tramps who dream and wander, the bums who drink and wander."[11] Cultural images of these itinerant laborers contain a tension between what I call the "vulnerable" and "volitional" types—those who are unwilling members of the capitalist "army of unemployed" versus those "hobohemians" who reject wage work and bourgeois society in favor of the freedom of the road. As their definitions suggest, these character types do not divide easily along political lines and are highly unstable, melding into one another and creating fascinating contradictions within hobo narratives. It is also important to note that these are discursive categories describing cultural types rather than social realities. Scottsboro defense literature, I argue, strategically represented the nine black boys as vulnerable transient youth, while using the image of the volitional hobohemian to explain the reactionary behavior of the white female accusers. These competing hobo types accounted for racism within the underclass while providing a language for narrating interracial unity among the unemployed.

The hobo narratives of the 1930s built upon a tradition that originated in the first decades of the twentieth century with the Industrial Workers of the World (IWW), a radical labor organization also known as the Wobblies. The

IWW was committed to organizing unemployed, itinerant, and unskilled workers along with skilled workers in "one big union." Wobbly publications such as *Hobo News* and the *Little Red Songbook* projected a radical version of the volitional hobo who was willing to work but rejected the capitalist wage system and bourgeois domestic values. Instead, this hobo embraced a mutualistic ethic.[12] An article in a 1914 issue of the IWW's *Solidarity* magazine, for example, marvels at the masculine proletarian hero who "promptly shakes the dust of a locality from his feet whenever the board is bad, or the boss is too exacting, or the work unduly tiresome" and has "no wife or family to encumber him."[13] The Wobblies put this image of the volitional hobo to radical ends, using it to imagine a proletarian counterculture steeped in working-class notions of white masculinity. The Wobblies' mythic hobo, according to historian Todd DePastino, was the "manly white pioneer of the industrial West."[14]

Although hobo jungles and urban lodging house districts known as the "main stem" were often hostile to African Americans, the cultural imagery of transient labor became more diverse in the 1930s. Popular folklorist George Milburn, for example, championed the hobo as an antiracist folk hero, writing in the song collection *Hobo's Hornbook* that "among the hoboes the Negro finds something approaching social equality. There is little, if any, discrimination against the dingy 'bo in the jungles."[15] Writing for the National Association of Colored People's (NAACP's) *Crisis* magazine in October 1932, Roy Wilkins similarly applauded the egalitarian ethic of the Bonus Marchers, a group of war veterans who, like hoboes, rode freights across the nation to demand insurance payments from the federal government. What is most striking to Wilkins is the absence of Jim Crow in eating and sleeping arrangements—domestic spaces where racial boundaries tended to be most stringently policed. He marvels sentimentally at "white toes and black toes sticking out from tent flaps" and at "Negroes and whites mixed together in line and grouped together eating." The accompanying photographs show a pair of Whitmanesque 'boes, shirts unbuttoned and faces unshaven, standing arm in arm, and a mixed-race group seated together with their dinners on their laps, foot to foot and shoulder to shoulder, forks poised midbite.[16] Woody Guthrie popularized this notion of interracial hobo fraternity in his postwar autobiographical novel *Bound for Glory*, which begins, "I could see men of all colors bouncing along in the boxcar. We stood up. We laid down. We piled around on each other. We used each other for pillows."[17] These images build upon the Wobbly mythology of the hobo jungle as a masculine, homosocial alternative to bourgeois domesticity, revising it to suit the racial inclusivity of the 1930s and postwar Left.

During the Depression, the romance of the road also called to the daring few who did not fit the almost exclusively white male profile of the hobohemian: women, lesbians and gay men, African Americans, and immigrants of color. The writers and artists among them revised the hobo figure accordingly. These new hoboes often sought work but also hoped to find in the boxcar freedom from the constraints of middle-class sexual mores, rigid gender roles, and strict racial segregation. Pauli Murray—an African American woman who became a Yale-educated civil rights lawyer and cofounded the National Organization for Women—rode the rails for adventure in the 1930s, often passing as a white boy. In 1931 Murray was discovered by Traveler's Aid workers in Bridgeport, Connecticut, when she entered the men's room at the railroad station while her female companion, also wearing boys' clothes, went into the ladies' room. Undaunted by police interrogators, Murray told them "it was real good fun while it lasted. It'll make great material for the book we are going to write. It was a noble experiment."[18] Indeed, Murray's story piqued the interest of Harlem Renaissance patron Nancy Cunard, who commissioned her to include a few pages of her "astounding career and all that marvelous journeying on foot and as a boy and the different jobs done." She assured Murray that "we won't tell the reader that you are a girl." The article would be accompanied by a photo of Murray as "the BOY itself" and signed by "Pauli Murray, a name for boy or girl."[19] This story—a wild adventure about the narrator and "his" friend Pete's hobo journey from California to New York—appeared in Cunard's *Negro: An Anthology* in 1934.[20]

The implication that the hobo *chooses* the freedom of the road highlights his or her active resistance to capitalist economic and social structures, racial hierarchies, and rigid gender roles. At the same time, however, the rhetoric of choice obscures the human cost of unemployment and its basis in capitalist labor demands: Who would choose homelessness? Carey McWilliams, a left-leaning lawyer and New Deal official involved in the California Popular Front, argued that the image of the volitional hobo sustained an exploitative system of capitalist agriculture. "A theory was evolved at an early date to rationalize the existence of these countless tramps," writes McWilliams in his scathing history of California agribusiness of 1939, *Factories in the Field*. "They were 'tramps,' shiftless fellows who actually *preferred* 'the open road' and the jolly camaraderie of the tramp jungle to a settled and decent life. . . . There was nothing you could do with these insouciant and light-hearted boys, you couldn't even pay them a decent wage for they would 'drink it up right away'"[21] While the IWW's *Solidarity* magazine championed the hobo's rejection of wage work, McWilliams points out how easily this subversive tactic could be misconstrued to sustain an exploitative labor system.

A competing image of the "vulnerable" hobo emerged in the 1930s as cultural commentators dealt with the changing demographics of itinerancy, particularly the influx of women and children. Boxcar Bertha, the heroine of Ben Reitman's "as-told-to" autobiography of a female hobo of 1930, noted that only a tiny fraction of female transients were "habitual hoboes" and announced the emergence of "a new order, certainly, from that of the old hard-boiled sister of the road who *chose* the road for adventure and freedom in living and loving!"[22] Journalists, social scientists, and government officials fretted that the older type of (white male) volitional hobo would corrupt women, children, and young, job-seeking male transients.[23] In a sociological interview excerpted in a 1934 issue of *American Mercury*, for example, a "lady hobo" describes in graphic detail several instances of being violently raped and coerced into sex in exchange for food, transportation, shelter, and protection. Most hobo women "wear pants," she reported, "so they won't be molested and pass off for men in getting on and off the trains."[24] In response to the problem of itinerancy, the New Deal administration established the Transient Program under the Federal Emergency Relief Administration in 1933. Relief camps specifically targeted new transients, particularly young men and families, who were susceptible to the corruption of "men of the familiar hobo persuasion."[25]

This dichotomy between the volitional hobo and the vulnerable hobo shaped film and literature as well. William A. Wellman's film *Wild Boys of the Road* of 1933 dramatized for mainstream audiences the vulnerability of poor hobo youth—male and female—to predatory hobohemians. When a white female hobo is raped by a railroad worker, an interracial group of hobo teenagers avenges her.[26] Over a decade later, Filipino American writer Carlos Bulosan described in agonizing detail the brutal gang rape of a young girl by "professional hoboes."[27] Like these texts, the Scottsboro stories were shaped by the tensions between the volitional hobohemian and the vulnerable hobo driven to the rails by the collapse of the capitalist economy. Although often placed in binary opposition, these categories overlapped. The hobohemian's status as an unemployed worker belied his volition, while freedom coexisted with poverty and social alienation in the experience of vulnerable youth. As public sympathy kindled for the more "deserving" kinds of transients, left-wing journalists defused the incendiary rape-lynch myth by recasting the Scottsboro boys as devoted, dispossessed sons and their accusers as wild "sisters of the road."

On 10 April 1931, the front page of the *Daily Worker* blared, "8 NEGRO WORKERS SENTENCED TO DIE BY LYNCH COURT." In its report on the Scottsboro trials, the CP's official newspaper cast the boys as unemployed *workers*, part of a growing and increasingly diverse transient population in the United States.[28] Likewise, Helen Marcy's dispatch from the *Southern Worker* reported that the boys hopped a Memphis-bound freight out of a desperate need to support their families. Beginning the article with a letter from Heywood Patterson to his "Dearest Sweet Mother and Father," Marcy details the economic conditions that propelled so many youths onto the rails in the 1930s. Mr. Patterson's "wages were cut and now for three days work he gets a measly $7 for a family of eight." Another Scottsboro boy, Andy Wright, "started work when he was 10," lost his job, and doggedly sought honest work: "Day after day, for a whole year, Andy hung around the firms [sic] windows until he saw it was no use." Unable to stand "being a burden on his mother," Andy and his pals "decided to go to Memphis to look for work" and "hopped on a train headed in that direction."[29] The *Labor Defender* authenticated this image of the boys as involuntary hoboes through the voices of the boys and their families. In an interview published in February 1932, Ada Wright remembered her son Andy saying, "'I'm going down [to Memphis] and send you back some money for to live on.'"[30] A year after the first convictions, the boys echoed this hobo narrative in their letters from Kilby Prison: "Our kinfolk was starving for food. We wanted to help them out. So we hopped a freight—just like any one of you workers might have done—to go down to Mobile to hunt work."[31] These texts cast the boys in the role, familiar in 1930s mass media, of the hobo driven to the rails by hard times and filial devotion.

While the Scottsboro defenders depicted the boys as vulnerable transient youth, they deployed the image of the volitional hobohemian to discredit the Scottsboro accusers, Ruby Price and Victoria Bates. This depiction of the Scottsboro "girls" fed into an existing media narrative of wild girl hoboes. Pauli Murray—the African American woman mentioned earlier who passed as a boy hobo—documented this phenomenon in a scrapbook of hobo life entitled "Vagabondia." Murray clipped articles bearing sensational titles such as "Girl Hobo Loses Both Legs under Wheels of Freight," "Girl 22 Years Old Dresses as Boy," and more sentimentally in *Scribner's*, "A Bride in a Boxcar."[32] Radical journalist Mary Heaton Vorse drew on similar images of girl hoboes in her *New Republic* article of 1933, "How Scottsboro Happened."

Vorse opens with sketches of "the three hobo children"—Bates, Price, and their male companion, Lester Carter, a.k.a. the "Knoxville Kid"—who entertained themselves with "promiscuous love affairs, whose playgrounds were hobo swamps and the unfailing freight cars."[33] While Vorse retains some of the elements of the vulnerable hobo in characterizing the Scottsboro accusers, making it clear that "poverty and ignorance" drove them to tramp and trump up lies, she relies on the image of the wild "sister of the road" to distinguish them from the defendants.

Constructing an image of the adventurous, promiscuous, cross-dressing "girl hobo," Vorse offers a colorful counternarrative to Victoria Price's tale of violated southern white womanhood. While Price claimed that she and Ruby Bates spent the night in a boardinghouse, Vorse contends that "in reality they had stayed all night in a hobo jungle, where they picked up Orval Gilley, alias Carolina Slim, another of the great band of wandering children, another of those for whom this civilization has no place. Here the boys made a 'little shelter from boughs' for the girls and went off to 'stem' for food." Identifying the boys by their hobo nicknames and making liberal use of hobo slang, Vorse recasts the rape-lynch myth as a hobo tale. Vorse concludes her article by placing Bates and Price in the larger context of "200,000 children under twenty-one wandering through the land" and emphasizing their volition: "These girls are part of a great army of adventurous, venal girls who like this way of life."[34] Notably, Vorse's article appeared two months after Ruby Price recanted her testimony and turned witness for the defense. In order to distance Bates from Price, Vorse characterized their relationship according to the hobo types of the predatory "jocker" and the vulnerable "punk." Whereas Bates looked girlish in her "cheap gray dress and a little gray hat," Price had a "hard face." Bates herself played on this duality, insisting that she falsely accused the boys because "Victoria had told her to."[35]

Not all Scottsboro literature relied on this dichotomy of the volitional hobo and the vulnerable hobo. Some, in order to imagine a counternarrative of proletarian unity, emphasized the black and white hoboes' shared status as unemployed workers. In his play *Scottsboro Limited*, Langston Hughes depicts both the black boys and their white accusers as vulnerable youths. The play opens with the eight black boys riding in a boxcar. Their dialogue emphasizes the class dynamics of the southern agricultural economy and downplays the divisive dimensions of race, gender, and sex:

6th Boy: (*In wonder*)
   Look a-yonder you-all, at dem fields

> Burstin' wid de crops they yields.
>
> Who gets it all?
>
> 3rd Boy: White folks.
>
> 8th Boy: You means de rich white folks.
>
> 2nd Boy:
>
>> Yes, 'cause de rich ones owns de land.
>>
>> And they don't care nothin' 'bout the po' white man.
>
> 3rd Boy:
>
>> You's right. Crackers is just like me—
>>
>> Po' whites and niggers, ain't neither one free.[36]

In declaring "po' whites and niggers, ain't neither one free," the 3rd Scottsboro Boy expresses a commonplace in liberal-Left discourse that the share-
cropping system was a form of economic slavery forced upon both poor
whites and blacks after Reconstruction. This line replaces the media image
of black and white youths on opposite sides of the law—the alleged rapists and the witnesses for the prosecution—with the notion of their mutual
enslavement. Moreover, Hughes interprets the false accusations of Ruby
Bates and Victoria Price as products of their class oppression. In the play,
the police and a corrupt judicial system manipulate the poor young women,
promising "you'll get paid for testifying, and your pictures in the paper." The
play ends with the black boys and their Communist sympathizers singing
"together, black and white, up from the darkness into the light!"[37] Hughes
elides the combustive issue of interracial sex by masculinizing the girls, describing them as "some girls getting off dressed in overalls." Hughes calls
attention to their class status and marginality in a male space rather than
their promiscuity. Scottsboro Limited counters the southern lynch myth by re-
structuring the triangle to cast both the accused and the accusers as victims
of racial capitalism.

Radical journalists and writers revised the volitional hobo of Wobbly lore
in light of mounting cultural anxieties about vulnerable youth forced into
a dangerous underworld. As ordinary Americans lost faith in capitalism in
the 1930s, they, too, began to see the hobo not as a free spirit but as a sympathetic underdog. The hobo provided a populist alternative to the self-made
man for American audiences seeking a new kind of hero. Freedom-loving
and independent-minded, he nevertheless lived communally and would
sooner share his wages than save them. He suffered from hunger, homelessness, and want like other low-paid and unemployed workers, yet he made

a home in the boxcar rather than tolerate the speedups and wage cuts that were the life support of a dying capitalist economy. In liberal versions of this myth, such as Wellman's *Wild Boys of the Road*, Roosevelt's New Deal comes to the rescue, offering sympathy and work relief for displaced youth.[38] In radical versions, like Hughes's *Scottsboro Limited*, white and black unemployed workers wave the red flag of communism. Both liberal and radical versions of the hobo narrative advanced the Popular Front project of building a class-based, interracial alliance. While the Scottsboro appeals dragged on into the late 1930s, Popular Front writers continued to use the dual hobo figures—the volitional and the vulnerable—to imagine interracial unity while confronting the intransigent issue of white supremacy within America's underclass.

Steinbeck's and Attaway's Hobo Novellas

Two hobo novellas—one a best seller written by a white liberal, the other a neglected first book by a radical African American—continue to use these unstable categories of vulnerable hobo and volitional hobo to replace the southern lynch myth with an antiracist hobo narrative and to explain the reactionary behavior of the white masses. John Steinbeck's *Of Mice and Men* tells the story of two lonely migrant agricultural workers, George and Lennie, who dream of owning their own farm. George acts as the caretaker of Lennie, who is physically powerful but mentally disabled. When read in light of the dual hobo figures in Scottsboro literature, Steinbeck's *Of Mice and Men* takes on new meaning. George is a hobohemian figure who leaves the vulnerable Lennie behind when he goes to town on a Saturday night. Lennie then expands his vision of the dream farm to include Crooks, the "negro stable buck" who is also left behind. The novella reaches its climax when Lennie accidentally kills the boss's wife, known only as "Curley's Wife." George then executes Lennie to spare him a more brutal death at the hands of a lynch mob made up of his fellow volitional hoboes. Thus, the novella explores the radical possibilities of the vulnerable hobo while attributing mob violence to the older type of volitional hobohemian. Steinbeck's novella provides a lens into *Let Me Breathe Thunder*, a fascinating, little-known hobo story written by a twenty-five-year-old African American writer, William Attaway. The narrator, a white migrant worker named Ed, envisions the boxcar as a version of Lennie's dream farm—a domestic, racially inclusive space that gives him a sense of belonging. Yet his ruthless hobohemian companion, Step, dashes this dream by beating a black man falsely accused of raping a white woman. Attaway thus extends Steinbeck's gesture toward the radical possibilities of the vulnerable hobo figure while making a more explicit critique of the hobohemian's fear of racial mixing as a kind of homegrown American fascism.

Of Mice and Men and *Let Me Breathe Thunder* are both set in the Pacific Northwest and depict intimate friendships between white migrant agricultural workers, Lennie and George, and Step and Ed, respectively. In each pair, one partner tends toward the volitional hobohemian, and the other resembles the vulnerable transient youth cast adrift by the Depression. In *Of Mice and Men*, George complains that Lennie constrains him: "God a'mighty, if I was alone I could live so easy. I could go get a job an' work, an' no trouble. No mess at all, and when the end of the month come I could take my fifty bucks and go into town and get whatever I want. Why I could stay in a cat house all night. I could eat any place I want."[39] George views his migratory status as a rejection of wage work and domesticity, yet his relationship with Lennie ironically reconstitutes the bourgeois marriage. In fact, both sets of hoboes have spousal qualities. Lennie and Ed play the feminine roles, seeking physical intimacy, nurturing children and animals, and deferring to George and Step in making decisions. Lennie initiates physical closeness by crawling "slowly and cautiously around the fire until he was close to George," but George reinforces a boundary, pretending "to be unaware of Lennie so close beside him" (13). Similarly, while waiting for a freight in the cold rain, Ed acknowledges that "it would have been better for all of us to have snuggled together in a heap, but Step and me were funny about things like that."[40] Only George and Step seek out sex with women: Lennie stays behind when "the boys" go to the brothel, and Ed joins Step on "double dates" with reluctance. Steinbeck and Attaway use the archetypes of the "jocker" and "punk" to represent their hobo pairs.[41]

These books also resemble each other in terms of form: They are novellas written for popular audiences, with a heavy use of dialogue in dialect, and are structured so as to be adapted easily to theater or film. Many writers of the 1930s turned to theater as a medium to express social concerns because, unlike the novel, it invites audience participation.[42] Hughes's play *Scottsboro Limited*, for instance, ends with the audience chanting, "Fight! Fight! Fight! Fight!"[43] In a letter to his agents, Steinbeck explained this hybrid genre: "The work I am doing now is neither a novel nor a play but it is a kind of playable novel. Written in novel form but so scened and set that it can be played as it stands."[44] *Of Mice and Men* was eventually adapted into a Broadway play and three feature films.

Building on this tradition of activist literature, Attaway wrote *Let Me Breathe Thunder* with an eye toward theater, a choice informed by his youthful experiences with the stage. He wrote his first play, *Carnival*, while a student at the University of Illinois in 1936. He then joined his sister Ruth, a Broadway actress, in New York, where he began *Let Me Breathe Thunder*. He was acting in the traveling production of Moss Hart and George S. Kaufman's *You Can't Take It with You* when he learned that his manuscript had been accepted by Doubleday.[45] A critic for the *Saturday Review* found fault with Attaway for "project[ing] too much of his dramatic experience . . . into his writing," by creating scenes that "are plainly stagy, seen as tableaus in terms of groups and gestures, or heard as dramatic speeches with an eye towards effective curtains and black-outs."[46] Yet Attaway probably intended the novella to be performed; in fact, producer-director Herbert Kline began working on a film adaptation of the novella in Mexico in 1960, but the film was never made.[47]

Published in 1939, *Let Me Breathe Thunder* received positive reviews in both the mainstream and the radical press. As Milton Meltzer proclaimed in the *Daily Worker*, "When William Attaway's first novel landed on the desks of the critics the other day they got excited. From left to right the reviews are alive with paragraphs punched out enthusiastically."[48] Attaway's novel may have appealed to critics in and out of the literary Left because it embedded radical themes—anticapitalism, antilynching, and even interracial sex—within the framework of a more conventional masculine road narrative like *Of Mice and Men*. As Stanley Young of the *New York Times* put it, "His tough and tender story of two young box-car wanderers and their love for a little Mexican waif who rides the reefers with them has some of the emotional quality and force of the familiar relationship of George and Lennie in 'Of Mice and Men.' We see two rootless men faced by hard reality yet still susceptible to dreams and affection."[49] Similarly, Evelyn Page of the *Washington Post* and W. N. of the *Los Angeles Times* focused on the relationship between the "boys of the road" and "the little Mexican, Hi Boy, the novel's chief joy," glossing over the novel's violence, sexuality, and social criticism.[50] Like Young, several critics noted parallels between Attaway and Steinbeck. Fred T. Marsh, a conservative critic writing for the *New York Herald Tribune Books*, drew the comparison less favorably: "The tale, in more respects than one, bears a superficial resemblance to 'Of Mice and Men.'" Whereas Young heralded Attaway as "an authentic young artist," Marsh dismissed him as "imitative of the imitators who have trailed in the wake of Hemingway, James M. Cain and John Steinbeck."[51] Far from imitating Steinbeck, however, Attaway challenges the older, more established white writer. He injects an African American voice into the predominately white tradition of the hobo narrative, not simply because he is an African American, but because he creates white characters who are distinctly racialized.

Critics in the 1930s plainly recognized the parallels between these novellas, but subsequent scholars have not pursued them. In fact, some critics have recently warned against comparing these kinds of texts because the authors, due to their different racial backgrounds, supposedly followed different political and literary traditions.[52] Attaway has received more critical attention for his second novel, *Blood on the Forge*, which is thematically and stylistically similar to Richard Wright's *Native Son*—the paradigmatic African American protest novel of the period. This critical preference is perhaps due to the tendency of scholars to define African American literature as literature *by and about* black people, literature that has a distinctly African American literary genealogy. What does one do with a book written by a black writer with white protagonists? A book that resembles *Of Mice and Men* more than *Native Son*? A comparative analysis reveals the cross-pollination of African American– and white-authored texts, which produced a bountiful harvest for the literary Left in this period. Both these texts are reformulations of the Scottsboro story that reveal the possibilities and limits of the hobo figure as a vehicle for the black-Left alliance in the Popular Front period.

Of Mice and Men opens with Lennie and George in a pastoral setting, having fled the trouble that the mentally disabled Lennie inevitably brings upon himself by acting on his impulse to touch soft, pretty things. According to their ritual, the pair reconciles by affirming their commitment to each other, which they express through their shared dream of a self-sufficient farm:

> "Someday—we're gonna get the jack together and we're gonna have a little house and a couple of acres an' a cow and some pigs and—"
> "An' *live off the fatta the lan'*," Lennie shouted. "An' have *rabbits*. Go on, George! Tell about what we're gonna have in the garden and about the rabbits in the cages and about the rain in the winter and the stove, and how thick the cream is on the milk like you can hardly cut it. Tell about that, George." (15, emphasis in original)

As itinerant agricultural workers dependent on wages, Lennie and George long to own their own farm, work their own fields, and live off the bounty they produce. This producerist ethic, as historian Michael Kazin explains, is the foundation of populist thought that has its origins in Thomas Jefferson's vision of a yeoman republic.[53] Yet Lennie and George's populist vision has a particularly domestic quality. Their dream farm comes to life more vividly through domestic imagery—the "little house," "garden," and "stove"—than through the agricultural production of the "couple of acres" surrounding it. Urging George to "tell about that" and taking over the narrative himself, Lennie tempers his partner's hobohemian individualism with a populist alternative to the bourgeois family.

What most critics have missed in their readings of this novella—perhaps the best example of mainstream populism in the 1930s next to *The Grapes of Wrath*—is the interracial character of Steinbeck's hobo community.[54] At the climax of the novella, Lennie invites Candy, the aging and crippled "swamper," and Crooks, the black stable hand with a disfigured back, to share in his populist dream. Critics' oversight may be due to the tendency to see George as the architect of the fantasy, even though Lennie creates a more inclusive version on his own. When George goes off with the other men to "blow their stake" in town on Saturday night, he tells Lennie to "'stay here an' not get in no trouble'" (67). The "hobohemians" leave behind the "weak ones," as Curley's Wife derisively tags them: "a nigger an' a dum-dum and a lousy ol' sheep" (75, 77). Yet their very marginalization allows them to break the code of segregation that governs the social relations at the ranch. Like the Scottsboro stories, *Of Mice and Men* draws the reader's sympathies toward the more vulnerable, reluctant hoboes and locates revolutionary potential in them.

Steinbeck sets the stage for interracial alliance by portraying Crooks and Lennie as doubles. Both men are said to have attained their disabilities by being kicked by horses, and both are inconsequential participants in the conversations of able white men: "Crooks laughed again. 'A guy can talk to you an' be sure you won't go blabbin'. . . . George knows what he's about. Jus' talks, an' you don't understand nothing.' He leaned forward excitedly. 'This is just a nigger talkin', an' a busted-back nigger. So it don't mean nothing, see? You couldn't remember it anyways'" (69). Crooks identifies a parallel between Lennie, who cannot comprehend, and himself, to whom no one will listen. Both characters live in a communication void. This common ground provides a foundation for an interracial friendship.

Steinbeck visually dramatizes the hoboes' crossing of racial barriers, calling attention to how their friendship transgresses racist social norms. When Lennie enters Crooks's room, he crosses both a literal threshold and a figurative racial barrier. In establishing the setting of this scene, the narrator emphasizes the division between interior and exterior space, describing the "open door that let into the barn" and the "small electric globe" that "threw a meager yellow light" from Crooks's room (66). Seeking companionship with Crooks, "Lennie appeared in the open doorway and stood there looking in, his big shoulders nearly filling the opening" (66). Crooks attempts to enforce the farmworkers' code of segregation, reminding Lennie that "'I ain't wanted in the bunk house, and you ain't wanted in my room'" (67). However, Lennie cannot comprehend the contradictory social meanings of the open doorway, which invites entry, and the threshold, which delineates a racial barrier. As soon as their conversation resumed, "he advanced a step into the room, then remembered and backed to the door again" (67). As a symbol of man in his natural state, Lennie exposes the artificiality of racial hierarchies through his utter incomprehension of the farmworkers' racial codes. When Candy, the maimed "old swamper," happens upon them, he also "stood in the doorway" and "made no attempt to enter" (73). "Looking blindly into the lighted room," he occupies the dividing line between not only black and white but also light and dark. Eventually crossing the threshold, Candy reflects upon the absurdity of the practice of segregation: "'I been here a long time,' he said. 'An' Crooks been here a long time. This is the first time I ever been in his room'" (73). For Candy, the racial boundary was invisible—taken for granted—until crossed. Crooks, Candy, and Lennie thus transform the space into the prototype of Lennie's dream farm—the utopian interracial collective.

The racial integration of Crooks's room is a pivotal moment in the narrative. It impels Crooks to abandon his initial skepticism about Lennie's dream farm and ask to "'come an' lend a hand'" (75). It is crucial to note, however, that Steinbeck falls far short of imagining a truly democratic collective; Crooks does not enter the community as an equal but, rather, offers to "work for nothing—just [my] keep" (75). As we shall see, Attaway challenges Steinbeck's timid interracial vision by imagining black hoboes who have sexual access to white women, and black women who own land and businesses. Attaway's black characters aren't willing to play a submissive role, to "work just for keep." In both novellas, the most vulnerable hoboes defy segregation, but Attaway's vision is more radically egalitarian—and violently explosive.

Steinbeck does not leave his readers with this promising, albeit limited, glimpse of interracial unity. *Of Mice and Men*'s tragic ending replicates what William Maxwell calls the "antilynch triangle" common in leftist literature, in which black and white men unite in shared disgust for the white female accuser.[55] Immediately following Crooks's halting appeal to join the populist fraternity, Curley's Wife barges in, standing "still in the doorway," the symbol of racial boundaries (75). When she makes a pass at Lennie, putting him at risk of lynching, since she is married to his boss, Crooks tries to throw her out of his room. "'You got no rights comin' in a colored man's room,'" he shouts at her, "'now you jus' get out, an' get out quick'" (78). Ironically, Crooks deploys the code of segregation to defend the interracial collective. Protecting Lennie from the threat of lynching, he acknowledges his friend's shared status as a racialized "other." Candy defends against her threats by invoking the power of their collective, telling her, "'an' we got fren's, that's what we got'" (77). In contrast, Curley's Wife mobilizes the sexist code of chivalry: "'Well, you keep your place then, Nigger. I could get you strung up on a tree so easy it ain't even funny'" (79). This painful exchange demonstrates the intersections of race and gender in maintaining white male power, and the circumscribed options of women and people of color who resist it. Unfortunately, the modicum of power that Crooks derives from segregation is no match for the racial privilege of a white woman who doesn't even have a name of her own.

As this close reading suggests, Steinbeck makes a key revision to the antilynch triangle: Crooks and Lennie double as the falsely accused. At the end of the novella, it is not Crooks who violates Curley's Wife, but Lennie. A child in a grown man's body, Lennie pets her too roughly because he likes to touch soft, pretty things, then inadvertently kills her while trying to stifle her screams. The other workers on the farm—the volitional hoboes who were George's companions on Saturday night—form a mob, and George shoots Lennie to spare him a more brutal death by lynching. Thus the rape-lynching triangle is figuratively enacted, with petting substituting for sex, and Lennie standing in for Crooks. These mirrored lynching triangles defuse the fears of miscegenation that fueled the fires of the Scottsboro prosecution. By doubling Lennie and Crooks, Steinbeck racializes Lennie's social marginalization. At the same time, he avoids the controversial issue of interracial sex that would have offended his mainstream readers.

Of Mice and Men offers a counternarrative to the Scottsboro story that was palatable to a mainstream audience. Steinbeck avoids dealing directly with interracial sex by envisioning an all-male collective, by creating a black character who is physically disabled and emasculated, and by having Lennie stand in as Crooks's double in the only sexually suggestive scene. Thus readers can cast a sentimental gaze on an interracial hobo collective and decry

Curley's Wife's threat to Crooks without having to entertain the possibility of sexual relationships between black and white people. That the novella stays within the range of permissible dissent may account for its canonical status and enduring popularity, unlike the writing of William Attaway. Attaway's hobo novella, Let Me Breathe Thunder, was received favorably by critics but did not sell well. Its reception may reflect a reading public offended by explicit scenes of interracial sex and who wanted their hobo heroes untarnished by indefensible acts of racial violence.

Like Steinbeck, William Attaway became interested in hoboes not because he experienced poverty himself but because he rejected the bourgeois values of his upbringing. Attaway was born in Greenville, Mississippi, in 1911 and migrated as a child to Chicago. His father, a physician, and his mother, a teacher, desired better opportunities for their children outside the Jim Crow South and encouraged their son to pursue a career in medicine. William, however, chose another path. He frequently skipped classes during high school, preferring to watch the planes take off at nearby Checkerboard Field. According to his own admission, "Teachers told their pupils to stay away from Bill if they wanted to go straight."[56] After discovering Langston Hughes in a high school English class, however, he yearned to write. Attaway continued his academic underachievement at the University of Illinois, with the notable exception of his creative writing course.[57]

In 1931—the same year as the Scottsboro incident—Attaway dropped out of college and hopped a freight headed west with forty dollars in his pocket. While desperate men, women, and children filled these westward-moving boxcars, Attaway's journey was more like Pauli Murray's volitional hobo journey: less a means to survive than a rejection of social conventions. Upon reaching San Francisco, Attaway realized he was too broke to follow his dream of traveling to the Far East, so he got a job as a stevedore. Lured once again by the romance of the road, he followed the crops northward through the western states, stopping for a few months at a farm in Kansas and again with a Japanese family back in San Francisco. "I had a hard job making it," Attaway reminisced to the Daily Worker in June 1939. "Going over the mountains in an empty [refrigerator car] I lost all sensation in my fingers for almost two years." Riding the rails as an itinerant laborer radicalized Attaway, and he worked as a union organizer upon joining his sister Ruth in Harlem in 1933. After struggling to find a job in the depth of the Depression, Attaway hit the road again, this time as part of a traveling theater company. He returned to Illinois in 1935 to finish his degree.

Attaway participated in the thriving community of African American writers on the Left in the 1930s. John Oliver Killens, known for his involvement in the Black Arts and Civil Rights movements of the 1960s, remembers Attaway "at a left wing session [in the thirties] to hammer out a liberation ideology for black writers."[58] In 1935 Attaway was hired by the Federal Writers' Project in Illinois, where he met Richard Wright, who became a kind of mentor to him. Attaway felt "deeply grateful" for Wright's "generous criticism" on his second novel, published in 1941, as well as a short story written while he was in college.[59] Attaway's interactions with Wright in this period shaped his sense of himself as an artist-activist whose job it was to jolt bourgeois readers out of their complacency. After attending a lecture Wright gave on trade unionism at the University of Illinois, Attaway invited him to speak at the college literary society. In recalling the incident to the *Daily Worker* several years later, Attaway presented himself and Wright as radical outsiders to the academic establishment: "[Wright] started to read that swell story ["Big Boy Leaves Home"] . . . and when he got the second paragraph, half the audience had fled. Dick went on, set on giving it to them, and at the end, the room was empty of the literary set and only Dick and I were there."[60] Through Wright, Attaway witnessed the power of literature—particularly a lynching story—to disconcert and provoke middle-class readers. His proud recollection of this experience helps to explain the overt sexual and racial violence that pervades both of his novels.

As *Let Me Breathe Thunder* is out of print and nearly untouched in academic criticism, a consideration of the central themes and plot is necessary before undertaking a closer analysis. Attaway drew from his hobo experience to write his first novella, yet its main characters, Step and Ed, are white. This choice—rare in African American fiction then and now—allowed Attaway to explore the similarities between race-based and class-based prejudice. Living outdoors and working on farms literally and figuratively darkens Step and Ed, prompting one contemporary reviewer to remark that they "might as well be Negroes; their experiences are colored throughout by the same problems that daily confront the Negro or any other member of a minority group."[61] On a lark, Step and Ed take a runaway Mexican child named Hi Boy under their wing. With the boy in tow, they stop to work for a few months at an apple farm in Washington's Yakima Valley, owned by a fatherly, populist figure named Sampson and his daughter, Anna. While living on the farm, they frequent a nearby roadhouse owned by a black female entrepreneur, Mag, and her partner in business and love, a black man named

Cooper. Mag's place sharply contrasts with Sampson's farm: It is a site of leisure, illicit sex, violence, and racial mixing as opposed to work, family, nurture, and whiteness. While Ed likes the tranquility of Sampson's farm, Step chafes under its domestic and labor routines and prefers the pleasures of Mag's roadhouse. Like George and Lennie, Step and Ed represent the volitional and the vulnerable hobo types.

Step—the ruthless, hedonistic, womanizing hobohemian—faces a moral dilemma in deciding whether to leave Hi Boy with Sampson, where he can have a stable, wholesome life, or bring him back on the road to fulfill his desire to take care of someone, a role formerly played by his pet dog. As Ed explains, Hi Boy gave them a sense of family and rootedness that was the price the hobo paid for his freedom: "[Sampson] had his land and his orchards. That made him into something. Step and me had each other and we had the kid, that was all. . . . They couldn't carry around orchards to hold them to the earth" (84). Eventually Step decides to leave Hi Boy in Sampson's care, but Attaway thwarts this redemptive ending. The worlds of the farm and the roadhouse—of white domesticity and interracial mobility—collide when Step brings Sampson's daughter to Mag's place and rapes her. The plot devolves from this point into a lynching narrative that, unlike the CP pattern, pits black men against white. Cooper, a black man, is unjustly accused of raping Anna, and Step and Ed readily join the posse in betrayal of their former friend. The price they pay for their hypocrisy is dear: Escaping the violence by rail, they have no time to take Hi Boy back to the farm, and he dies a miserable death in the boxcar.

By writing about white migrant workers in Washington, Attaway fell into Steinbeck's literary orbit (in an intellectual sense) more than other African American writers interested in the radical potential of the southern black folk. The western context distances the story from the black nation thesis—the lynchpin of CP theory on race that promoted a separate African American nation in the southern states. The CP proposed this theory in the "Resolution on the Negro Question" of 1928, which marked a dramatic shift from its previous color-blind view of the class system. An impractical solution, the black nation thesis nevertheless validated the nationalist impulses so prominent in African American politics and thus attracted many black workers and intellectuals to the communist Left. Poet Sterling Brown, for example, valorized the southern black peasantry as the heart of the black nation.[62] Yet Attaway revises Steinbeck by offering a more biting critique of racism in the U.S. West that anticipates Chester Himes's postwar migration novel discussed in Chapter 5. Attaway's characters contrast the multiple axes of racism in the West to the black-white binary of the South. According to Cooper, the black manager of Mag's roadhouse, "It don't make no difference where you go . . . they always hating somebody somewhere. All along from Texas through New Mexico they hate Mexes worse'n a snake; down in lower California they get like mad dogs if you mention Japs; I ain't never been far east, but they say that out there everybody hates everybody else" (58). Furthermore, Attaway calls attention to the anti-Mexican sentiment that raged in the Southwest, resulting in the repatriation of hundreds of thousands of people and aggressive deportation drives.[63] It may have been such a raid that left Hi Boy an orphan. Asked about his parents, the child replies in mixed English and untranslated Spanish, "Family over there. . . . *Están allá, pero no encontrarlos. . . . Los molestaría mucho*" (7). [They are over there, but I can't find them. . . . They bothered them very much.] Yet this multiracial context presents opportunities as well. The black and white characters drink saki together, and the Mexican child transforms a pair of lonely hoboes into a family. Mag compares the western lynch mob favorably to its southern counterpart, as it is "just as ready to run white out of town as well as black, once they get riled" (58). She thus offers an ironic example of racial egalitarianism in the West.

In addition to offering a sharper antiracist critique, Attaway responds ambivalently to Steinbeck's agrarian populism. Sampson's place is Attaway's version of the dream farm in *Of Mice and Men*, replete with Edenic symbolism (it's an apple orchard). The narrator, Ed, is attracted to Sampson and the populist virtues he represents. Rather than operating a "factory in the field," Sampson works his own land. His face is "reddened and crinkled," a sign that "wind and shine must have been in his face for many a long morning before breakfast" (18). He treats Step and Ed like the sons he lost in the war, and his relationship with his workers is familial, not transactional. Moreover, he expresses the oppositional politics rooted in nineteenth-century Populism when he claims, "An apple sure is a beautiful thing. Makes a man think about guns and revolutions when he sees them rotting on the ground" (45). Sampson even speaks Spanish, which helps him to bond with the Mexican orphan. Attaway's fiction suggests that the producerist ethic appealed to African Americans in the 1930s, even though most scholars contend that populism had little to offer people of color.[64] Yet Attaway acknowledges its limits as an oppositional language. Sampson maintains his social position by policing sexual boundaries, refusing to let his daughter, Anna, "mix with the usual run of pickers that come along this way" (79). Sampson's farm is a setting that is productive and nurturing as well as racially hierarchical and paternalistic.

Attaway suggests the boxcar as a more egalitarian alternative to Sampson's farm and, by implication, Steinbeck's agrarian ideal. Like the dream farm, the boxcar is a domesticated space that shelters the transient workers. When the threesome hop a freight to escape the rain and cold, Ed transforms the empty refrigerator car into a domestic tableau: "Six fellers in a 'reefer,' clicking along in the night. We sat shoulder to shoulder, our damp clothes steaming. It was pleasant to be in out of the weather; it made me drowsy. The next thing I remember was waking with my head on Step's shoulder, the kid half across my lap. Someone had lit the stump of a candle and all eyes were strung to the flame. The air was thick with human steam and smoke. It all smelled good" (30). Ed describes the boxcar—emblematic of mobility and masculine freedom—as a male domestic space. The air, "thick with human steam and smoke," is not rank as one would imagine but, rather, has the coziness and pleasant aroma of a kitchen. Ed renders the physical arrangement of their bodies into a harmonious triangle, the feminine resting against the masculine, the child connecting them. The boxcar provides shelter from the elements, recalling the feminine home of sentimental novels, as well as Lennie and George's dream farm in *Of Mice and Men*.

The boxcar is a site of more radical social equality than the dream farm. According to the black hobo in the story, "Guys on the road ain't got prejudice like other folks" (32). Whereas Steinbeck desexualized his black character, Crooks, Attaway's black hobo asserts his racial equality by bragging about his sexual encounter with a white woman: "There was a yeller-haired girl in the empty with a bunch of us. Some of them gave her money. She let me love her up all the way in to Chi for a piece of cake. . . . Black or white, it's all the same on the road" (32). His sexual access to white women a "piece of cake," the black hobo sees the boxcar as a democratic utopia where he can violate the powerful taboo that whites had used to justify lynching for more than half a century.

This boxcar scene pushes far beyond Steinbeck's socially-acceptable vision of integration, calling to mind communist expressions of social equality between the races. Although Attaway's official membership is unknown, his social and artistic circles and Marxist perspective in his writing align him with the organization. At this time, the CP was unparalleled among white-led organizations in its commitment to African American social equality. Several black Party leaders in Harlem, including vice presidential candidate James Ford, were married to white women, and interracial dancing and dating were commonplace at Party social events.[65] In fact, the most dramatic instance of the CP's effort to eliminate white chauvinism from its ranks was the sensational, staged trial of August Yoniken, a Finnish janitor accused of ousting black comrades from a community dance in Harlem.[66] Lauding antiracist practices such as these, the *Chicago Defender* in 1933 declared the Communist Party the only "political, religious, or civic organization in the country that would go to such lengths" to prove its commitment to racial justice.[67]

Not surprisingly, the CP's acceptance of interracial sex made it vulnerable to attack. Until 1948, thirty states had antimiscegenation laws on the books, which prohibited marriage between white and black people, and Congress did not deem these laws unconstitutional until 1967 in the landmark case *Loving v. Virginia*. Anticommunists vilified the Party by linking it to interracial sex, miscegenation, and promiscuity. The Birmingham *Labor Advocate* warned its readers of insidious agitators who snuck around "under the cover of darkness" "preaching free love [and] intermarriage."[68] Even outside the South, commentators asserted that black men defined "complete equality" as "*free possession of White women.*"[69] The sight of interracial groups of men and women protesting together often incited police to violently repress unemployment demonstrations in the early 1930s.[70] In a segregated nation that claimed to be classless, policing sexual boundaries was easier to justify than the repression of class-based protest. Even on the Left, interracial cooperation was difficult to achieve. Fears of racial mixing stymied CIO efforts to organize interracial unions; many activists avoided the subject for strategic reasons. Furthermore, workers who might have tolerated interracial unions violently resisted the integration of neighborhoods and recreational spaces, as the Detroit riot of 1943 so painfully attests. As historian Gary Gerstle explains, violent conflicts between black and white workers in overcrowded cities make "unionized workplaces . . . seem like oases of enlightenment and interracial fraternity."[71] Even writers as radical as Nelson Algren elided interracial sex. Taking James Farrell's suggestion, Algren expunged from the original manuscript of his novel *Somebody in Boots* the redemptive relationship between the white hobo protagonist and a black woman named Val, who offers him a way out of his vagrant life and motivates him to get his first legitimate job.[72] Interracial sex was a taboo subject in mainstream, liberal, and sometimes radical discourses, and these widespread fears of miscegenation impeded political and literary expressions of working-class equality.

Yet while interracial sex may have been a kind of litmus test for one's commitment to racial equality, it risked reducing the African American freedom struggle to sexual access to white women. Writing in 1951, Zora Neale Hurston dismissed CP interracialism as the deluded belief "that the highest ambition of every Negro man was to have a white woman."[73] Similarly, the narrator of Ralph Ellison's *Invisible Man* asks in exasperation, "Why did they [the Communist characters] insist upon confusing the class struggle with the ass struggle?"[74] While Hurston and Ellison's anticommunism must be understood as a product of the Cold War and thus an unreliable and misleading index of African Americans' relationship with the Left before the war, these concerns were nonetheless relevant in the 1930s. As Maxwell points out, Ellison's narrator repeats a well-known Harlem joke of the earlier period.[75]

Moreover, black female communists were not impressed by CP displays of social equality, especially since the vast majority of interracial relationships involved black men and white women. West Indian Communist Grace Campbell led a group of Harlem women who objected to the interracial marriages of black Party leaders on the grounds that they reinforced the common misconception that black women were socially and morally inferior to white women.[76] The CP's response—to give white men dancing lessons to encourage them to socialize with black female comrades—is laughable not only for its odd observance of racial stereotypes but also for its assumption that what black women wanted was more attention from white men.[77]

While Attaway's boxcar scene follows the conventions of CP interracial literature, the novella concludes with a lynch triangle that warns of the reactionary tendencies of the white underclass, and it does so without ignoring black women. When Step hears (falsely) that his African American friend Cooper attempted to rape Sampson's white daughter, he violently attacks him. His betrayal is all the more egregious for its hypocrisy: Step himself had had violent sex with the underage girl, prompting Cooper to warn him that "they can put you under the jailhouse for rape" (62). Step exemplifies Marx's notion of the *lumpenproletariat*, "the 'dangerous class,' the social scum, that passively rotting mass thrown off by the lowest layers of old society" who swing unpredictably from revolutionary proletarians to "a bribed tool of reactionary intrigue."[78] Marx saw these beggars and unemployed who existed outside the wage system as victims of capitalism, but nonetheless a potentially counterrevolutionary force due to their alienation and utter dependency. Many radical writers of the early to mid-1930s drew on the concept of the *lumpenproletariat* to depict the hobo's underworld as the dank dumping ground of capitalist society. In his seminal 1956 study, Walter Rideout dubbed this subcategory of proletarian literature "bottom dogs," based on the title of Edward Dahlberg's 1930 novel.[79] For example, Cass

McKay, the hobo figure in Nelson Algren's novel of 1935, *Somebody in Boots*, is violently beaten by the police and his fellow hoboes when he expresses empathy for dark-skinned men. These acts of violence enforce a compulsory whiteness, teaching him that "a white man who walked with a 'nigger' was a 'nigger' too."[80] William Maxwell argues that Algren's novel warns communist readers that their antiracist organizing competed with violent "lessons in white racism."[81] Similarly, Attaway highlights the susceptibility of the dispossessed to white supremacy—a kind of fascist collective that offers them a sense of power and manhood.

Step and Ed's participation in a lynch mob suggests the vulnerability of the *lumpen* figure to fascist collectives. As he joins a lynch mob, Ed is intoxicated by the "spirit of the crowd" (102). He easily abandons his loyalties to his black friends. Participating in the lynching frenzy gives him a sense of power and belonging: "There was a glorious feeling of being strong as God Almighty in the very air . . . of having a thousand hands and feet. I laughed crazily and tried to push my way to the steps of Mag's house" (103). With "a thousand hands and feet," Ed surrenders his individual identity to the group. Steinbeck depicts the psychology of the lynch mob in a very similar manner in his short story "The Vigilante."[82] Just as Ed feels like an all-powerful being, Steinbeck's protagonist "hardly felt it" when "a driving line of forty men deep had crashed [him] against the door like the head of a ram" in their efforts to kidnap a black prisoner.[83] In exploring mob psychology, Attaway and Steinbeck highlight the vulnerability of the dispossessed masses to the fascist promise of collective power through white supremacy. Later, both writers would represent the unity of "the people" as progressive forces in their novels *Grapes of Wrath* and *Blood on the Forge*. These dark novellas, however, reveal the fine line between the populist community and the fascist lynch mob.

The grim ending of *Let Me Breathe Thunder* warns readers that fears of racial mixing are a form of homegrown American fascism as formidable as the rising crisis in Europe. Observing the atrocities of Hitler and Mussolini but unwilling to intervene, the American public in the 1930s feared a fascist takeover from within. In *Forerunners of American Fascism*, published in 1935, journalist Raymond Gram Swing boldly predicted that "America is heading for fascism." His treatise analyzed five rising demagogues—the "radio priest" Father Coughlin, Louisiana politician Huey Long, Mississippi senator Theodore Bilbo, and reformer Dr. Townshend—who were amassing power by fanning the frustrations of the disaffected lower middle class.[84] In his novel *It Can't Happen Here*, published in 1935, Sinclair Lewis made an American fascist movement seem plausible by basing his demagogue protagonist,

Buzz Windrip, on the real-life figure Huey Long. Like Long, Windrip builds a mass following from middle-class people who feel the ground crumbling beneath them. The liberal *New Republic* monitored the fascist movements over the course of the 1930s, making antifascism central to its agenda by the time Hitler had solidified his power in 1935.[85] California—the setting of Attaway's and Steinbeck's novellas—was widely viewed as a breeding ground for fascism. In his muckraking history of California agriculture, *Factories in the Field*, Carey McWilliams compares the powerful growers' organization, the Associated Farmers, to "organizations of like character in Nazi Germany." McWilliams carefully documents the "rise of Farm Fascism": control of the legislature, banks, utilities, and police; a sophisticated espionage system; a propaganda machine; the violent repression of workers; and the segregation and disenfranchisement of dark-skinned peoples.[86] Most commentators in the 1930s and after interpreted fascism as a middle-class phenomenon—either a tool of industrial capitalism or a reaction against it by the disaffected petite bourgeoisie. In his *Revolt of the Masses* of 1932, however, José Ortega y Gasset proposed that fascism emerged from the collapse of the class structure and rise of the "masses."[87] American writers of the "bottom dogs" hobo narratives point out the appeal of fascism to destitute transient and unemployed workers. In particular, lynching tropes highlight fascism's irrational, visceral appeal to the dispossessed.

The lynching scene that occupies the dark climax of Attaway's novella departs from the conventions of Party literature not only by eliminating white male allies but also by refusing to ignore black women and to reduce the African American social struggle to black male sexual access to white women. A final twist in the plot reveals that Cooper, the black man accused of rape, is impotent. Cooper wanted to leave his African American partner, Mag, so she could find a better man, but he was afraid that his departure would reveal his shame. So he made a pass at Anna to give Mag a reason to throw him out. Notably, Cooper uses Anna to satisfy the sexual needs of his black female lover, not to assert his racial equality. "It never crossed my mind," he claims, "that the little gal would holler" (114).

This convoluted plotline not only disconnects black male equality from sexual access to white women; it also incorporates, to some extent, black women into the larger Popular Front discourse of interracialism. While Attaway's representation of women in general is misogynistic regardless of color, Mag is a notable exception. Having heard Step admire Mag and her business acumen, Ed assumes she is white and is "knocked off [his] feet" when he discovers otherwise (34). Mag mystifies Ed, who has never seen a black female entrepreneur, nor an older woman who keeps a lover (at fifty-three, Mag would have been more than twice the age of Attaway and his youthful protagonists). Through this twisting plot, Attaway targets fear of racial mixing as the foremost obstacle to class-based alliance, even though, needless to say, sexual access to white people was a low priority for African Americans. He does so, however, without elevating white women as the "prize" of racial equality at the expense of women of color.

Both Steinbeck's and Attaway's grim novellas question the suitability of the hobo as an icon of the Popular Front. Yet to entirely dismiss the hobo from Popular Front iconography fails to consider the multiple variants of this figure, both within Attaway's novel and in liberal-Left discourse more generally. The tension between the volitional hobo and the more vulnerable transient youth, a duality embodied by Step and Ed as well as George and Lennie, shaped the Scottsboro story—arguably the grand narrative of the radical Left. Far from rejecting the hobo, writers like Vorse and Hughes employed the language and forms of the hobo narrative to imagine proletarian unity while accounting for its alter ego, the white working-class lynch mob. While the hobo had its roots in the largely white male transient labor force of the post–Civil War era and was mythologized as such by the IWW, African American, ethnic, and white-leftist writers revised this figure in the 1930s and '40s. Preserving the themes of freedom-seeking and rejection of wage work and domesticity, writers like Pauli Murray, William Attaway, Nelson Algren, Richard Wright, Jack Conroy, Woody Guthrie, and Carlos Bulosan countered the white male hobo icon with African American, Mexican, and Filipino variants.

Thus the fascist tendencies of Attaway's hobo are less an indication of its failure as a Popular Front icon than its role in critiquing Popular Front interracialism in the wake of Scottsboro. Attaway's experience as a hobo cultivated his anticapitalist politics and gave rise to his vision of the boxcar as a racially egalitarian space. For Attaway, the migratory worker in California linked the agrarian roots of American populism—an idea enshrined by Steinbeck—to the multiethnic base of the CIO. But stories of multiethnic protests and migrant camp life too often elided issues of racial mixing. Attaway used the hobo's association with illicit sex to represent sexual relations between black men and white women, thus forcing his readers to confront the seemingly insurmountable barrier to working-class unity. Rather than rejecting the hobo as a Popular Front icon, Attaway revises the Scottsboro narrative, as well as Steinbeck's liberal reformulation, by exposing the sexual and racial construction of white masculinity.

CHAPTER 2 AN OKIE IS ME

While the reactionary tendencies of the hobo made him a problematic icon for the Popular Front, the migrant family held more promise. In particular, government photographers produced images of dust bowl migrants in California that rallied support for New Deal programs. These unemployed workers had advantages over the Scottsboro boys in terms of public appeal: They were white, they traveled in family groups, and most of them would have little to do with the Communist Party. When vigilantes hired by the corporate growers beat white strikers during a lettuce strike in Salinas in 1936, the incident made national news.[1] Readers far from California who may have turned a blind eye to violence against Mexican workers bridled at economic and physical abuses against people from the American heartland, who embodied the national frontier myth of hard work and self-sufficiency. The stunning popularity and policy impact of Steinbeck's *Grapes of Wrath* testifies to the power of the image of the migrant family to provoke public outrage over unchecked capitalism, corporate power, labor exploitation, and the inadequacy of government relief.

The cultural imagery of migrant families in California was produced mainly by liberals like Steinbeck who envisioned the federal government as a mediator between labor and capital. Scholars debate whether these documentarians portrayed dust bowl migrants sentimentally, as deserving victims in need of the paternal care of a liberal state, or whether a more radical vein penetrates these texts. In his seminal *Documentary Expression and Thirties America*, William Stott argues that migrants "come to us only in images meant to break our heart . . . helpless, guiltless as children."[2] More recent work challenges this view. Joseph Entin argues that left-wing writers and photographers developed an aesthetic of "sensational modernism" that jolted middle-class audiences through visceral images of bodily suffering, while Will Kaufman and Mark Allan Jackson have cut through Woody Guthrie's folksy persona to uncover his radical political commitments.[3] In my view, radical writer Sanora Babb is an undiscovered star in this constellation of documentarians of California's agricultural labor crisis.[4] Babb was born in Oklahoma Territory, lived as a small child in an earthen dugout in the arid high plains of eastern Colorado, and then moved from town to town throughout Oklahoma, graduating from Forgan High School in 1924. She migrated to California in 1929, where she became involved in radical political and artistic circles. When fellow midwesterners surged into the state in the mid-1930, she documented their struggles by writing articles in the radical press and a novel, *Whose Names Are Unknown*. In these writings, Babb combines the indigenous populism of the midwestern plains with the politics of the communist Left and her own incipient feminism to produce an alternative, radical vision of the migrant family.[5] After placing Babb's writing in the context of the California labor crisis and her own activism, I will examine the gender and racial politics of her novel.

The dust bowl migrants entered California's agricultural labor force on the heels of militant agricultural uprisings that prompted unprecedented federal intervention. Forty-two thousand workers—predominately of Mexican descent—participated in twenty-three strikes in California in 1933 and 1934, many of which were successful in raising wages.[6] Although they were officially organized by the Communist-led Cannery and Agricultural Workers' Industrial Union, the workers themselves provided the leadership and tactical support on the ground. The growers' violent response—such as the shooting of unarmed strikers and their families in Pixley in October 1933— generated public sympathy for the strikers, despite their "foreign" and "radical" associations.[7] The National Labor Board mediated a settlement between the union leaders and the growers, resulting in a new wage rate of 75 cents per hundred pounds. Although many farmworkers hoped the state would continue to empower them—especially as white citizens swelled their ranks—the government did not intervene in subsequent agricultural strikes. Instead, the growers combined forces to establish the Associated Farmers, a powerful bloc of industrialists and corporate farmers that manipulated the press, pressured politicians, and resorted to vigilante violence. The rights of agricultural workers took another serious blow in 1935, when they were excluded from the protections of the National Labor Relations Act, which guaranteed the right to organize.[8] The CP dissolved the Cannery and Agricultural Workers' Industrial Union in 1935, choosing to direct its resources toward recognized unions.[9] The dust bowl migrants arrived in the wake of the greatest agricultural strikes the United States had ever known, strikes that had already aroused public sympathy for the plight of migrant workers. Yet market forces, a timid federal government, exclusionary legislation, labor organizing strategies, and a highly organized and power-ful opposition formed formidable barriers to their class struggle.

By 1936 white workers, many of them dust bowl migrants, comprised two-thirds of the agricultural workforce in California, displacing Mexicans, who had been the majority, and Filipinos, who had been the largest minor-ity.[10] This influx of white, native-born migrants, while precipitating a pub-lic health crisis and the ruthless exploitation of desperately poor people, seemed to augur a new day for agricultural labor relations, and possibly the inclusion of farmworkers in the National Labor Relations Act.[11] Liberal commentators such as labor advocate Carey McWilliams saw the migrants' white citizenship as an asset: "These despised 'Okies' and 'Texicans' were not another minority alien racial group (although they were treated as such), but American citizens familiar with the usages of democracy." Stein-beck similarly cautioned that "with this new race the old methods of repres-sion, of starvation wages, of jailing, beating and intimidation are not going to work; these are American people."[12] This hopefulness, however, rested on the assumption that the "whitening" of the California agricultural labor force was relatively permanent, and that the Okies would use their status as white citizens to improve conditions in the fields. "This new race is here to stay," wrote Steinbeck in a series of articles published in the *San Francisco News* in 1936, "and heed must be taken of it."[13] In other words, liberal ag-ricultural reform relied upon Okies' remaining in the fields long enough to develop a consciousness as workers and push for change. "Will . . . the Okies realize," liberal sociologist Paul Taylor asked readers of *Survey Graphic*, "that they are definitely a part of the under-employed labor army—white Americans, Mexicans, Negroes, and Filipinos—mobile and restless, which has engaged in strike after strike?"[14] As Taylor's question suggests, Okies had a different view of their status as agricultural workers. They would pick cotton and peaches for next to nothing just until they got on their feet, until they could find decent jobs or a plot of land. As it turns out, the Okies were right—their place in the agricultural workforce was temporary. Their win-dow of opportunity opened unexpectedly when the United States entered World War II in 1941. Western defense industries demanded Okie labor to build ships and airplanes. The Okies did not use their status as white citi-zens to improve conditions for agricultural workers, but rather, as historian Debra Weber points out, they seized the first opportunity to escape this sub-merged caste, as did immigrant workers before and after them.[15]

However, it is only clear in hindsight that the Okies' position on the bot-tom rung of the agricultural economy was temporary. In the spring of 1935, public officials feared that California was on the brink of social upheaval. The California Emergency Relief Administration sent Paul Taylor to the state border to investigate the in-migration. The agency was considering building federal labor camps in order to stave off social unrest, as poor housing was one of the main grievances of the 1934 strikes.[16] Taylor's report, illustrated by Dorothea Lange's arresting photographs, won $200,000 in federal funds to build the camps. Taylor reworked his report for the July 1935 issue of *Survey Graphic*, whose readership consisted of social workers and others interested in liberal reform. His article "Again the Covered Wagon" begs the reader to sympathize with the migrants, humanizing them through moving quotations that highlight their pride, despair, and reluctance to go on relief. Critical of the CP and confident that the migrants "neither understand nor profess to favor communism," Taylor favored reform through a "protecting government" that enlightened vulnerable citizens rather than equalizing class relations.[17] "The trek of drought and depression refugees to California is the result of a national catastrophe," proclaimed Taylor in an address to the Commonwealth Club in September 1935. "The succor of its victims is a national responsibility."[18]

Both Sanora Babb and Woody Guthrie offered more radical analyses of the labor crisis in California. Yet although Guthrie is hailed as an exemplar of Popular Front antiracism, Babb arrived to these antiracist commitments earlier, expressed them more forcefully in her dust bowl writings, and incorporated an incipient feminism that stands in sharp contrast to Guthrie's masculine style. Guthrie's fierce commitment to racial equality grew out of the class struggle, but his racial consciousness did not awaken until after he left California for New York in 1940. In fact, he exhibited blatant racism in his performances on KVFD radio in Los Angeles in the late 1930s that he would later regret. His comedy routine was littered with ethnic slurs, such as "darkies," "niggers," "Chinamen," "Japs," and "pepper bellies."[19] After Guthrie performed the song "Run, Nigger, Run," an African American college student wrote him a letter expressing his resentment and letting him know that "no person . . . of any intelligence uses that word over the radio today."[20] Guthrie's response indicates his ripeness for reform: He apologized on the air, tore up the offending song sheet, and promised that he would never use the offending word again.[21] Guthrie experienced a full transformation of racial consciousness when he moved to New York with actor Will Geer in 1940. Guthrie was influenced by Geer's progressivism as well as his experiences living and working with black musicians such as Brownie McGhee, Sonny Terry, and Huddie "Lead Belly" Ledbetter. African

American listeners and musicians forced Guthrie to confront his racism, and he proved remarkably teachable. Yet his views did not change considerably until he left California and was transformed by the war and the Popular Front's antifascist crusade. Sanora Babb, in contrast, understood that the dust bowl migrants were part of a larger interracial class struggle. Moreover, while Guthrie's sexual politics continued to be problematic throughout his life, Babb incorporated women's issues and female leadership into her writings.

Babb's subject matter was close to her heart; she wrote about rural people in her native region of the high plains. "These were the people I knew all my life," she wrote shortly after finishing her novel; "I knew them and lived with them through the hard pioneering days of breaking new land, of more prosperous days, of the early depression years."[22] While Babb's early life shared characteristics of many of the poor dust bowl migrants, her life in California was far from typical. A budding journalist, Babb migrated to California in 1929 to become a newspaper reporter, but the stock market crash stymied her career aspirations. Jobless and intermittently homeless, she eventually found work as a secretary for Warner Brothers, a scriptwriter for KFWB radio in Los Angeles, and then as a reporter on labor conditions in the Southwest. Babb built a career as a short-story writer in the 1930s and '40s, publishing in left-wing magazines such as the *Daily Worker*, *New Masses*, *Anvil*, *Black and White*, and the *Clipper*; in regional magazines such as *Kansas Magazine* and *Midland*; and in other smaller periodicals. She continued to publish regularly throughout her life. She was well known and highly respected in an artistic circle that could boast some of the major voices of radical, ethnic, and African American literature at midcentury, including Carlos Bulosan, Ralph Ellison, Meridel Le Sueur, Dorothy Parker, William Saroyan, Genevieve Taggard, Nathanael West, and Chinese American cinematographer James Wong Howe. She fell in love with Howe in the early 1930s and married him in Paris in 1936 while he was on film location in England. Babb and Howe faced discrimination as an interracial couple, both in the United States and abroad. California banned interracial marriage until 1948, at which time they legalized their union and proudly posted their wedding photo in the newspaper. Babb later described their union as "a stormy marriage, a loving marriage and finally a fully healing marriage." Its storms were due to Babb's fierce independence and intense (though rarely sexual) relationships with other men. Babb had a brief, passionate love affair with Ralph Ellison during the League of American Writers conference in 1941 that nearly broke up both their marriages.[23] Babb and Ellison remained friends, and Ellison's criticism of her manuscript is the only contemporaneous response available, since the novel was not published until decades later.

By the time Babb married Howe (for the first time) in 1936, she was a Communist Party member and organized her social life and literary ambitions around her commitment to radical anticapitalism. After Howe expressed jealous concerns over her relationship with Filipino writer Carlos Bulosan, Babb asserted her independence, asking him to "let me have my friends in the movement. . . . I have to have some friends who are interested in literature, in economics and political events."[24] In the summer of 1936, Babb traveled through eastern Europe and Russia. Accompanied by filmmaker Herbert Kline and several other tourists, she attended a monthlong film festival, seeing plays every night in Kiev, Moscow, and Leningrad. Babb stubbornly refused to cancel her Russian tour even though her appendix was near bursting and doctors warned her against having surgery there. Although the occasion for her Russian tour was ostensibly the theater festival, she was also motivated by "sincere political interests," as she confided to Howe.[25] She was impressed with working conditions in the Soviet Union, remarking, "Kiev is very nice and the workers look happy—they have eased faces beside the others we have seen in Germany and Poland."[26] Her primary focus, however, was the lives of Russian children, an interest that would carry over to her work among the migrants. "It must be very satisfying to rear children under communism," she wrote to Howe.[27] Babb's sense that communism promoted better family life and more equitable gender relations was reinforced by Party literature. The 30 April 1934 issue of the Working Woman, for example, included a photograph of children with the caption, "BEST CARED FOR CHILDREN IN THE WORLD: Soviet Children at Play in the Garden of the Nursery While Mothers Work."[28] Like many American literary radicals, Babb admired Russia for its seeming economic vitality amidst the Depression, social equality, and commitment to a revolutionary culture that provided a central role for artists.[29]

Returning to California in 1938, Babb turned her attention to the conditions of migrant workers in California, focusing, as she did in Russia, on maternal and child welfare. She organized a strike in Modesto after discovering child laborers who were harvesting walnuts without pay. The United Cannery, Agricultural, Packing, and Allied Workers of America (UCAPAWA), the CIO's new agricultural union, turned down Babb's request for help, directing its limited resources toward more centralized and stable workers in the food processing industries. Babb forged ahead on her own to help the children get the money they had earned.[30] Her involvement in strike activity was threatening enough to attract the attention of police and the Associated Farmers. She spent a night in jail along with CP organizer Dorothy Ray Healey and once received death threats by hired thugs.[31] Yet these were isolated incidents; Babb did not devote her energies to labor organizing in California but, rather, worked for the FSA as an assistant to Tom Collins, director of the federal camps for migratory workers. The camps provided shelter, sanitation facilities, health clinics, and community centers for the migrants with the aims of averting a public health disaster and stabilizing the workforce. In the winter of 1938, Sanora Babb and her sister, Dorothy, traveled along Highway 99, from the pea fields in the Imperial Valley to the orchards of the Sacramento Valley. Sanora took notes in her journal during the day and composed sketches in the evenings, while Dorothy, an amateur photographer, took pictures. Between February and October 1938, Babb visited nearly 800 migrant families, registering over 300 of them into the government camps.[32] Working from her field notes, she published articles in the radical press and crafted her novel, *Whose Names Are Unknown.*

Babb saw revolutionary potential in the migrants and their experiments with grassroots democracy in the camps. She helped Collins implement a project he called "Democracy Functioning," which aimed to cultivate self-governance and restore pride. Residents elected camp councils that enforced regulations, negotiated disputes, and served as liaisons between residents and the government officials who managed the camps. An array of subcommittees organized social events, athletic contests, child care, clubs, camp newsletters, and other social networks. Collins saw the "D.F." groups as a training ground for the CIO and eventually a broader labor front. He described Babb in almost messianic terms as a link between the migrant camps and a broader movement: "It was she who bridged the chasm between the D.F. and the next move, the C.I.O. It was she who raised aloft, the bigger banner for the united front. Of such stuff are the real leaders of men made."[33]

While Collins promoted workers' rights under the auspices of the New Deal, Babb envisioned the D.F.s as springboards to more revolutionary action. In 1938 she wrote an essay, "Migratory Farm Workers in California," that appears to be addressed to CP organizers in the region.[34] Babb reported that the Okies are "to the point of a near-revolutionary state."[35] They "have begun to realize that the 'D.F.' is not enough" and have joined forces with the CIO "as a step" toward more radical solutions.[36] Babb believed that Collins could also be persuaded to "accept the logic of Communism," since he shared her principles and "in many ways uses our own tactics without knowing it." Babb advised the CP to recruit Collins: "I should like to recommend him for this 'education' and I feel sure he would be invaluable working among the agricultural workers. . . . Some concentrated training should make him very useful in a larger way."[37] Babb's work with the FSA, then, does not mark her a New Deal liberal but, rather, locates her on the Left edge of the Popular Front coalition.

While Babb hoped she could nudge Collins toward revolutionary organizing, she felt that she could best contribute to the movement herself as a writer. Collins agreed that she could effect change through "the power of the written word." "The field is rapidly being filled with organizers," he wrote in 1938, "I would like to see you WRITE and WRITE. . . . We all HOPE YOU WILL. WE WANT YOU TO DO SO."[38] Even though Babb did her best work in the short-story form, she chose to write a novel and sought a major publishing house with national distribution, which suggests she aimed for the widest possible audience even at the risk of losing working-class readers. By the time Babb was writing in the late 1930s, Marxist critics more or less agreed that a novel's "perspective" determined whether it was "proletarian," as opposed to the class status of its author, audience, or characters. Writing to Babb in 1943, Ralph Ellison praised her for achieving this working-class "perspective": "Steinbeck was never for the workers in GOW, but was pleading subtly for the big shots to stop their wrong-doing. You, however, have been for the workers, showing his rebirth into a new consciousness."[39]

Babb embraced the role of spokesperson for the dust bowl migrants by incorporating their writings and viewpoints into her novel. Both poor tenants in the midwestern plains and those who migrated to California implored Babb to write, and they influenced the story she told. Babb gathered information from her parents about dry farming and daily life in the Great Plains. While Walter Babb answered her questions about cultivating winter wheat, Jennie Babb described the human cost of crop failure, livestock depletion, and debt. A "half starved" neighbor urged Jennie Babb to pass on to Sanora "facts on farmers here" so she could "write them up and publish."[40] Migrant workers in California were also eager to help Babb document their struggles. In October 1938, while cotton workers struck in Kern County, Babb returned to Los Angeles to write her novel. Riley Dixon invited her back to the Arvin camp so she could "look around you might see something that would help you in your work."[41] Henry Selb offered to show her around the camps and to "take some snapshots of some of the other camps that we didn't get to visit . . . so you can show your friends how a cotton picker has to live to get to work for John farmer in this part of Calif." Selb not only saw

Babb's literary talents and access to middle-class audiences as a weapon in the movement, but he also claimed the role of the documentarian, using meager resources to photograph the camps himself.[42]

Babb's novel had an auspicious beginning: Random House gave her an advance contract after reading the first four chapters and moved her to New York so she could finish the manuscript. But when *The Grapes of Wrath* took the nation by storm in 1939, they suddenly reneged. Chief editor Bennett Cerf told Babb he had received "exceptionally fine" reports on her manuscript, but "obviously, another book at this time about exactly the same subject would be a sad anticlimax!"[43] The similarities between the novels were striking. As another editor noted, "It would almost seem as if Sanora Babb and John Steinbeck had thoroughly discussed an identical theme and set out to write their separate books—so similar are GRAPES OF WRATH and WHOSE NAMES ARE UNKNOWN."[44] It is no wonder that these novels resemble each other—Steinbeck borrowed Babb's field notes, and both writers worked closely with FSA camp manager Tom Collins. In fact, Steinbeck even makes a cameo appearance in *Whose Names* as "the famous writer" who advocated on behalf of a poor migrant who stole some radiators in order to feed his starving mother.[45] The similarities in the content of these two novels—not aesthetic considerations—scared editors away from publishing what is arguably the best novel of the dust bowl migration. Editor Charles A. Pearce contended that Babb was "a more capable and exciting writer than Steinbeck," and an anonymous editor at Random House agreed: "Whereas GRAPES had color, excitement, and humor, Babb's book is more uniformly intense. . . . If there hadn't been a GRAPES, I would say unreservedly, here is something new, something fine, we must publish. Moreover an unusual talent is displayed in this first novel."[46] Babb approached several other publishing houses, but they gave her the same response. Babb seems to have continued to work on the novel as late as 1942; in that year, Ellison gave her feedback on the manuscript, imploring her to finish: "I hope you have gotten back to the novel and that it is completed for fall publication. You must."[47] Sadly, Babb eventually filed away her masterpiece, where it would remain for over sixty years. *Whose Names Are Unknown* was published by the University of Oklahoma Press in 2004.[48]

The novel tells the story of the Dunne family—Milt, Julia, and their two daughters—who live in an earthen, underground dugout on their grandfather's barely subsistent broomcorn farm on the arid high plains of the Oklahoma panhandle, miles from the nearest town. In Part 1, Babb uses the tools of literary regionalism to immerse the reader in the haunting landscape of the high plains and to give voice to rural women's labor, which, in its re-petitiveness, resists narrative. The family survives repeated crop failures and apocalyptic storms by relying on their neighbors and bridles under the economic control of large landowners and banks. After years of starvation and Julia's devastating miscarriage, the Dunnes join two of their neighbors in the trek to California. Part 2 takes place in California, where the family follows the crops up the California central valley. Homeless, hungry, and hated, they ally with white, Filipino, and African American migratory work-ers in a cotton strike. Although the strike fails, the workers vow to "stand together as one man" (222). I will focus first on the gender politics of the novel. Babb depicts women as populist heroes and places their domestic routines and reproductive experiences at the center of a narrative about political transformation. In a unique twist to the conventional proletarian novel, her characters not only gain class consciousness at the end but a new gender consciousness as well. Second, I will discuss Babb's vision of inter-racial unionism, which stemmed from her own life experience in interracial communities and entailed a reckoning with the Okies' whiteness.

Populism, Regionalism, and Gender in *Whose Names Are Unknown*

Babb's activism and art call us to take seriously the oppositional populism of the 1930s rather than dismissing it as an early sign of working-class racial and political conservatism. While historians attribute the failure of agricul-tural unionism in California mainly to political and economic structures, they also vigorously debate how elements of the Okie culture were incom-patible with the organized labor movement.[49] Historians James Gregory and Devra Weber offer a litany of conservative cultural traits—what Greg-ory calls "plain folk Americanism"—that impeded labor organizing: racial prejudices, religious fatalism, fervent patriotism, staunch anticommunism, an ethos of individualism, and an abiding faith in the political process and agrarian ideal.[50] They reject the notion that Okies brought with them po-litical traditions rooted in nineteenth-century agrarian radicalism, arguing that populist and socialist egalitarianism was annihilated by the resurgence of nativism, racism, and fundamentalism in the 1920s.[51] Gregory concludes that the Okie subculture stood at midpoint between "the agrarian radicalism of an earlier era and the flag-waving conservatism of the next."[52] However, white working-class conservatism was not foreordained, and the trajec-tory of Left-labor movements in California and white migrants' role within them were not so clear at the time. Sanora Babb's grandfather subscribed to the Socialist paper *Appeal to Reason* and inculcated the socialist and populist political culture in his granddaughters.[53] Once in California, Babb spoke with migrants who were receptive to her ideas about the class interests they shared with Mexican and black workers. She had also come from a rural white community in Oklahoma, yet she embraced communism and loved a man from China. Whereas social historians like Gregory focus on what he calls the "majority trend," cultural critics can turn to the "variation" for insight into how writers and activists tried to reimagine and remake social relations despite the odds against them. The populist impulses and the co-operative spirit of rural life prepare her protagonists—male and female—for militant, interracial labor protest once they reach California.

The Dunnes' journey toward proletarian class consciousness begins in Oklahoma, where the family develops an oppositional politics nurtured by the indigenous populism of the region. Broadly speaking, populism is a political culture that celebrates the "people"—particularly small farmers, craftsmen, and other "producers"—and opposes corporate power, banks, and other private creditors.[54] The rural society Babb depicts does not divide easily along lines of landowners and farmworkers, as a Marxist analysis of class would have it. Rather, it distinguishes between producers—those who do tangible work—and parasites who live off the work of others.[55] The wealthiest landowner, Brennerman, owned "thousands of acres he had bought up from farmers who had proved up government land" and was also "a power in the Flatlands Bank, which held the farmers' loans" (4). Another neighbor family, the Brownells, fits into the middle category that populism allows for but Marxism does not. Lucky enough to have a creek running through their property, they operate a self-sufficient farm. Their hard work gives rise to generosity rather than greed, and they invite their poorer neighbors to share meals with them. Their college-educated sons, Max and Pete, connect nineteenth-century Populism to the Popular Front vision of labor unity, advising their neighbors that "farmers have got to realize that they belong with others who work" and telling them of the "farmers' Grange and farm cooperatives"—institutions forged by the nineteenth-century Populist movement (103). The grocer, Flanery, also illustrates the populist understanding of class. As a small business owner, Flanery and the farmers "are all in the same boat" (118). Although the Brownells and Flanery own land and businesses, they work to sustain them, and it is this tangibility of work that aligns them with the tenant farmers in their community.

The bankers, on the other hand, represent the ultimate parasites in the populist worldview. The fundamental tenets of populism, characteristic of both the agrarian revolts of the 1880s and '90s and the rural unrest of the 1930s, are opposition to banks and their legal privilege, monopoly over credit, and the acquisition of capital through nonproductive means.[56] Just as the Oklahomans in *The Grapes of Wrath* feel terrified and infuriated by the "monster bank," the Dunnes and their neighbors bristle within a system of modern finance in which they are at the mercy of nameless, faceless, institutional creditors. Characters in *Whose Names Are Unknown* actively defy the banks. Old "Granny Cyclone," for example, meets the bank representatives armed with a shotgun, warning them, "'What are you buzzards sailing around my farm for? Got your greedy hawk eyes on my wheat, eh? And your manikerred claws ready. Well, you ain't gonna git none of it. Just put that in your craw'" (66). Granny Cyclone's reference to "manikerred claws" emphasizes the nonproductive nature of the bankers' work and codes the bourgeoisie as effeminate.

Yet as the tough-talking, gun-toting grandmother suggests, Babb's novel does not code *women* as bourgeois. Instead, Babb revises the populist category of "producer" to include women. The nineteenth-century Populists viewed women (and African Americans) as dependents. Rather than being welcomed into the fraternity of producers, working women were seen as a sign of men's failure to earn a living for their families.[57] In the 1930s the family wage ideal persisted, marginalizing women in the labor movement. Advancing a working-class feminist consciousness, Babb constructs women as populist heroes. They labor alongside men in both productive and reproductive ways and defy a financial system and its elite managers who would rob them of the fruits of their labor. The Dunnes' neighbor Mrs. Starwood, for example, confronts the bank manager who threatens to foreclose on her farm. Mrs. Starwood, who "had been up and working for almost five hours before the bank opened," is more entitled in a moral sense to her farm than the white-collar bankers who own the mortgage (111). In presenting her case to the bank manager, Mrs. Starwood emphasizes her gender equality as well as her fiscal integrity: Even though her "husband is dead" and she's "got a houseful of children to raise," she can "work in the field like a man, and when there's a crop, [she'll] pay [her] debts" (112). In an act of defiance as audacious as Granny Cyclone's, she drops a dead skunk on the bank manager's desk.

The populist political culture of the Great Plains finds literary expression through the regionalist mode of Babb's fiction.[58] As Douglas Wixson notes, Babb "was determined to write of the High Plains people, who at that time were without a literature and too new to the land to create a history."[59]

While only the first four chapters of *The Grapes of Wrath* take place in Oklahoma, Babb devoted more than half of *Whose Names Are Unknown* to life in the dust bowl on the eve of migration. "Almost all of it is taken up with the Midwest, and the last is going to be concentrated stuff on California," she wrote to Collins, indicating the value she placed on these white settlers of the high plains beyond their role in the California labor crisis.[60] Devoted to telling the story of a people and a place as well as a political crisis, Babb emphasized setting and character in Part 1 of the novel. The narrative follows the slow and cyclical rhythms of the seasons, rather than following a plot punctuated by events. The relatively short novel is divided into forty-five chapters; these vignettes reflect Babb's predilection for short fiction, which is the preferred mode of regionalists.

Yet the novel differs from 1930s regionalism (and its nineteenth-century antecedent) in crucial ways. Less local color or regionalist by genre, the novel incorporates regionalist aesthetics into its social realism.[61] In nineteenth-century regionalist texts, a middle-class, worldly narrator mediates between like-minded readers and the static "folk" subjects, whose sentimental appeal lies in their pristine primitivism, untouched and untainted by modern life.[62] Long considered a minor form, regionalism has recently sparked the interest of critics who have reconsidered these texts as tools of nation building and U.S. imperialism in the postbellum era. Although 1930s regionalism was inspired by the Left and was more explicitly political (the idea for the Federal Writers' Project originated with the CP-led Author's League), it also constructed a national narrative of belonging that elided class conflict and racial differences.[63] As critics Lauren Coats and Nihad M. Farooq argue, writers who strove to "give voice" to the American people often wound up perpetuating stereotypes and speaking *for* marginal subcultures in a paternalistic way.[64] One editor implied that Steinbeck's regionalism was hampered by such caricatures, praising Babb's book for being "more honest, moving, and human than much of the stuff in THE GRAPES OF WRATH."[65] Steinbeck's flat characters and condescending anecdotes of migrant life irked dust bowl migrants at the time and account for the critical depreciation of the novel in more recent years.[66] Like Babb's editor, Ralph Ellison was moved by Babb's evocation of place: "In re-reading your novel I had the same feeling of an emotionally dense atmosphere I experienced during our first conversation, (coming up Park Avenue in the dark) that was more of Kansas and the plains than of a taxi and New York."[67] Unlike government-sponsored regionalists, Babb was free from the editorial constraints and ideological pressure of the Federal Writers' Project, and unlike Steinbeck, she had a reciprocal relationship with the people she represented. In her hands, literary regionalism was a female-centered strategy of resistance against the capitalist exploitation of farmworkers' productive *and* reproductive labor, rather than a tool for constructing an isolated, unchanging "folk."[68]

The high plains landscape is a powerful presence in the first half of the novel. Babb is at her best as a writer in her ability to find language that evokes a landscape characterized by the *absence* of physical features. For example, the landscape figures prominently in Babb's description of the events surrounding the premature birth of Julia Dunne's baby. Julia and her little girls traveled miles to buy milk from a wealthy neighbor, who sent her home despite an impending storm in order to avoid feeding them dinner. Julia gets caught in the terrific storm, which induces early labor, and the baby dies. As this scene suggests, storms are belligerent forces that antagonize humans, blowing rain "against them in sharp little spears" (36) and dust "against their shoes in a low flurry" (78). Babb uses sublime imagery to capture the extremeness of storms on the high plains, a characteristic of a region with no natural barriers to tame the wind. A summer storm is a sentient, malevolent being, "whipping the rain into a great swishing silver tail that lashed across the plains" (36). Likewise, an April dust storm "was an evil monster coming on in mysterious, footless silence . . . magnificent and horrible like a nightmare of destiny towering over their slight world that had every day before this impressed upon them its vast unconquerable might" (78). After the storm, Julia's husband, Milt, goes out to the fields to bury his son. The sublime Oklahoma sky transforms his personal grief and resentment into an aesthetic experience tied to a particular geography. When he finished covering the grave, Milt "stood still looking at the pure circle of earth around him, the far, smooth, lonely plain. The earth was very clean and fresh after the rain. He could see the long straight fences miles away. They were frail and small so far beneath the great clear morning sky" (45). In this passage, Babb uses the language of geometry—a "pure circle," "smooth" and "clear"—to render this geography of apparent emptiness, with its "vast," "immense" arid plains that "seemed unpeopled and deserted," marked only by fence posts (129). As Milt Dunne stands under an open sky, he contemplates his son's stillbirth, which was induced not only by a sudden summer storm but also by poverty and social inequality. Babb creates a sense of place that shapes the consciousness of her characters as profoundly as their economic conditions and political culture.

The regionalist aesthetics of Part 1 of the novel highlight a sense of place rather than the action of the plot, allowing Babb to foreground Julia Dunne's domestic experience. Contesting the assumption that space is a fixed and static category, Hsuan L. Hsu reconceptualizes "regions" as "dynamic and flexible units of production" that "can be as dialectical as time."[69] Regional literature thus gives expression to the repetitive routines of rural women's daily lives, which are dynamic in relation to space but less so in relation to time, and thus marginalized in the plot-driven realist novel. For example, Julia speaks directly to the reader in one chapter through diary entries, a form that allows for repetition and thus the textual representation of activities like housework, child-rearing, and waiting out a monthlong dust storm. Babb borrowed the language, structure, and content of her mother's own diary, written in April 1935. The diary records the worst of the dust storms to plague the high plains, a storm that blackened the skies of Oklahoma and Kansas and sent grit as far east as Washington, D.C. Babb copied much of the diary verbatim into the novel, editing her mother's run-on sentences for readability but preserving much of her language. While the novel's narrator evokes the enormity of a prairie storm with sublime imagery, the diary entries (both historical and fictional) convey the enormity of a dust storm through relentless repetition: "a fierce dirty day," "dirt still blowing," "blowing all night again," "still blowing," "blew all night," and so on (90–93). The diary entries lengthen during breaks in the storm, detailing housework that creates a sense of a feminized retaliation against the natural world in which the armaments are, in Jennie Babb's words, "dust rags and brooms and electric sweepers."[70] Babb recognized the social and literary value of her mother's diary, incorporating it into the novel to give expression to rural women's domestic labor.

Babb's female perspective on the dust bowl crisis contrasts with Woody Guthrie's masculine perspective in *Dust Bowl Ballads*. Guthrie recorded the album with RCA Victor in 1940, riding the popularity of Steinbeck's *Grapes of Wrath* to garner support for tenant farmers and migratory workers. The song "The Great Dust Storm (Dust Storm Disaster)" describes the storms of April 1935 and culminates with an image of utter destruction. Dust "covered up our fences, it covered up our barns / It covered up our tractors in this wild and dusty storm." Guthrie focuses on the storm's impact on the masculine spaces of the fields, buildings, and tractors. In contrast to Babb's image of housewives armed with brooms, Guthrie's domestic space is passive. Gripped by fear, the family "was crowded into their little room, / They thought the world had ended, and they thought it was their doom."[71]

Another song, "Dust Can't Kill Me," expresses "stubborn resistance to defeat in the face of America's greatest ecological disasters," according to Mark Allan Jackson, but it is also a particularly masculine resistance.[72] The male speaker laments that the dust kills "my baby," "my family," "my homestead," "my home," "my house," and "furniture"—all domestic entities—while proclaiming his own survival: "dust can't kill me."[73] Similarly, in "Dusty Old Dust (So Long, It's Been Good to Know You)" and "I Ain't Got No Home," the male speaker loses his wife and home, and he is left "driftin' along."[74] In Guthrie's dust bowl ballads, dust storms and equally brutal economic forces dispossess male speakers of home and family. Underlying this dispossession, however, is a sense of liberation of a male individual unencumbered by domesticity.

Although Babb made few changes to her mother's diary, she did significantly alter the final entries in order to use Julia's domestic struggles as the family's motivation for leaving the dust bowl. Whereas Jennie's factual diary ends on a positive note with an April morning "warm and nice," Julia's fictional diary concludes with the death of a neighbor and the "dust still blowing" (95). The dust storm wreaks its destruction both physically and linguistically, killing neighbors and silencing the diarist. The last entry reads, "No use to keep on writing dust, dust, dust. Seems it will outlast us" (95). By modifying her mother's diary, Babb shows how the environmental crisis impacts Julia's home as well as Milt's crops. Her fictional rendering of the "push" factors in the dust bowl migration thus balances the masculine implications of an agricultural bust with the domestic image of a home besieged by dust.

Sanora Babb is a recent addition to an ever-expanding cohort of radical women writers from the 1930s—Tillie Olsen, Meridel Le Sueur, Marita Bonner, Josephine Herbst, Ramona Lowe, Fielding Burke, Myra Page, Grace Lumpkin, and many others—whose work has been recovered, reprinted, and reconsidered by feminist critics in the past few decades. These women writers investigated the relationship between gender oppression and capitalism, stimulating debates within the CP at the time and building a foundation for feminist thinking of a later generation.[75] The CP's record on the "Woman Question" is mixed: While it replicated the sexist, androcentric assumptions of the dominant culture and marginalized female members, it also offered women political opportunities, organized female workers, supported housewives' boycotts and community organizing, and advocated for day care, maternity leave, and birth control.[76] The Party's women's magazine, the Woman Worker (renamed Woman

Today in the Popular Front period), was the principal publishing outlet for radical female writers, and it urged militant strategies for addressing working women's issues. Three female Party members, Grace Hutchins, Mary Inman, and Rebecca Pitts, were instrumental in developing a class analysis of women's work and subordinate social status. Hutchins's book *Women Who Work* (1934) popularized the notion of a woman's "double yoke" of wage labor and domestic duties. Inman and Pitts insisted on the centrality of housework and child-rearing to capitalist production. Published serially in the Party's West Coast magazine, *People's World*, in 1939, Inman's *In Women's Defense* argued that housework produces and reproduces labor power and therefore cannot be considered separately from male wage labor. Party leader Avram Landy disagreed, claiming that "it is because the husband is exploited that the housewife's position is wretched and miserable."[77] Women on the Left articulated a working-class feminism that was met with uneven responses from the CP. Lacking the language and infrastructure of an organized women's movement, Babb articulates an incipient feminism that challenges this view of women's struggles as derivative of the exploitation of male wage labor.

In her California writings, Babb shows how capitalism demands both wage labor and reproductive labor from women. In addition to her novel, Babb wrote articles on migrant labor conditions for radical magazines such as the *New Masses*. In her article "Farmers without Farms" published in the *New Masses* in June 1938, Babb described in vivid detail how women suffer the physical brunt of poverty as they struggle to earn wages as well as carry, bear, and breastfeed children. Babb reported the shocking disparity between the national average infant mortality rate of 52 per 1,000 births and the rate in the San Joaquin Valley of 139 per 1,000 births.[78] Babb's article walks the reader through the migrant camps, offering a personal glimpse of the residents' privation, devoid of condescension or voyeuristic thrill. Babb's essay is an example of radical reportage, which Marxist critics considered to be the most effective genre in effecting social change. They characterized reportage as "three-dimensional reporting" that allowed the reader to "see and feel the facts." It aimed to narrow the gap between writer, reader, and working-class subject. These concise, breathless articles were published quickly, connecting readers to the revolutionary movement as it unfolded.[79] While the majority of Babb's article emphasizes the pride and dignity of migrants, the final two paragraphs shift to an alarming tone as she recounts migrant women's reproductive struggles: "Many of them have no other choice than giving birth to their already malnourished babies without proper medical care, lying on a dirty mattress or a spring on the ground floor, with newspapers for sheets and possibly the help of the camp neighbors. Such a mother must suffer the heightened pains of an underfed body, and often find that she has no milk for her child."[80] Babb's outrage over the health crisis faced by childbearing women is evident in her field notes as well. She recorded the grisly story of a woman who gave birth to a premature baby at home. While she was "too ill to know" what was happening to the baby, the "grasshoppers chewed it." The parents took the baby to the hospital, where doctors conducted highly invasive and inhumane experiments, denying her milk and water, until her "tongue was like dry leather." When they brought the baby home, she was "covered with needle holes" "crusted with dirt," and "infected where slashes had been made."[81] The baby died after a few days. A photograph of a starving infant taken by Dorothy Babb matches Sanora's fiery indignation over the utter lack of health care for expectant mothers and their children (see Figure 1). According to Joseph Entin, such visual and textual images of "wounded proletarian bodies" reveal the limits of literature and photographs to represent the material conditions of poverty, and their grotesque forms reflect the efforts to transcend these limits.[82]

Babb's experimentation with what Entin calls "sensational modernism" seems to be more pronounced in her unpublished field notes and reportage, receding as she reaches toward a more mainstream audience in her novel and stories. Reportage allowed Babb to link personal narrative, a traditionally feminine form of writing, to the masculine realm of political economy.[83] This genre particularly suited Babb, who felt connected to the dust bowl migrants through her personal history, and whose empathy toward her subjects animates her writing.

In her novel, Babb softens the grotesque imagery of miscarriages and dying babies that appears in her reportage. Nevertheless, scenes of failed birth play a crucial role. The novel has two tragic birth scenes: In Oklahoma, the Dunnes' baby dies shortly after his premature birth, and in California, a migrant woman's malnourished baby dies within minutes of being born. Both these incidents are key events in the development of the characters' political consciousness. United by tragedies such as these, the migrant workers form a union and organize a strike. Although the strike ultimately fails, it portends class revolution in embryo. As Ralph Ellison put it in a personal letter to Babb, "It is [Julia's] 'misscarriage' that forshadows the 'stillborn strike.'"[84] Scenes of failed birth serve as female-centered counterparts

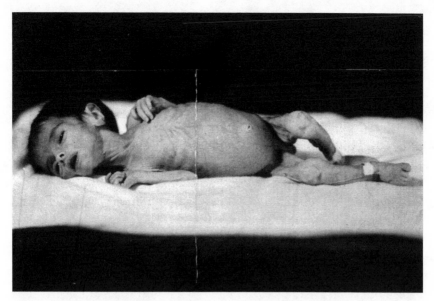

Figure 1. Photograph of a starving child of dust bowl migrants, by Dorothy Babb (ca. 1938). Courtesy of Harry Ransom Center, University of Texas at Austin.

to the strike as a catalyst for conversion to class consciousness. Like strikes, births bring the community together in a common cause, then raise class-consciousness and incite political action when this cause fails.

In the migrant camp in California, the failure of a literal birth delivers a figurative birth of class consciousness and collective action. The Dunnes arrive in California hungry and homeless and seek shelter at a government camp. While Milt desperately seeks food for his starving family, one of their neighbors goes into labor. Forced to deliver the baby in a dirty tent because the hospital would not admit her, the laboring woman screams: "'I have to suffer like this because we're poor, that's why, only poor!'" (141). The woman's travail motivates Milt to think beyond his own family and to join his neighbors in a collective effort. When the camp manager gives him a task, he "forgot his hunger and his hungry children. . . . In a little while the whole street had come alive, and women were rushing about, speaking to neighbors they had not met before, finding rags, asking for baby clothes" (141). Like the occupational accidents or strike violence common in male-authored proletarian novels, childbirth in Babb's novel generates the community solidarity—spearheaded by women—that forms the foundation of organized protest. Using reproductive metaphors, Babb feminizes the discourse of class.

While reproductive experiences prompt changes in class consciousness, the conditions of migrant labor in California prompt changes in the *gender* consciousness for both female and male characters. High food prices and low wages force all family members to work in the fields, which violates the Dunnes' customary division of labor. At first, Milt defies his boss by refusing to let his wife pick cotton. He experiences class exploitation as a threat to his masculinity and resists by asserting control over Julia's labor. Julia, however, insists on picking, and her wage labor gives her greater voice in the family: "'Oh shut up!'" she fires at Milt when he claims derisively that her wages have made her "feel [her] oats" (182).

While Julia feels empowered by wage work, she also transforms her traditional role of feeding the family into a radical act. The struggle for food is a driving force behind the novel, reflecting the centrality of Julia's consciousness in the narrative. The family's economic decline is measured by the declining nutritional value of their meals: buttered bread and chicken at a neighbor's house during a good harvest, a scanty feast of tiny snowbirds during a lean winter, crusts of bread dipped in pepper tea in California. While the strikers demand higher wages, Julia demands food for her children by stealing bread. She imagines herself as a Robin Hood figure as she "dreamed for a moment of taking the basket and bringing it back for the camp" (213). Her awareness of class inequality transformed not only her moral outlook on property rights but also her gender consciousness. "It would not be wrong" to take the bread, she thought, but only to "suffer in silence, and wait—the way she had always done, erasing herself" (214).

Perhaps the most radicalized woman in the novel is Frieda, the daughter of the Dunnes' prosperous neighbors, the Brennermans. Though economically secure, Frieda left Oklahoma because her marriage prospects had dwindled as she aged, and she sought something more out of life than to be an old farmer's wife. Although Babb marries Frieda off in the end, she is no ordinary wife but a budding labor organizer, jailed for her strike activity. An activist in training, she "wants to know as much about her business as the people who hire us do about theirs" (208). Finally, the strike also prompts a transformation in the gender consciousness of Milt. In the final pages of the novel, Milt has an epiphany that is not a conversion to class consciousness but a commitment to an egalitarian marriage: "He made up his mind to talk to [Julia] in a new way, and she would be able to talk to him. They had been hard-pressed for a long time, or maybe they had never really known each other very well. It startled him to think like this" (217). While Milt's conversion to class consciousness happens rather quietly earlier in the novel, his adoption of a more egalitarian model for marriage is climactic. By fore-grounding Julia's domestic labor, using reproductive metaphors for class struggle, and envisioning gender equality as a prerequisite for class solidarity, Babb places the CP's Woman Question at the center of the class struggle.

Babb's Vision of Interracial Unionism

Babb stands out among dust bowl documentarians and radical writers more generally not only for her incipient feminism but also for her commitment to antiracism. Babb drew explicit parallels between regional and ethnic subcultures, attributing to the dust bowl people "some cultural rawness . . . that has not been overcome, and shows up clearly in neighborhoods of foreign-born and Americans together."[85] As a member of a regional subculture, Babb identified with ethnic and African American workers in California and recognized their centrality to the agricultural industry and labor protests. Babb felt marginalized by members of the eastern literary establishment who used the "stinging word" "regional" "to try to keep writers outside of NY in their places."[86] Throughout her life, moreover, Babb lived in interracial communities. In the beginning of her memoir, *An Owl On Every Post*, Babb remembers leaving the Indian community in which she lived as a child: "All the way on the train from the Indian country of Oklahoma to the flat plains of Colorado east of the Rocky Mountains, my mother and I were sad; she to leave household and friends, and a town, however small; I, to leave my pinto pony and the Oto Indians near Red Rock, my other family, my other home."[87] Long after leaving Oklahoma Territory, Babb still answered to the name the Oto Indians had given her, "Little Cheyenne Who Rides Like the Wind."

Babb's cross-racial empathy not only welded friendships but also inspired literary creation. In his semiautobiographical narrative *America Is in the Heart*, Filipino writer Carlos Bulosan based the characters Alice and Eileen Odell on Sanora Babb and her sister, Dorothy. As Michael Denning explains, Bulosan's narrator shares a similar family background, migration experience, and literary talent with the Odell sisters, and their friendship is an exception to the violent, broken relationships that pervade the narrative. Dorothy Babb's fictional persona embodies the promise of America for Bulosan's narrator: "She was undeniably the *America* I had wanted to find in those frantic days of fear and flight, in those acute hours of hunger and loneliness."[88] Bulosan professed his love to Sanora in a series of letters in 1936, thanking her profusely for "this human love you gave me, this tenderness I felt in you, this loveliness I gathered from you, this understanding I noted from you."[89] In turn, it is likely that Babb based the character of Pedro, the Filipino strike organizer in *Whose Names*, on Bulosan, who wrote Babb several letters from the labor union office near Santa Maria during the "Salad Bowl Strike" of 1935. In these letters, he draws parallels between the art of writing and manual labor, and Babb uses similar techniques to represent labor organizers' planning sessions in her novel.[90] Babb's lived experience of integration may explain one of the crucial differences between her novel and Steinbeck's *Grapes of Wrath*: its racially and ethnically inclusive representation of the California agricultural strikes of the mid-1930s. Whereas Steinbeck erases workers of color from both *Grapes* and *In Dubious Battle*, Babb recognizes Mexican and Filipino leadership in these protests.

In order to envision racially inclusive mass unionism, Babb had to deal with the issue of the Okies' whiteness—the interlocking forces of their identity as white citizens, racist attitudes, and racial privilege.[91] She was troubled by the prejudice of white migratory workers in California, particularly because the farm owners manipulated these views to keep their workers divided. In the journal she kept while working for the FSA in 1938, Babb stressed the "necessity of unity with Filipinos and Mexicans and all other racial minority groups," and she confronted the white dust bowl migrants about their attitudes toward workers of color. Babb continued: "After discussing this [problem of racial prejudice] with them, stressing the question as to whether they were fighting among themselves as workers of one race or another, or fighting together successfully against the big growers and corporation owners who were pleased with their squabbling, they seemed to have no difficulty understanding this problem. It was a fine thing to hear them explaining this to others, and encouraging friendly relations."[92] Proximity and shared class interests did alter the racial views of some migrants. In the FSA camp in Arvin, for example, a group of migrants from Texas demanded the expulsion of Mexican camp residents, but after a couple of months they elected Mexican representatives to the camp council.[93] More common, however, were Okie efforts to delineate a color line that had been blurred by their dire economic circumstances, outsider status, and performance of jobs usually relegated to African American and foreign-born workers. Okies clashed with African American migrants in the San Joaquin Valley, for example, when they were faced with the prospect of sending their children to integrated schools.[94] These tensions escalated into full-blown hostilities in the 1940s as white and black migrants competed for industrial jobs, housing, and recreational space during the war.

In light of these circumstances, Babb's optimism seems overblown. Labor historians now take it as a given that American workers had competing interests, and that white workers benefited economically from racial hierarchies.[95] Whiteness studies transformed labor history in the 1990s, as labor historians turned their attention to the racial identities of white workers and the structures of racial privilege they navigated, reviving a field that had fallen by the wayside as race replaced class as the preferred category of analysis in American studies and historical scholarship. Yet just as racial hierarchies cannot be reduced to a matter of economic interests, it is reductive to explain workers' beliefs and behavior solely based on race. A monolithic understanding of "whiteness" fails to explain why unions integrated before other institutions, for example, or the vilification of white migrants in California.[96] Viewing working-class history through the single lens of race tends to flatten a complex cultural landscape. Mexican, white, Filipino, and African American migratory workers interacted with one another, with growers, with the organized Left, and with the state in ways that were shaped by this complex web of market forces, racial ideologies, and political contingencies. Babb's novel may not help us make sense of questions of political economy, but it does shed light on the cultural discourses that shaped them. Babb creates a vision of Popular Front unity not only by insisting on the shared class interests of migrant workers but also by suggesting their shared status as ethnic outsiders. While her liberal peers defended the Okies' rights as white citizens, Babb highlighted the permeable boundaries of whiteness in order to make room for class-based unity.

The narrator of *Whose Names* acknowledges the racial division of labor, as well as housing segregation and the lack of due process of the law for nonwhite agricultural workers. Yet whereas Steinbeck and McWilliams saw the white citizenship of the Okies as a political asset, Babb saw it as tenuous, outweighed by the harsh prejudice they encountered in California. In fact, she highlights the migrants' lack of *state* citizenship, which made them ineligible for relief. A resident of a migrant camp laments, "'If we ain't citizens a this state we ain't nothin' by their way of thinkin.'"[97] Babb recognized that whiteness has varying degrees and thus considered the Okies a kind of ethnic minority without full access to the cultural and material benefits of differential treatment based on race. In her 1938 missive to CP organizers in southern California, Babb claimed that the Okies would not abandon the labor movement once their economic conditions improved because the type of discrimination they faced was actually racial in nature. "There are any number of reasons why a relief check or a job will not slow them up," she writes. "The Jim-Crowism practiced against them and their children in school as 'Okies' is one of them."[98] As her term "Jim-Crowism for the worker" suggests,[99] Babb uses African American experience as a model for understanding the experience of dust bowl migrants. In the field notes upon which Babb based the novel, she observed "the thousands of women who are continually asking that migratory workers' children not be permitted to attend public schools along with their children, that the men and women be sterilized because they are poor, that they be driven out, and so on."[100] Babb's sense of the Okies as "not quite white" recognizes the variations within this racial category, thus anticipating "whiteness studies" by half a century. While some critics may see Babb's vision of interracial solidarity as an example of the Old Left's subordination of race to class, I see it as her effort to demonstrate the inseparability of these categories.

Babb explicitly racializes the label "Okie," which marks the migrants as inferior outsiders. Paralleling a common motif in African American literature, the migrant children experience a sudden awareness of their social difference upon hearing the ethnic slur. *An okie. Something bad?" the children wonder. "An okie is me. Why does it hurt?"*[101] When the Dunne family reaches California, a state resident yells, "'This goddamned okie got fresh with my wife,'" spurring on a posse that shouts, "'Get out of the way, okies, or we'll give you some. . . . Git outa the way, you white niggers!'" (154). The term "white nigger" dates back to the 1850s and was a white-on-white slur used when poor white people accepted work usually relegated to black people, or when they crossed political or behavioral boundaries separating white and black people.[102] In accusing the "okie" of making a pass at his wife, the vigilante invokes the same triangular lynch myth that was used to terrorize black men. This scene creates a common ground for black and white migrants through shared oppression. Yet Babb's use of the lynching trope risks downplaying the unique racial terror experienced by African Americans. Moreover, the term "white niggers" may actually reinforce the color line, particularly for readers whose sympathy for the Okies is heightened by the idea that white Americans are being treated like black people. Yet as Matt Wray has recently argued, the term "white trash" is a "boundary term that speaks equivocally and ambivalently to the question of belonging and membership in the category *white*, and one that mobilizes a wide array of social differences to do so."[103] "Okie" is a similar boundary term that mobilizes differences of region, culture, religion, and class to question white migrants' membership in the broader white community.

For Babb's protagonist, Milt Dunne, the experience of being called an "okie" erodes his sense of racial superiority and awakens him to class consciousness. Introducing himself to a black worker named Garrison as they worked side by side picking cotton, "Milt waited automatically to hear the 'suh' and when it did not come, he was relieved. He had been wondering how he would say it, tell him not to. *We're both picking cotton for the same hand-to-mouth wages. I'm no better'n he is; he's no worse.* The memory of being called a white nigger in Imperial Valley lay in his mind unforgotten, sore, like an exposed nerve. Milt looked at him. Garrison looked back, his eyes straight, and there was no difference" (185, emphasis in original).[104] This passage highlights Milt's memory of ethnic name-calling as a formative moment that paves the way for an interracial alliance. As a migrant, Milt learns what it means to be an outsider, and he recognizes the common ground he shares with a black man along lines of class. Perhaps counterintuitively, white workers in *Whose Names* must first acquire a kind of ethnic identity based on regional origins in order to advance a class-based movement.

Milt's individual transformation soon translates into collective action. After the cotton pickers initiate a spontaneous walkout, Milt and four others gather in Garrison's home and meet with the union leaders, a white American named John Lacy and a Filipino man named Pedro. Babb creates a tableau of interracial and cross-gender alliance: "[Pedro] began to question the men, and in a few minutes they were all talking in turn, suggesting, questioning, explaining, planning. Sweat broke out on Lacy's forehead, and Pedro took off his leather jacket. Smoke lay above the table like a fog bank. Garrison talked in his slow, sensible way, and sometimes Phoebe spoke, reminding them of something they had forgotten" (195). This passage depicts the unity of the black, white, and Filipino workers through visual, sensual, and aural images. Gathered around a table and ensconced in a smoky "fog bank," they merge into a collective entity. Their bodies respond in unison to the heat generated by the summer night and the intensity of their discussion. Above all, the act of speaking, the interplay of voices "all talking in turn," symbolizes the egalitarianism of the moment. The succession of verbs in the present progressive ("suggesting, questioning, explaining, planning") emphasizes the physical action of conversing. Speech is an active force. The strong, articulate voices in this passage stand in sharp contrast to the repeated representation of the characters in other points in the novel as "wordless" (38). They do not gain a voice until this moment, when they join with others across boundaries of ethnicity, race, and gender. This tableau attests to the central role of migration in bringing about interracial working-class solidarity: Each figure converged upon California from a different homeland—the American South, the Great Plains, and the Philippines.

Although we do not hear her voice or the content of her comments in this passage, the African American woman leader, Phoebe, participates in the planning. Garrison, her husband, calls her "Madame Chairman" when he thanks her for her input, but it comes across as patronizing, since there is no explanation of this reference. Phoebe's character is based on a woman Babb encountered while working in the migrant camps. Babb wrote in her field notes, "Be sure to put in novel about Negro committee with woman chairman—and conversation." Babb was inspired by the black female chairman's comments to a labor organizer: "You ain't white and you ain't yellow and you ain't brown—youse all them colors in one!"[105] Babb also saved a handwritten note, signed by Bettie Steward, that offers a glimpse of black female leadership in the camps: "We colored people and hour manager don't seam to be cooperation together so good I don't know what the trouble are We have tried in every way we knowed to do hour deauty and obey the camp roolr but it seam like we just can't please the manager of coarest we might be wrong but he never give us a smile If he will only smile we will smile with him."[106] Though a mere fragment of the historical record, this short note captures an instance of black women's political activism. Steward writes in a confident tone that asserts her leadership and her moral authority. In claiming that "we colored people" "tried in every way . . . to do our [duty]," Steward makes a claim for citizenship based on unfettered opportunity to fulfill responsibilities, rather than on entitlement to state resources. In framing black citizenship on the notion of "responsibility" rather than "rights," Steward draws on a strong tradition in African American history that is often misconstrued in public debates about African Americans and their relationship to the state.[107] Phoebe is remarkable as a black female presence in a scene of interracial unionism. Yet we see more of black women's participation in camp politics in Bettie Steward's note than we do in Babb's novel. Responding to Babb's unpublished manuscript in 1943, Ellison noticed Babb's timid handling of African American characters in the novel, advising her, "Don't be afraid of the Negro, you know enough to give a deeper insight into Garrison even though he doesn't demand much attention."[108]

The underdevelopment of Garrison's character may have less to do with Babb's racial unease than with a larger structural weakness of the novel. Part 1, which takes place in the high plains, is more textured and vivid than the California portion of the novel. This unevenness has consequences for the gender politics of the novel, as Julia's consciousness recedes in the second half. As Ellison noted, the novel "would have had an even greater impact upon me had you organized it more closely around Julia's consciousness, since it is her 'misscarriage' that forshadows the 'stillborn strike' and the frustrations which lead up to the migration and accompany it, since her journey from bread (bakery) to breadlessness (pepper tea) furnishes the pattern for the whole."[109] When Babb wrote of the Dunnes' struggle to make a living in the arid plains, she wrote out of deep personal experience. The lyrical descriptions of the natural world, the sensitive evocation of family relationships, the innovative depiction of housework, and the lively vignettes of rural culture suited the episodic, regionalist form of the first half of the novel. The California portion seems rushed, and Babb may have done more justice to the dire conditions of migrant labor in her hard-hitting reportage.

In the resolution of the novel, Babb offers a vision of working-class solidarity that is predicated on the populist dissent and cooperative culture the migrants brought with them. Yet there is a didactic quality to the ending that tarnishes an otherwise subtle treatment of a multifaceted social struggle. In the final lines of the novel, the narrator gives poetic voice to the workers' vow to stick together: "One thing was left, as clear and perfect as a drop of rain—the desperate need to stand together as one man. They would rise and fall and, in their falling, rise again" (222). Ellison criticized this resolution, which "should have been . . . given in terms of their voices, their idioms, their emotions, not yours."[110] Ellison implies that Babb had committed one of the "didactic sins" of radical literature by imposing her consciousness on her characters and fulfilling her "wish" for revolution through an optimistic ending.[111] Of all the debates surging through the Left press in the 1930s, the issue of didacticism perhaps loomed largest. In 1937, the editor of the *Partisan Review*, Philip Rahv, broke with the Communist Party and launched through the pages of his magazine an attack on proletarian literature, which he deplored as "the literature of a party disguised as the literature of a class."[112] Rahv coined the term "leftism," by which he meant the use of art as political propaganda, and he accused Granville Hicks and the *New Masses* as its chief practitioners. Liberal critics also dismissed proletarian literature as sterile, didactic, and stifled by its quasi-religious adherence to a party line. Marxist critic Edwin Seaver vigorously rebutted this charge in his piece "Sterile Writers and Proletarian Religions," published in the *New Masses* in 1933. Seaver insisted that "the revolutionary orientation of the younger writers is not . . . a sign of their sterility. It is, on the contrary, a sign of rebirth and rededication of creative energies that were in danger of evaporating completely. It is the repudiation of sterility."[113] More recent scholarship suggests that Rahv's attack on the *New Masses* was sectarian and overblown. In *Radical Representations*, for example, Barbara Foley argues convincingly that despite the ingrained perception of proletarian fiction as propagandistic, Marxist critics deplored didacticism, and the CP issued no clear "party line" on aesthetic matters.[114] These debates often focused on the endings of literary works, which seemed to have a special role in moving the reader. "Anybody can write the first two acts of a revolutionary play," wrote Mike Gold in 1934. "It is the last act, the act that resolves the conflicts, that has baffled almost every revolutionary playwright and novelist in the country."[115] Worker-writer Jack Conroy agreed that one of the "major concerns" of the proletarian writer was to convince readers of the "reality and inevitability" of a revolutionary climax, and he gave for an example an ending in which "the strike is lost but the workers, undaunted, pledge themselves to continue the struggle." His example indicates the clichéd quality of Babb's ending.

Yet a letter from a migrant worker, Henry Selb, calls into question the charge that Babb lapsed into didacticism by resolving the conflict too neatly and imposing her consciousness on her characters. Accounting for the failure of the cotton strike, Selb assured Babb that his fellow strikers vowed to "get to gather and work harder to organize than ever before" and to "stick together like brothers and sisters should in a union."[116] A migrant character in the novel paraphrases Selb: "I reckon we feel kind of like brothers and sisters, as we say in the union . . . and we can get to where we're going together" (218). Arguably, Babb gave voice to Selb's consciousness rather than imposing her own. Ellison's critique nevertheless indicates the challenge of meeting the aesthetic demand of realism to "show, don't tell" while advancing a political goal. Babb's otherwise subtle prose and three-dimensional characters caused Ellison to remark, "It is ironical that one of the most mature novels of a strike was not published."[117]

There is much to be gained from this lost novel of the dust bowl migration. In the past two decades, scholars of the literary Left have nearly exorcised the ghosts of Cold War anticommunism, offering more positive evaluations of the aesthetics of proletarian and Popular Front literature, its racial and gender politics, and the relationship between women and minorities and the Left. As "one of the most mature novels of a strike," Babb's work can take its rightful place at the center of this revisionist project. But it does more than validate 1930s political art as worthy of scholarly attention; it revises our understanding of 1930s politics and culture. First, recovering

Sanora Babb challenges the perception that populism impeded the more radical antiracist and anticapitalist goals of the Popular Front. The dust bowl migration dominates American popular memory of the Great Depression, yet scholars tend to dismiss its cultural representations as emblematic of mainstream populism that elided racial conflicts by using white rural families to symbolize "the people." Many scholars of the 1930s Left tell a story of decline, beginning in Scottsboro in 1933, the height of Third Period interracial radicalism, and ending in California in 1939, a moment of whitewashed, patriotic, Popular Front unity.[118] Babb's novel complicates this assessment, as it melds midwestern populism with Marxism and crafts a racial-and gender-inclusive image of "the people" that also recognizes structures of privilege. Second, Babb's novel, field notes, and reportage reveal the migrant crisis in California as an important chapter in Left feminism, the contours of which remain to be fully explored. By connecting women's reproductive struggles to the issues of unemployment, depressed wages, and welfare policy, Babb reoriented the Left discourse of gender from its focus on the exploited male worker and his dependents to the family as an integrated source of labor power. Finally, the connections between Babb's novel and William Attaway's novel of the Great Migration, *Blood on the Forge*, to which we turn next, challenges critical categories that place "proletarian" novels and "African American literature" into separate categories. The tensions and continuities between African American and white migration narratives call for an integrated approach to understanding the 1930s Left and its literary production.

CHAPTER 3

STEEL MILL BLUES

Like Sanora Babb, William Attaway was both insider and outsider to the Great Migration that he depicted in his novel *Blood on the Forge*. Attaway was six when his middle-class family migrated to Chicago from Mississippi in 1911. The Attaways could afford to leave the South before labor-starved northern factories opened their gates to southern workers during World War I. A doctor and a teacher, Attaway's parents provided him with a college education that they hoped would launch his medical career. Economic stability and education gave Attaway the freedom and skills to become a writer, while his rebellion against his parents' bourgeois values led him to seek a different kind of learning. Attaway left the University of Illinois after two years to ride the rails and work as a labor organizer. When he returned to Chicago in 1935, he landed at the epicenter of the black Popular Front.

African Americans were hit the hardest during the Depression, and Chicago was among the hardest-hit cities. Half of the black workers in Chicago were out of work, and the city's emergency relief funds were tapped out by 1932. Former sources of support, such as the Urban League and African American charities, buckled under the burden of this overwhelming poverty.[1] Provoked by this economic collapse and sustained by the vitality of the black Left, African American writers and artists fought for a better society. "I want to do murals and paintings, to influence people," painter Bernard Goss reported to novelist Willard Motley in 1940. "I might be called a revolutionary painter. I'm not satisfied with social and economic conditions. My aim is to do something about them."[2] The African American fellow travelers that Attaway met in Chicago wrestled with the tensions between race and class. Would class-based organizing adequately address racial discrimination, lynching, barriers to voting, and other violations of African American rights? Was the black bourgeoisie an ally or an enemy of working-class African Americans? Was the nationalist character of African American culture at odds with the goals of proletarian revolution? Whereas Babb strove to expand the dust bowl migrants' often nativist populism into a more racially inclusive, Marxist vision of an egalitarian society, Attaway struggled to reconcile African American migrants' nationalistic impulses.

The black Popular Front in Chicago was sustained by New Deal programs, African American institutions, and informal networks. According to writer Arna Bontemps, a luminary of the Harlem Renaissance who also moved to Chicago in 1935, "Harlem got its renaissance in the middle 'twenties, centering around the *Opportunity* contests and the Fifth Avenue Awards Dinners. Ten years later Chicago reenacted it on WPA without finger bowls but with increased power."[3] Attaway was among the two dozen or so African American writers employed by the Illinois Federal Writers' Project, which provided crucial financial support for emerging authors and fostered interracial exchange.[4] Another New Deal–sponsored center for creation, exhibition, instruction, and interaction that sustained the black Popular Front into the 1940s was the South Side Community Art Center (SSCAC). In 1941 artists employed by the Illinois Art Project created the art center from the ruins of a broken-down house in Chicago's largest black neighborhood. Artists at the SSCAC connected their art to the social conditions that surrounded them. Charles White, for example, validated the role of the artist during an urgent social crisis: "Paint is the only weapon I have with which to fight what I resent. If I could write I would write about it. If I could talk I would talk about it. Since I paint, I must paint about it."[5] In addition to these New Deal programs, African American institutions provided crucial publishing outlets and social networks for radical writers and artists in this period. The flagship black newspaper, the *Chicago Defender*, under new leadership after the passing of Robert S. Abbot in 1940, provided fertile ground for the African American Left by publishing editorials, advertisements, news stories, and poetry that supported radical causes. African American little magazines, such as *Negro Story*, also published fledgling radical writers who may otherwise have struggled to find an outlet for their work. The *Defender*'s staff members and contributors, many of whom, such as Jack Conroy, Langston Hughes, and Margaret Burroughs, were Communists or fellow travelers, worked closely with the SSCAC and *Negro Story*, cultivating personal and institutional networks that provided a solid base for African American social art.[6]

Attaway belonged to a circle of talented, radical writers that Bontemps described as a "writing clan," which included Richard Wright, Frank Marshall Davis, Margaret Walker, Willard Motley, and Gwendolyn Brooks.[7] Wright formed the South Side Writers' Group in 1936, which nurtured and politicized these young writers. Attaway recalled fondly to a *Daily Worker* reporter how Wright frightened a room full of straight-laced academics when he read his antilynching story "Big Boy Leaves Home." By the end of the reading, the audience had fled, Attaway remembered, "and only Dick and I were there."[8] Like Attaway, many of the writers in this circle were southern migrants, and they gave expression to the transformative power of this experience for themselves, their people, and the broader culture.[9] Wright left Mississippi for Chicago in 1927 and chronicled the experience in his autobiography, short stories, and photo-book, *12 Million Black Voices.* Margaret Walker and Arna Bontemps, both from Louisiana, sought higher education in Chicago. Walker's poem "For My People" traces the movement of "playmates in the clay and dust and sand of Alabama" to "47th Street in Chicago" where they fill "cabarets and taverns and other people's pockets."[10] Bontemps's history, *They Seek a City,* offers a long view of African American migration, narrating its history from the eighteenth-century settlement of the Midwest to the wartime migration to California. Although Attaway was only a child when he arrived in Chicago on the eve of the Great Migration, he became the "outstanding interpreter," the "one superbly deliberate, conscious artist" of this movement that changed America.[11]

Blood on the Forge is a historical novel set during the great steel strike of 1919, in which the socialist Left abandoned and vilified African American workers. It responds to present concerns about race and labor by revising the optimistic trope of the "New Negro" that proliferated during the Harlem Renaissance of the 1920s. The novel tells the tragic story of three brothers from the rural South who migrate to the steel mills near Pittsburgh in 1919. Their journey begins after Big Mat, the eldest brother, nearly kills a white man—a poor sharecropper like himself who had been raised to the ranks of "riding boss" by the landowner. Desperate, Big Mat and his brothers take up a labor agent's promise of higher wages and flee to the North. For a while, the brothers enjoy the camaraderie of their fellow workers—black and white—and revel in the pleasure of spending their wages. The sudden eruption of a labor strike, however, pits white unionists against black strikebreakers. Big Mat seizes the opportunity to become a police deputy so he can exercise power over white men. At the novel's climax, Big Mat suddenly sees his shared class interests with white workers, realizing that landowners and mill owners manipulated racial hatreds to divide them. But the realization comes too late: He then dies at the hands of a terrified white striker. Spiritually lost and grieving, his younger brother Melody abandons his guitar, which was his only connection to his revitalizing folk culture and means for adjusting to his new world. The novel closes as Melody observes the youngest brother, blinded from a mill accident, fumble with a cigarette with a blind World War I veteran as they ride the train toward the "running sore" of a Pittsburgh ghetto. This final image connects industrial capitalism with imperialist war and questions whether American workers can attain the vision necessary to overthrow this powerful system.

Attaway's grim memory of the Great Migration sharply contrasts with a powerful visual narrative that also made its debut in 1941: Jacob Lawrence's *Migration of the Negro*. Both Lawrence and Attaway viewed the Great Migration of 1919 through the lens of the present, yet Lawrence maintained the optimism of the New Negro and displayed less ambivalence about the promise of modernity. Lawrence's *Migration* series consists of sixty panels, each featuring a small format painting accompanied by a short caption, that comprise a historical narrative of African American migration during the 1910s. Although radical artists tended to prefer murals or reproducible graphic arts that could reach large audiences, Lawrence brought modernist art to the people by combining abstraction with simple, educational captions and representational forms. In comparing these literary and visual texts, one must consider how genre shapes the contours of meaning. As Stacy Morgan notes in his study of African American social realism, novelists and visual artists of the period aimed to reach the masses but did so in different ways. Muralists, graphic artists, and painters like Lawrence who produced art for the people often turned to historical allegory to comment on the root causes of social problems. Although critical of social injustice, their work tended to ring a hopeful note due to the public venues in which it was often exhibited. In contrast, social novelists like Attaway drew on the forms of literary naturalism to express the interior lives of poor, often politically naive characters and to examine the social forces that entrap them.[12] These genre conventions help to explain the divergence in tone in Lawrence's and Attaway's representations of the New Negro.

Though Lawrence was only twenty-three years old when he completed the *Migration* series, he was already an established professional artist, and the series received immediate critical acclaim. *Fortune* magazine published twenty-six panels on an eight-page spread in its November 1941 issue. The series toured the country the following year, finding permanent homes at the Museum of Modern Art and the Phillips Collection in Washington, D.C.[13]

Lawrence moved to Harlem at age thirteen in 1930 and was nurtured as an artist over the course of the decade by the Harlem Art Workshop, the YMCA, the WPA-sponsored Harlem Community Art Center, and the communist American Artists School.[14] Socially engaged artists opened their studios to young talents like Lawrence as well, providing space to work and to discuss political and social issues. Lawrence met William Attaway along with other left-leaning writers, artists, dancers, actors, and musicians at Charles Alston and Henry Bannarn's studio at 306 West 141st Street, known as "306." "At sixteen it was quite a learning experience," remembered Lawrence in an interview, "hearing [Attaway and others] discuss the topics of the day—as well as philosophy and creative processes pertaining to their own fields."[15] Lawrence's *Migration* series reflects the influence of the populist Left in its focus on working-class experience, its representation of everyday life, and its effort to inspire ordinary viewers.

Whereas Attaway's protagonists flee the South due to the threat of lynching, crammed into an overcrowded boxcar under the cover of darkness, Lawrence's migrants weigh their choices carefully, impelled mainly by economic opportunities. As art historian Patricia Hills notes, the first few panels discuss the economic push-pull forces that caused the migration; lynching and discrimination are not mentioned until panel 14.[16] The *Migration* series represents ordinary African American people as historical agents in a collective, grassroots movement. Lawrence emphasizes this sense of collectivity in the first panel of the series, which depicts a crowd of migrants at a train station with the caption, "During the World War there was a great migration North by Southern Negroes" (see Figure 2). The figures in the crowd form a solid mass of alternating green and black accented by splashes of bright red and yellow. Several formal elements convey the cohesion of the crowd: The limited palette creates a sense of uniformity; the figures face in the same direction; and their backs form parallel diagonal lines. The crowd crests into three peaks where the migrants file through doors marked by the destination cities of Chicago, New York, and St. Louis. This wavelike pattern infuses the image with motion and energy. This visual motif of the triangular mass repeats in panels 12, 18, 23, 35, and 40, forming a refrain reinforced by captions: "The migration gained in momentum" (panel 18); "And the migration spread" (panel 23); "They left the South in large numbers and they arrived in the North in large numbers" (panel 35); "The migrants arrived in great numbers" (panel 40). Lawrence's complex narrative captures the contradictions of the migration—its promises and its perils—and this refrain ties it together. Whereas Attaway's fugitive migrants are motivated by fear and violence, Lawrence's New Negroes act collectively in a mass movement.

Another difference between Attaway's novel and Lawrence's visual narrative is their representations of modernity. As the title *Blood on the Forge* suggests, Attaway imagines the steel industry as a destructive force that violates the natural environment and crushes men in its greed for profit. "It's wrong to tear up the ground and melt it up in the furnace," admonishes Smothers, an injured worker who serves as a kind of doomsday prophet. "Ground don't like it. It's the hell-and-devil kind of work. Guy ain't satisfied with usin' the stuff that was put here for him to use—stuff of [sic] top of the earth. Now he got to git busy and melt up the ground itself. Ground don't like it, I tells you."[17] In contrast, Lawrence represents modern life—and the steel industry in particular—in terms of progress. Panel 37 explains, "The Negroes that had been brought North worked in large numbers in one of the principal industries, which was steel" (see Figure 3). Whereas Attaway uses apocalyptic imagery to depict the industrial forges and highlights the bodily suffering of workers due to heat and exhaustion, Lawrence celebrates the molten metal as a symbol of modernity. In this minimalist image, bright yellow liquid steel cascades from a ladle. Lacking human figures, the image highlights the industrial product rather than the human labor that produced it, and transforms this commodity into an object of beauty. Lawrence painted the molten metal using thin, straight brushstrokes in a cheerful yellow streaked with blue, a color scheme and technique he also used to paint the grass in panels 39 and 40. These echoes suggest the compatibility of modern industry and the natural environment. Moreover, Lawrence depicts Pittsburgh as a site of opportunity for migrants. Whereas Attaway's Moss brothers are killed and maimed by industrial warfare and retreat to the "running sore" of Pittsburgh, Lawrence depicts an intact extended family arriving in Pittsburgh in panel 45. The family members look at one another with joyful expressions on their faces, their figures interlinked through touch and gazes. The smokestacks outside the train window echo the ribbons on a woman's straw bonnet, suggesting a smooth transition from their rural folk culture to the urban industrial environment. Although Lawrence treats at length the discrimination, race riots, and overcrowded housing that the migrants faced (panels 46–53, 55), the series concludes with images of schools and voting. *The Migration of the Negro* reproduces the New Negro for the next generation of African Americans. As we shall see, Attaway also imagines a New Negro figure in the character of Melody, making his novel more richly complex than most critics have allowed. Nevertheless, there is more continuity in Lawrence's *Migration* series between the New Negro of the 1920s and the Red Negro of the 1930s than there is in Attaway's novel.

Figure 2. *The Migration of the Negro*, panel 1, by Jacob Lawrence (1940–41). "During the World War there was a great migration North by Southern Negroes." Courtesy of The Phillips Collection, Washington, D.C. © 2013 The Jacob and Gwendolyn Lawrence Foundation, Seattle / Artists Rights Society (ARS), New York.

The *Migration* series's optimistic view of African American participation in urban life also appealed to the editors at *Fortune*, who offered a preview of the series to its business-oriented readership on the eve of America's entry into World War II. Eager to quell the racial conflicts that threatened to obstruct wartime production, *Fortune* featured Lawrence's positive images of African American industrial workers and warned readers to heed their demands to desegregate shop floors. This message took on special resonance under the looming threat of A. Philip Randolph's March on Washington Movement to protest segregation in the military and defense industries.[18] Attaway's novel, in contrast, depicts class warfare morphing into race war as black strikebreakers battle white unionists. Lawrence's stated purpose in creating the *Migration* series was to educate black youth and the white public about African Americans' major contributions to American society and culture, and his Marxist education may have caused him to balk at *Fortune*'s use of his paintings to advance their explicitly procapitalist agenda. Nevertheless, his narrative of progress served both these purposes and helped launch the *Migration* series into the public spotlight.

Attaway shared a similar social purpose—to bring about economic and racial justice—but adopted different political and aesthetic strategies.

Figure 3. *The Migration of the Negro*, panel 37, by Jacob Lawrence (1940–41). "The Negroes that had been brought North worked in large numbers in one of the principal industries, which was steel." Courtesy of The Phillips Collection, Washington, D.C. © 2013 The Jacob and Gwendolyn Lawrence Foundation, Seattle / Artists Rights Society (ARS), New York.

While Lawrence captured the hope of the Great Migration, Attaway reignited the painful memory the "red summer" of 1919, when race riots erupted throughout the country. Attaway thus reminded his allies on the Left that socialist revolution depended on their commitment to black freedom. The novel responds to the pervasive stereotype of the black migrant as strikebreaker, which obscured black workers' attempts to organize and resist the racist practices of unions and mill owners. Notably, Lawrence also counters the image of the black strikebreaker, albeit more subtly, by highlighting the structural forces of the labor market in panel 29: "The labor agent recruited unsuspecting laborers as strikebreakers for northern industries." According to American studies scholar Kimberley Phillips, even during the 1919 strike, "black men actively participated in shop floor organization, street activism, and efforts to deter the importation of strikebreakers," and the vast majority of black workers walked out with their white peers in Chicago and Cleveland.[19] Although black workers were as amenable to organization as white workers, the unions' racist policies excluded them and bred deep distrust.

As the National Urban League put it in the late 1920s, "Negro men are not kindly disposed to the unions—not because they do not believe in unionism but because they feel that one of their greatest enemies is the white union man."[20] This image of the "black scab" was also the result of the manipulations of mill owners. When 400,000 steelworkers, most of whom were immigrants from southern and eastern Europe, walked off the job in 1919, the steel companies retaliated by mercilessly exploiting racial hostilities. In Gary, Indiana, the steel company imported unsuspecting black workers from the South and paraded them through town, mocking the strikers with their show of resilience.[21] City police forces hired black deputies to threaten the strikers, so the image of the black worker as class traitor was seared into the memories of white unionists.[22] Although the company loyalty of skilled white workers may have done more to hamper the strike, white unionists and their company managers believed that "Niggers did it," and the stereotype of the black strikebreaker became rampant.[23] In his historical novel, Attaway set out to set the record straight. As he explained in his "plan of work" for the Julius Rosenwald Fellowship, "Nobody took into consideration the fact that the strike issues in the mills were to the Negroes trivial by contrast to the terrible labor conditions under which they had so lately suffered."[24] The novel highlights not only the racist practices of unions and mill barons but also the wordview of African Americans new to the industrial environment.

These antagonistic cultural memories of the "white man's union" and "black scab" were still very much alive in the 1930s. Attaway provides a fictional backstory to these antagonisms, placing the onus on unions to build bridges across the racial divide. Memories of 1919 stymied the CIO's effort to organize African American workers in the steel industry in 1936 and 1937. The CIO's Steel Workers' Organizing Committee struggled to recast the relationship between African Americans and the union. Writing for the *Pittsburgh Courier*, a prominent black newspaper, George S. Schuyler assured his readers that the committee's campaign was "a different kind of union drive from that to which America is accustomed." The committee further strengthened its credibility among African Americans by forming alliances with the National Negro Congress, hiring black organizers, and appointing as its director Philip Murray, former vice president of the United Mine Workers, which was unparalleled for its racial egalitarianism.[25] This racially inclusive, highly popular campaign reaped its rewards. After a year, union membership soared to 350,000, and in western Pennsylvania, the majority of black workers joined the United Mine Workers, reportedly in greater proportions than white workers.[26] The Steel Workers' Organizing Committee achieved an astonishing success in March 1937 when it signed a collective bargaining agreement with U.S. Steel, the largest company in the steel industry.

The old racial antagonisms resurfaced, however, in the failed "Little Steel" strikes later that spring. Rather than following the lead of U.S. Steel, the smaller independent companies (Bethlehem, Republic, Youngstown Sheet and Tube, and Inland) refused to sign an agreement with the union, triggering a strike involving 75,000 workers. While the majority of black workers supported the strikes in Chicago and Cleveland, few joined the picket lines in the smaller steel cities in Ohio. Some black workers served as police deputies, a particularly painful reminder of 1919. In order to combat this image of the black scab, African American unionists volunteered to repel the strikebreakers, preempting the misconception that the conflict was racial in nature. African American women made meals for the strikers in the kitchen at the union headquarters and marched on picket lines, where their support of the strike was highly visible.[27] Schuyler depicted black workers as loyal unionists in dozens of articles in the *Pittsburgh Courier* and other black newspapers. Directly confronting the scab stereotype, he asserted that "the enthusiasm with which the black steel workers in the Great Lakes area have aligned themselves with their white fellow workers in the great drive to organize the steel industry belies the oft-repeated charge that Negroes are not susceptible to unionization appeals and are inclined to strikebreaking activities."[28] This resurgence of the black scab stereotype in 1937 helps to explain why Attaway returned to 1919 to tell the story of the Great Strike from the point of view of the black migrant strikebreaker.

A strike story embedded in a migration narrative, *Blood on the Forge* has invigorated recent scholarly debates over the relationship between African Americans and the Left. Concerned with how Attaway negotiates the competing ideologies of black nationalism and Marxism, critics focus on the character of Big Mat, a strikebreaker who rejects militant racial separatism in favor of class consciousness only in the throes of death at the end of the novel. This scene seems to confirm Alan Wald's contention that "the experience of national and racial oppression was vivid, real, and overwhelming for Black writers. Full-blown interracial class solidarity was by comparison almost a leap forward to a quixotic chimera." Similarly, Robert Bone found Big Mat's conversion to class consciousness unconvincing, arguing that Attaway "tries to endow his protagonist with his own consciousness" when the logic of the narrative demands Big Mat's "death in perpetual blindness."

Yet Barbara Foley contests the idea that nationalism is a more "authentic" mode for black writers. She argues that Big Mat's contradictory behavior reflects the contradictions of CP theory itself, which combined nationalist and integrationist strategies.[29] In my view, critics have focused too narrowly on Big Mat in their readings of Blood on the Forge, neglecting the role of Melody as co-protagonist. Big Mat's actions determine the plotline, but we view the world of the novel through Melody's perspective and gain more access to his interior self.[30] In downplaying the interracial exchanges that happen outside the workplace, contemporary scholars have missed Melody's transformation into a modern figure. Reading Blood on the Forge with a focus on Melody complicates Morgan's characterization of the novel as an antibildungsroman—a novel of failed conversion.[31] While "failed conversion" describes Big Mat's belated awakening to class consciousness, Melody's trajectory is more open-ended, ambiguous, and improvisational, reflecting his role as a blues musician and the modern condition itself. Whereas Big Mat gains class consciousness in one dramatic moment, the experience of migration slowly awakens Melody to new ways of thinking about race and class, which he registers through his music. Shifting our interpretive lens to Melody highlights the role of blues music as a metaphor for the relationship between nationalism and integration, as a site of interracial exchange, and as a catalyst for changes in consciousness. Attaway's novel, I submit, offers a more complex view of the interplay of nationalism and integration than critics have acknowledged.

The African American blues figure appeared in the first African American Great Migration novel of the twentieth century, Paul Laurence Dunbar's Sport of the Gods (1902). Known only as "Sadness," this urban musician belongs to "a peculiar class" "that prides itself upon its well dressed idleness" and lives interdependently with others of its kind, forming a "fashionably uniformed fraternity of indolence."[32] Similarly, Melody thrives on art and idleness; his muscles "did not sing" like his brother's but, rather, "cried for long, slow movement" (80). As a blues musician, Melody is a counterpoint to the hypermasculine proletarian worker. In fact, the industrial environment stifles his creativity. The overwhelming "rhythms of the machinery played through his body," displacing his own music (80). After a long night shift, "he was so worked up that his voice was high and thin, like a knife running over an E string in his throat" (83). In characterizing Melody as a feminized artist who shuns hard labor, Attaway departs from Popular Front iconography of masculine interracialism. This is perhaps why his exploration of interracial friendship has been downplayed by Marxist critics and

Figure 4. *Automobile Industry.* Mural study, Detroit, Michigan, Post Office, by William Gropper (1940–41). Courtesy of Smithsonian American Art Museum, Museum acquisition.

scholars of the Left. An example of this interracial imagery is found in William Gropper's mural of Detroit autoworkers, which he created for the WPA at the same time Attaway was writing his novel (see Figure 4). Two male workers, one black and one white, occupy the focal point of the mural. Both bodies have exaggerated masculine features—wide shoulders, narrow hips, bulging muscles, and square jaws—and they are fused into a single figure. The white worker's left arm is extended, creating a diagonal through the center of the composition that extends organically into the left shoulder of the black worker. Laboring together, their bodies work as one. This iconography linked black and white workers through their shared masculinity and their role as producers.

Melody, a feminized artist, is the antithesis of the masculine producer, but his musical sensibility allows him to cross cultural barriers. Dreaming up blues lyrics one hungry evening in Kentucky, for example, Melody articulates a nascent integrationist sensibility: "At night the hills ain't red no more. There ain't no crab apple trees squat in the hills, no more land to hoe in the red-hot sun—white same as black" (11). Attaway's depiction of the southern folk figure as an integrationist departs from the tendency of black Left writers, such as Sterling Brown, to depict the South as a "black nation" and the

site of "authentic" black culture.[33] In Melody's lyric, the darkness of night is an equalizing force that blends the races. Once in the North, Melody connects with white immigrant workers through music. Although he "hadn't understood one word" of the Ukrainian songs he heard on the streets, "he didn't have to know the words to understand what they were wailing about. Words didn't count when the music had a tongue. The field hands of the sloping red-hill country in Kentucky sang that same tongue" (98).

In contrast to Melody, Big Mat is a worker who employs nationalist strategies to deal with the hostile industrial environment. Big Mat, "blacker than his half brothers," was taunted mercilessly by the "white share croppers' kids" and "had learned to draw a safe distance within himself everything that could be hurt" (11–12). Viewing the urban industrial world solely through the lens of race, he enjoys demonstrating his superior strength over the white mill workers. His strength and courage earn him the respect of the white immigrant steelworkers, who call him "Black Irish" (92). The relationship between Big Mat and the Irish workers resembles Lenin's notion of "the equality of nations" that is a precursor to international unity under socialism.[34]

Big Mat and Melody also diverge in terms of gender and sexuality. Melody compares favorably to his hypermasculine brother, suggesting that Attaway connected violence and misogyny to nationalist separatism. Big Mat asserts his patriarchal dominion, imagining the land as a fertile woman whose body and its issue belong to him. Far from being a gentle steward, however, Big Mat beats the bodies of women in subsequent passages that are gruesomely misogynistic.[35] Melody, on the other hand, rejects the notion of ownership, which has a social leveling effect. He respects the land, and to some extent, he respects women. He refuses to sleep with fourteen-year-old Anna when he first meets her in the whorehouse in Mex Town, seeing all the oppressed, sexually objectified women he had ever seen "shackled in her eyes" (74). Anna calls Melody a "sissy fellow" (74, 76), while Big Mat fulfills her fantasy of finding a man with "a pine tree on his belly, hard like rock all the night" (76, 103). Whereas "violence came" to Big Mat "as a thunderblast" (93), Melody sickened at the sight of a dogfight (94). Governed by his feelings, Melody exhibits traits coded as female. He "was full of emotions that fell and rose like clouds rolling in a still evening sky" (183) and sought education to enable him to transform his feelings into art, to "say what he's feelin'." Big Mat, on the other hand, had "simpler meanings" "that he might, if he chose, take in his hands" (183). Nonintellectual and rooted in the material world, Big Mat is the archetype of the masculine worker.

Understanding the dynamics between Big Mat and Melody sheds light on Attaway's response to CP theory, as their relationship stands for the dialectic of nationalism and integration that emerged from communist debates on the "Negro Question." In their differing perspectives, Big Mat and Melody engage one of the most pressing challenges to the American Left in the 1930s and '40s: how to address the distinct national experience of African American workers within an interracial class-based movement. V. I. Lenin first introduced the notion of African Americans as a "dependent and underprivileged nation" in his Preliminary Draft of Theses on the National and Colonial Questions (1920), which posited that national liberation movements of oppressed minorities were necessary before "complete unity" under socialism could be achieved.[36] In his acclaimed visit to Moscow in 1922–23, African American writer Claude McKay transformed CP thinking on race by insisting that the black freedom struggle was central to the class struggle.[37] He reminded his comrades in Russia that a purely class-based identity was untenable for African Americans, as "the Negro in America is not permitted for one minute to forget his color, his skin, or his race."[38] In 1928, when the Comintern entered its radical Third Period (1928–35), it made a dramatic departure from its "color-blind" approach to class struggle, which assumed that racial oppression was a by-product of capitalism and would simply disappear with the socialist triumph. The "Resolution on the Negro Question in the United States" posited a two-pronged approach. Its "black nation thesis" promoted "national self-determination in the southern states" and mandated an organizing campaign in the South, the first of its kind. Meanwhile, it took an integrationist approach in the North, focusing on recruiting black industrial workers into trade unions and grooming them for leadership. The resolution also vowed to fight "white chauvinism" in the Party and in industrial unions.[39]

Despite the fact that forming a separate black nation within the United States would have been virtually impossible, this idea validated the nationalistic impulses of black Americans and attracted many African Americans to a political organization that heretofore had had very little to offer them. The black nation thesis corrected a fatal flaw of Marxism—its subordination of race to class. Instead, it insisted that socialist revolution depended on black liberation. It demanded that white workers aggressively attack racism within their ranks and see antiracist struggles as fundamental to their own revolutionary struggle.[40] While the black nation thesis gave way to the emphasis on unity in the Popular Front period, it still resonated strongly with black writers. Wright's seminal "Blueprint for Negro Writing," written in 1937, was "the most extended discussion of the literary applications of the Black Belt Thesis," according to James Smethust.[41] Wright implored black writers to "accept the nationalist implications of their lives, not in order to encourage them, but in order to change and transcend them. They must accept the concept of nationalism because, in order to transcend it, they must *possess* and *understand* it." In *Blood on the Forge*, Attaway grapples with what Wright called the "bewildering and vexing" question of nationalism, exposing its destructive tendencies while acknowledging its logic within Jim Crow America.[42]

Big Mat's nationalism is destructive and blinding, perhaps reflecting Attaway's fear that the masses are susceptible to fascism and other reactionary influences. However, within the same text, Attaway offers another view of nationalism and integration as complementary rather than contradictory. Big Mat and Melody's fraternal relationship functions as an analogy for the complex dynamic between these political strategies. Attaway uses the grammar of music to convey the dialectical relationship between Big Mat and Melody and, by extension, between nationalism and integration. Although the following dialogue does not express the rhythm or meter that is characteristic of the blues, it has a structure that parallels this musical form in a striking way. Consisting of exactly twelve lines, the dialogue corresponds to the twelve-bar progression that is the most basic structure of blues music. The three harmonies in the blues progression are the tonic (I), which provides stability; the subdominant (IV), which departs from the tonic and builds tension; and the dominant (V), which creates a climactic feeling of energy and unrest. The chord progression plays in a constant loop in a blues song in the following pattern: I-I-I-I, IV-IV-I-I, V-IV-I-I. I have annotated the passage to mark the harmonies, which are the single chords found in each of the twelve bars:

I   "Muck ground git big every year jest like a woman oughta."
I   "Mat, I got a big feelin' like the ground don't belong to the white boss—not to nobody."
I   "Maybe muck ground my woman."
I   "You know, Mat—wish I'd 'a' had a chance to sit at a schoolhouse like the white kids—all year round."
IV "Muck ground jest a woman."
IV "Man oughta know book learnin'—"
I   "Only muck ground never fail if you plows it—"
I   ". . . so's he kin know how to say what he's feelin'."
V   "Git big if you plows it."
IV "Guess I oughta been white."
I   "Jest as well I was born a nigger. Got more misery than a white man could stand."
I   Melody had to look at him. His voice was so deep it was like a slow roll on a drum (23).

The dramatic structure of the dialogue follows the dramatic structure of the twelve-bar blues progression.[43] The blues progression begins with a calm, harmonious mood set by four stable tonics (I); in the passage, the long opening lines, as well as Melody's direct address to Mat, establish a sense of calm and continuity. The progression then builds energy in the middle section as the subdominant harmonies tease a departure. At this point in the dialogue (line 5), lines get shorter, repeating the themes in the first section in a more punctuated manner. These lines also proceed in parallel, as Mat and Melody continue their individual thoughts without responding to each other. The climax occurs with the entry of the dominant harmony in the ninth bar (V), which corresponds to Big Mat's emphatic, "Git big if you plows it." It then unwinds to the subdominant harmony (IV), Melody's resigned "Guess I oughta been white." The progression finds resolution in the stable tonics of the final two bars. Correspondingly, the final two lines are long, restoring a sense of calm. Big Mat's tongue-in-cheek comment lightens the mood with humor while recognizing the condition of racial oppression that ripples beneath each man's reverie. In the final line, the narrator resumes, leaving us with the image of a slow-rolling drum. The blues structure for Melody and Mat's conversation allows for both harmony and dissonance, calm and tension, in the brothers' relationship, providing a model for the synthesis of nationalism and integration in CP theory and practice. Their dialogue suggests the inseparability of nationalism and integration, violence and love, masculinity and femininity, matter and ideas, actions and feeling, work and art, and rhythm and melody.

Attaway's use of the blues form to express CP theory is a fascinating twist on the slogan for the League of Struggle for Negro Rights: "Promote Negro Culture in its Original Form with Proletarian Content."[44] Whereas Harlem Renaissance practitioners aimed to transform African American folk culture into high art, communist writers wanted to preserve the folk form but infuse it with radical content. For example, organizers in the South changed the spiritual "Roll the Chariot On" to "Roll the Union On."[45] The CP saw African American music as the authentic revolutionary voice of the people. In his dialogues, Attaway reveals the blues form to be the perfect expression of Marxist dialectics. He challenges the distinction between nationalist form and proletarian content, showing how the form itself expresses Marxist dialectical thinking on the Negro Question.

The dialogue structured by a dialectical blues progression expresses the synthesis of nationalism and integration. Melody's story of interracial exchange and artistic development also strikes a balance with Big Mat's tale of nationalism and industrial labor. Yet critics dismiss Melody's experience of interracial exchange as an exception, a qualification to their overall interpretation of the novel as pessimistic about the ability of African American migrants to transcend the "nationalist implications of their lives." "While Blood on the Forge does offer some limited instances of interracial identification among workers," concedes Morgan, "Attaway also suggests that these tentative identifications do not tend to bear up in moments of socioeconomic crisis."[46] Morgan's point is well taken (the novel ends in race war), but Melody's interaction with ethnic workers is not incidental. Reading the novel as a migration narrative (rather than a strike story) makes room for new interpretations.

In Blood on the Forge, the move from the rural South to the industrial North is accompanied by a shift in the language of social categories from race to ethnicity. Along with the immigrant narratives that preceded them, domestic migration narratives of the 1930s helped to shape the theories of multiculturalism and ethnicity that emerged in the 1940s. In 1940, Carey McWilliams and Louis Adamic established the journal *Common Ground*, which was the primary vehicle for the new concept of "multiculturalism." The term "ethnicity" appeared for the first time the following year.[47] A list of notable contributors to *Common Ground* contains a plethora of migrant writers, including Arna Bontemps, Margaret Walker, Zora Neale Hurston, Ralph Ellison, Gwendolyn Brooks, Chester Himes, Carlos Bulosan, and Woody Guthrie. In the American context, ethnic distinctions have tended to be less divisive than racial distinctions, creating the myth of America as a "nation of nations."[48] While the Moss brothers continue to use racial categories to understand their environment, the workers in the Monongahela Valley use ethnic labels. A veteran steelworker gives the newcomers words of advice, peppered with ethnic slurs such as "hunkies" and "mick" (44). On their first day on the job, they meet an Italian "with a good heart"; their work crew is "half Slavs" led by an Irish boss named O'Casey (55). Even the southern white migrants are labeled by their fellow workers, who "called all the young white fellows who were Americans and new to the mills 'hayseeds'" (90). Each of these ethnic characters speaks in a slightly different vernacular, distinguishing them along lines of culture rather than color. When Melody injures his hand on the job, the words of consolation by the stove gang read like a sympathy card from the United Nations:

> "Work back in easy, kid. Work back in easy," said the Irishmen.
> "How your hand do for himself?" asked the Slav.
> "You stand pain like anything," said the Italian. "I tell fella on night crew that you Italian. I say you gone back to Italy."
> The hayseed just took Melody's hand and parted his freckles in a grin (135).

Whereas the poor white sharecropper who lived next to the Moss brothers in Kentucky colluded with the landowner to keep them down, his migrant counterpart learns to have compassion for Melody. Attaway's positive portrayal of a white southern migrant is remarkable, considering that the African American and Left press often blamed them for exacerbating racial hostilities. For example, in his article "The Negro in 'Little Steel'" published in *Opportunity* following the failure of the "Little Steel" strikes in 1937, Romare Bearden described a striker who raised a knife to black workers passing by the CIO headquarters and "said in a long Southern drawl, 'I bet if I stick one of them black bastards with this, he'll howl.'"[49] It just so happens that

Bearden and Attaway were roommates in Harlem, where Attaway lived while he was finishing the novel. While Bearden reports the transplantation of Jim Crow to the North, Attaway tentatively imagines southern-born whites and blacks trading divisive racial identities for more pluralistic ethnic identities.

While Attaway's migration novel departs dramatically from the New Negro spirit of previous decades, depicting the North as a kind of hell rather than a site of vitality and redemption, migration nevertheless prompts a change in consciousness that fosters interracial exchange. Melody befriends an old Slav named Zanksi, "a good guy to be with" (136). They find common ground as migrants, as introspective men, and as workers: Melody's image of their clasped hands, Zanski's "hooked over his own to lift a slag hunk from the pit floor," symbolizes their bond (136). When Zanski gets hurt on the job and is forced to retire, emotionally sensitive Melody feels the urge to cry for his friend, but instead he finds pleasure in imagining the blessing in disguise: "Now the old hunky could sit in his courtyard and watch his kids and his kids' kids go to work in the mills" (125). Even though this kind of domestic stability is unavailable to African Americans in the novel, Melody is able to empathize with the old man. When Melody's relationship with his brother Big Mat disintegrates, becoming "casual, half strangerlike" (104), he confides to Zanski that he feels "all balled up here," in his head (138). Their dialogue is also structured by the twelve-bar blues progression, making a parallel between Melody's brotherhood with Big Mat and his friendship with Zanski. However, the labor strike ultimately divides the white and black workers. The friendship between Melody and Zanski suggests the possibility for interracial alliances, but these kinds of personal bonds are not enough to forge an interracial labor movement. Without a union equipped to support them, fledgling alliances like Melody and Zanski's struggle against a powerful economic system and social structure determined to keep them apart.

If social change relies on collective organizing rather than personal relationships, why would Attaway dwell on the friendship between Melody and Zanski? Although the opportunity for advancement was a top priority for African American steelworkers, they viewed the unions' commitment to social equality as proof that the organizations would fight to end racial discrimination on the job.[50] In Horace R. Cayton and George S. Mitchell's book *Black Workers and the New Unions*, reviewed favorably in the *Negro Quarterly* in 1939, the sociologists describe "warm friendships" developing between black and white workers. One union officer fought for the integration of the local bowling alley so that African Americans on the team could participate.

Unionists reported attending integrated meetings in workers' homes, and white workers' wives even hosted a birthday party for the Negro president's wife. George Schuyler's article on a successful union drive in a tire plant concludes with an image of social integration: "The workers ate, played, and danced together and had a fine time" in defiance of the practice of segregation in theaters and restaurants in the town.[51]

While commentators touted these displays of social equality, black workers had their doubts. Labor historians have recently challenged the notion that racial conflicts originated primarily with employers who wanted to keep their workers divided, showing how the formation of working-class identity in the United States went hand in hand with the development of white racial identity.[52] The rhetoric of inclusivity coming from CIO leadership was often aggressively resisted by the white rank and file. Most famously, 25,000 autoworkers staged a walkout of Detroit's Packard plant in 1943 to protest the promotion of three African Americans. The CIO was particularly successful at interracial organizing in the steel industry, but integration of the workplace did not often extend to the realm of home, neighborhood, and community.[53] A black worker in Chicago interviewed by Cayton and Mitchell pointed out white unionists' hypocrisy: "You know I've been to a couple of open meetings of the CIO. The white men get up and talk about unity, about how a black man is just as good as a white, how the restriction and segregation, both inside and outside the plant, must be broken down. But what happens? When I want to rent a house on Buffalo Avenue, you know this place ain't fit to live in, I go to that same union man who owns a house on Buffalo, but does he rent to me? No sir! He doesn't. They don't practice what they preach."[54] While white workers compartmentalized economic and social equality, black workers viewed access to jobs and housing as inseparable.

Similarly, Attaway's analysis of the promises and limits of working-class unity insists on the inseparability of political and social equality, and of the public space of the union and the private space of the home. Attaway points to the domestic arena as a seemingly insurmountable wall between black and white workers. Interracial camaraderie flourishes in the masculine spaces of the workplace and bunkhouse but deteriorates in the realm of family and neighborhood. While the actions of union organizers remain vague in Blood on the Forge, filtered through the minds of its politically naive protagonists, the hostility of white women and families is painfully clear. When Melody and his younger brother wander away from the bunkhouse and into a neighborhood of eastern European immigrants, they encounter a place "full of hatreds that they did not understand," where children throw rocks, women glare, and men spit at the sight of them (49).

While migration opens limited possibilities for interracial friendship in the novel, it also transforms Melody's consciousness as an artist. African American migration narratives like *Blood on the Forge* came into fruition in the late 1930s, when the CP shifted its emphasis to organizing African Americans in urban centers and became more engaged with mass culture as a site of resistance. Previously, it had turned to the South as the site of an authentic black culture, suspicious that commercialized music such as jazz was bound up in the capitalist market and tainted by bourgeois patrons and consumers. In a book on folk music he published in 1967, Attaway contests this earlier view. "Too tough to die," the blues was not diluted by mass culture but, rather, transformed into gospel, modern urban folk, jazz, and rock.[55] Attaway's depiction of Melody reflects this Popular Front reassessment of urban music as a potential site of resistance. Melody's art is tied to place; a new landscape demands a new sound. Back in the "red-clay hills of Kentucky," Melody liked to "slick" his guitar, but up in the milltown, "he didn't try any slicking. That was for back home and the distances in the hills. Here at the mills it felt right to find quick chords with the fingers—a strange kind of playing for him, but it was right for that new place" (62). In his books on music written long after the Popular Front, Attaway gives a sense of folk music as the voice of the migrant, "continually evolving" as it is passed "down the generations from one singer to another, and spread across the world with our wandering minstrels."[56] The CP's shift from its Third Period emphasis on southern folk culture and the black nation thesis to its Popular Front emphasis on urban culture and class unity mirrors the process of migration itself. As such, Melody embodies this dynamic relationship between South and North, folk and urban, and race and class.

Melody's search for a new music is thwarted by the end of the novel. Race war and other manifestations of the capitalist industrial environment threaten to engulf him. In his despair, Melody deliberately injured his picking hand. Although doctors said his hand would heal, he "left his guitar behind" on his journey to Pittsburgh (234). Yet I argue that Attaway leaves Melody's migration experience open-ended; his art does not necessarily die in the crucible of steel. The following passage, overlooked by scholars, is the analog to Big Mat's conversion scene in that it dramatizes Melody's shift in consciousness as a result of migration: "There was a deep pain in Melody. He was never happy. He thought about the first months in the Allegheny Valley. Then he had been fearful of the greatness around him, the endless clash of big forces playing up and down the banks of long rivers. This place had been a monster, beautiful in an ugly strength that fascinated a man so that it made him sing his fear. It was a new, big world. Right now all of Melody's world was little, dull pain. He had left his guitar behind" (234). Melody's world is sublime, invoking terror and awe, a "monster, beautiful in an ugly strength" that "fascinated" him. The term "fascinate" conveys the double-edged quality of the sublime, which impresses both pleasure and terror upon the beholder. The "endless clash of big forces" threatens to destroy him, but they also offer the creative possibilities of "a new, big world" whose very terribleness elicits music, making him "sing his fear." Melody's art is not a weapon—at least not yet—but, rather, a means of negotiating a new world. Whereas Big Mat awakens to a new consciousness through violence, Melody does so through aesthetic experience. Big Mat's conversion points toward a future revolution, but Melody's despair exists in the present moment, "right now." This phrase, I believe, is crucial for understanding the passage because it locates Melody's despair in the present moment, leaving his future open to question. Attaway resists teleology, refuses to predict a revolutionary outcome for Melody. Yet he does not necessarily miss the folk's "rebirth on a higher level," as Ellison charged. Instead, he describes the agony of the modern condition. In his 1928 essay "Human Migration and the Marginal Man," University of Chicago sociologist Robert Park argued that the movement of populations liberated an individual from the yoke of tradition but created an unstable, culturally hybrid, and racially mixed individual. This "marginal man" is the emblem of modernity, "the first cosmopolite and citizen of the world."[57] Caught between cultures, an artist who transcends racial barriers through music, Melody is a quintessentially modern figure. Attaway's historical novel revises the New Negro paradigm of the 1920s to meet the needs of the present. Whereas Alain Locke and his Harlem Renaissance contemporaries downplayed class differences in favor of "the race," Attaway locates the Negro artist within the black working class. Moreover, he refigures the North as a site of race and class conflict rather than integration and opportunity, pressing for revolutionary change.

In writing *Blood on the Forge*, William Attaway dramatized the Great Migration as a transformative event for the American working class. Racial oppression and class struggle are inseparable for his characters. Attaway's novel thus urges us to reconsider critical categories that separate "African American" and "proletarian" literature into distinct narrative traditions. Following Bill Mullen and others, my reading of the novel insists that African American literature and experience are deeply imbued with class consciousness.[58] It reveals the significance not only of the Left to African American literature but of African American literature to the Left. By reopening the wound of 1919, Attaway reminded readers that the labor movement needed African Americans, that white racism was the true class betrayal, and that any revolutionary movement must prioritize antiracist struggles.

In imagining the black strikebreaker's conversion to class consciousness, *Blood on the Forge* reflects a Marxist perspective. However, its tragic ending is also a stern demand that the Left renew its commitment to black freedom. Attaway's pessimism disconcerted Marxist critics who first reviewed the book. By the time the novel was published in 1941, Hitler had invaded Russia, and the CP renewed its call for unity against fascism with special urgency.[59] These international developments may have dampened the critical reception of Attaway's novel. In a review in the *Daily Worker*, Ralph Warner laments that "nowhere does Mr. Attaway express hope for the final unity of black and white workers."[60] Ralph Ellison's critical reactions to both Sanora Babb's and William Attaway's novels—one private, one public—reflect the emphasis Marxist critics placed on interracial unity during the war. In April 1942, Ellison dashed off a note to Babb urging her to publish her dust bowl novel. "I hope you have gotten back to the novel and that it is completed for fall publication," he wrote on the stationary of the *Negro Quarterly*. "You must."[61] Around the same time, Ellison published an influential review in the same journal on Attaway's *Blood on the Forge*. While Ellison praised Babb for showing the workers' "rebirth into a new consciousness," he took Attaway to task for being unduly pessimistic about the destructive effects of migration and industrialization on black folk.[62] "Conceptually, Attaway grasped the destruction of the folk, but missed its rebirth on a higher level," wrote Ellison, echoing the language he used to praise Babb's novel. "The writer did not see that while the folk individual was being liquidated in the crucible of steel, he was also undergoing fusion with new elements." In its bleak outlook on the events of 1919, continued Ellison, Attaway's novel missed the opportunity to impart an important political lesson. Even at this racial nadir, a few black workers saw past the virulent racism of white workers and bosses to envision the revolutionary potential of trade unionism. These visionaries "established those values embraced by a growing number of Negroes today. Serious writing about the Negro must spread this hard won consciousness."[63] The Popular Front crusade for unity escalated during World War II, alienating black Marxist writers like Attaway, Wright, Ellison, and Chester Himes, who refused to compromise in the struggle for African American equality.

Attaway's literary warning would take organizational form as the Double V campaign during World War II, in which African Americans insisted that the fight against fascism abroad depended on the eradication of Jim Crow at home. Just as Marxist critics failed to embrace *Blood on the Forge*, the CP opposed the Double V campaign and the March on Washington Movement. In focusing on Melody's interracial and aesthetic experiences in the novel, my reading does not intend to downplay Attaway's sharp, insider critique of Marxist ideals of class unity. Instead, it shows how Attaway maintained a larger social vision within his grim narrative. In his "Blueprint," Richard Wright gave the following advice to the black Marxist writer: "He may, with disgust and revulsion, say *no* and depict the horrors of capitalism encroaching upon the human being. Or he may, with hope and passion, say *yes* and depict the faint stirrings of a new and emerging life. But in whatever social voice he chooses to speak, whether positive or negative, there should always be heard or *over*-heard his faith, his necessity, his judgement."[64] Like Wright himself, Attaway chose to speak in a negative "social voice." Yet Melody's blues allows us to hear Attaway's larger faith over the clash of these capitalist horrors.

CHAPTER 4 BEYOND THE MIGRANT MOTHER

As the preceding chapters suggest, Popular Front depictions of interracial alliance often focused on the male worker. Yet the iconography of migrant motherhood was also widespread in Popular Front culture. Maternal imagery was rhetorically versatile, appealing to middle-class audiences contemplating the efficacy of the New Deal as well as to radicals pushing for deeper change.[1] The photograph that came to be known as "Migrant Mother" is perhaps the most enduring icon of the Great Depression (see Figure 5).[2] Dorothea Lange took the picture of Florence Thompson and three of her children while on assignment at a pea pickers' camp in California for the FSA. As Robert Hariman and John Louis Lucaites argue, the migrant mother icon places the middle-class viewer in the role of the provider for this deserving family. It calls for a collective response to their poverty, justifying the intervention of a protecting government.[3] The FSA used gendered symbols— 'Madonnas of the Fields," in the words of scholar Wendy Kozol—to elicit public support for New Deal programs that would alleviate their need, rather than overturn the structural conditions that produced it.[4] Lange's Migrant Mother series, which consists of six images, moved audiences from its initial publication, garnering relief for impoverished migratory workers after appearing in the *San Francisco News* in 1936. Although not included, surprisingly, in the *News* articles, the photograph known as "Migrant Mother" soon became famous. It was featured in *Survey Graphic* the same year, and U.S. *Camera Annual* included it in its exhibition of the year's outstanding pictures. By 1941 it had made its way to the Metropolitan Museum of Art.[5]

Dorothea Lange's training as a portrait photographer is evident in the framing, composition, and emotional intensity of the photograph. Lange had a knack for capturing her subjects at moments when their faces were particularly expressive. Florence Thompson wears a look of pensive worry, accentuated by the lines around her mouth and brow, the cupped hand raised to her cheek, the straightness of her lips, and the direction of her gaze, which looks off to the side of the camera lens. Lange highlighted Thompson's face by moving close to her subject, eliminating the background cluttered with

LEFT Figure 5. *Destitute pea pickers in California. Mother of seven children. Age thirty-two. Nipomo, California.* Photograph by Dorothea Lange (February 1936). Courtesy of Library of Congress, Prints & Photographs Division, FSA/OWI Collection, LC-DIG-fsa-8b29516.

RIGHT Figure 6. *Mother and Child.* Lithograph by Elizabeth Catlett (1944). Courtesy of the Metropolitan Museum of Art, Gift of Reba and Dave Williams, 1999 (1999.529.34). Image © The Metropolitan Museum of Art. Art © Catlett Mora Family Trust/Licensed by VAGA, New York, N.Y.

the utilitarian implements of camp life. While this artistic choice worked against the documentary aims of FSA photography, it allowed for a more aesthetically powerful and emotionally moving image. In the preceding photographs in the series, the older children face the camera, distracting the viewer, but in the iconic image they are nestled tightly at the mother's side with their heads turned away. This positioning enhances the symbolic power of the image: When we see the children's faces, we relate to them as specific children belonging to a specific mother, but when we see only the back of their heads, they take on a more abstract meaning as an "every child" dependent on a universal mother. The children frame Thompson, forming a pleasing pyramidal symmetry. Most importantly, this stylized composition resonates powerfully with the Christian iconography of the Madonna and child. In tapping into this Christian symbolism, it offers the nation hope of redemption through the maternal bond.[6]

Like Steinbeck's *Grapes of Wrath*, Dorothea Lange's "Migrant Mother" casts a long shadow over the cultural memory of the Great Depression, and the dust bowl migration in particular. Lange's photograph continues to be reproduced, sold in exclusive galleries and on mass-produced T-shirts.

However, there were other representations of migrant motherhood that were more racially varied, aesthetically challenging, and politically charged. The popularization of Lange's iconic image of a white family even obscured her own racially inclusive approach; it is one of scores of her FSA photographs that feature a highly stylized mother-and-child motif in depicting families from a variety of ethnic groups. Writers and artists pushed beyond Lange's redemptive, palatable icon to create grotesque images of migrant mothers (both literary and visual) designed to startle their audiences and impel more radical change.[7]

The variety of genres and media used to depict migrant mothers calls us to consider the differences between fiction and nonfiction, photography and imaginative art, and word and image. During the 1930s, many writers and artists placed value on forms that claimed to have special access to reality, such as photographs and reportage. Even novelists turned away from the modernist abstractions of the 1920s to bring about a resurgence of social realism. But the restriction of nonfiction to verifiable facts is both a representational asset and a limitation. On one hand, the factual basis of nonfiction lends it a certain power as "truthful" storytelling, even though these narratives are also carefully staged. On the other hand, the evidentiary constraint often prevents nonfictional forms from accessing the human interior, especially for those populations who are unlikely to leave introspective accounts of their lives. While nonfictional forms like sociology effectively represent social patterns and group experience, fiction zones in on individual, often idiosyncratic experiences. Both have a kind of truth to tell. Documentary photography and more imaginative visual forms share a similar dynamic. While luck and good timing played a role in Lange's ability to capture the pensive gaze of the migrant mother, Elizabeth Catlett, whose work I'll consider shortly, experimented with angles, tonal contrasts, and abstraction to create the moving faces of her mother figures.

One way that writers and artists in this period attempted to transcend the limits of nonfictional forms was by mixing media. "Interartistic" texts, such as the photo-essay, humanized sweeping sociological accounts with intimate images of individual people and particular environments.[8] In turn, the written text linked individual images to a broader context, allowing them to tell a story. As we shall see, Richard Wright and Edwin Rosskam's photobook 12 Million Black Voices gave a radical edge to FSA migrant mother photographs by placing them in a series to form a narrative about urban poverty and by juxtaposing them with grotesque language. Realizing that their literary works were outmatched by the popular appeal of commercial mass

ABOVE Figure 7. *Mother and child, FSA (Farm Security Administration) clients, former sharecroppers, just before moving to Southeast Missouri Farms.* Photograph by Russell Lee (May 1938). Courtesy of Library of Congress, Prints & Photographs Division, FSA/OWI Collection, LC-USF33-011418-M2.
LEFT Figure 8. *Young Indian mother and baby, blueberry camp, near Little Fork, Minnesota.* Photograph by Russell Lee (August 1937). Courtesy of Library of Congress, Prints & Photographs Division, FSA/OWI Collection, LC-USF33-011257-M2.

culture, many writers integrated journalism and performance through the "Living Newspaper" plays of the Federal Theater Project and by incorporating mass media into their literary works. According to critic Laura Browder, John Dos Passos's trilogy U.S.A. provided a new model of radical fiction that mobilized the power of the mass media in its blend of narrative, "newsreels," and biographical vignettes.[9] Thus writers' and artists' experiments with mixing media accorded with the larger goals of the Popular Front to engage working-class audiences and represent the voices of the dispossessed.

Both Dorothea Lange and her FSA colleague Russell Lee were particularly interested in the mother-and-child motif, replicating this highly stylized composition with subjects from a variety of racial and ethnic backgrounds, including people they identified as "Negro," "Indian," "Japanese-American," "Mexican," and "white" (see Figures 7–10).

Like Lange's iconic photograph, these images tap into the Christian symbolism of the Madonna. The composition is nearly identical in each: The mother figure is seated with the child in her lap and closely framed. Lange and Lee's migrant mother photographs offered a racially inclusive symbol of the American "people" that celebrated motherhood as a universal experience that transcends race, ethnicity, class, region, and creed. However, in deriving solely from a European aesthetic tradition, these photographs suggest that mothers of color are mere variants of the white Madonna. This idea of universal motherhood elides the historical experiences of colonialism, slavery, segregation, and internment that gave rise to vastly different meanings of motherhood and different priorities for social change.

Black Women on the Left and the Militant Migrant Mother

The work of Elizabeth Catlett, an African American artist and sculptor prominent in Popular Front circles in Chicago, Harlem, and Mexico City in the 1940s, challenges this notion of universal motherhood. Along with other black female writers and activists, Catlett offers a more militant vision of black womanhood than can be found in the FSA file. The mother and child was a dominant theme in Catlett's work over the course of her long career. Her sculpture *Negro Mother and Child*, which she completed for her master's thesis at the University of Iowa in 1940, won first prize at the American Negro Exposition in Chicago the following year. Catlett observed women and children in her community to prepare for her work. She found that when the mother and child were seated or kneeling, "the two always seemed closer, always more compact," which suited her aim of creating "a

ABOVE Figure 9. *Japanese mother and daughter, agricultural workers near Guadalupe, California.* Photograph by Dorothea Lange (March 1937). Courtesy of Library of Congress, Prints & Photographs Division, FSA/OWI Collection, LC-USF34-016129-C.
LEFT Figure 10. *Mexican mother in California.* Photograph by Dorothea Lange (July 1935). Courtesy of Library of Congress, Prints & Photographs Division, FSA/OWI Collection, LC-DIG-fsa-8b26837.

composition of two figures, one smaller than the other, so interlaced as to be expressive of maternity, and so compact as to be suitable to stone."[10] Yet Catlett took issue with the notion of universal motherhood with her Russian teacher, Ossip Zadkine. Favoring abstract forms, Zadkine urged her to eliminate ethnically specific details from a terracotta sculpture. Catlett explained that she was sculpting a racially specific mother and child "because I'm a black woman" and insisted that black people would not relate to a white or even a race-neutral mother and child.[11] Catlett reconciled this tension between abstraction and racial specificity by drawing on African aesthetic traditions, such as the mask, to render African American figures in a less representational manner. "After all," she commented, "abstraction was born in Africa." While studying with Zadkine, Catlett developed a hybrid style, balancing accessibility of representational features with "the extra strength and force that you can get from an abstract form."[12]

Catlett's 1944 lithograph *Mother and Child* reflects these mixtures of representation and abstraction, and of Western and African influences (see Figure 6). Catlett's piece borrows from Western Madonna iconography: The child is safely ensconced in his mother's arms, creating an idealized sense of intimacy and nurturance. Like Lange, Catlett emphasized the physical and psychic strength of the mother—a quality that distinguishes the tranquil Renaissance Madonna from her Depression-era descendants. In both Lange's photograph and Catlett's print, the mother's arm is a vertical plane that structures the composition—a formal and metaphorical ballast for the family. Yet Catlett's image speaks to the historical specificity of African American motherhood. As art historian and Catlett biographer Melanie Herzog notes, the masklike shape of the mother's face, the angular planes, and the drapery of her garment reflect the influence of African art.[13] Catlett also uses symbolic elements to evoke racial terror. The mother's hair morphs into the tapering branches of a bare tree, which raises the specter of lynching. (Catlett's peer in Harlem, Jacob Lawrence, included a similar image of a bare, thin-limbed tree with a noose hanging from in it in his series *The Migration of the Negro*, which Catlett reviewed in the *People's Voice*). A triangular plane extends from the child's shoulder to the tree, suggesting a road receding into the horizon. The mother's arm forms a larger, inverse triangle and seems to restrain the child from being drawn toward the ill-omened tree. Finally, dark horizontal bands across the mother's upper arm, though ostensibly abstractions of the folds in her sleeve, also resemble strands of rope or lashes from whipping. Thus, Catlett's abstracted planes and lines carry symbolic meanings that evoke African American social experience. While

Catlett's image retains the redemptive symbolism of the mother-and-child icon, it challenges the universality of motherhood, bringing to the fore the particular historical experience of black families.

In recent decades, Catlett has been recognized by art historians as "one of the most significant African American artists in history."[14] Her participation in Popular Front organizations and artistic networks, in both the United States and Mexico, provided the foundation for a career that spanned two nations and eight decades, reaching its height during the Black Arts Movement of the 1960s and '70s. Catlett was a middle-class African American woman raised in Washington, D.C. She studied art at Howard University and the University of Iowa, where she received an M.F.A. in sculpture. Her artistic and political horizons widened when she spent the summer of 1941 studying ceramics and printmaking at the SSCAC in Chicago. Catlett met a vibrant circle of African American artists who viewed themselves as workers in the class struggle. Although Catlett did not officially join the CP, her political commitments intensified when she moved to Harlem in 1942. She studied with Russian sculptor Ossip Zadkine, became chairman of the Russian War Relief, joined the Arts Committee of the National Negro Congress, and taught ceramics at the George Washing Carver School, a center for Marxist education. Having received a fellowship from the Julius Rosenwald Fund, which was a crucial sponsor of African American art and literature in the cash-strapped 1930s and '40s, Catlett left the distractions of the Carver school and moved to Mexico, which had a strong tradition of people's art. Catlett connected with the Taller de Gráfica Popular, an artists' collective dedicated to meeting the aesthetic and political needs of the people and cultivating a sense of *mexicanidad*, or Mexican identity based on indigenous heritage and social struggles. The collective was familiar to radical artists in the United States; the *New Masses* featured articles on Mexican artists, and they interacted with U.S. artists through the Artists' Union and American Artists' Congress, to both of which Catlett belonged.[15] Mexico provided Catlett with the creative and political context she needed to create a visual narrative of African American motherhood.

Catlett's work was critically well received early in her career. In *Modern Negro Art* (1943), Howard University professor James Porter described his student as "one of the brilliant graduates" and offered a glowing evaluation of her sculpture *Negro Mother and Child*.[16] She was included in the National Survey of Contemporary American Artists in 1945 and had her first major solo exhibit in 1947–48 at the Barnett-Arden Gallery in Washington, D.C. She married Mexican muralist Francisco Mora in 1947 (after divorcing African

American artist Charles White, whom she met in Chicago) and made a permanent move to Mexico. During the anticommunist purges of the 1950s, the U.S. embassy harassed Catlett and joined forces with the Mexican government to arrest her as a "foreign agitator" in 1959. She subsequently became a Mexican citizen and was summarily declared an "undesirable alien" by the U.S. State Department. She remained in exile in Mexico until 1971, when finally she was allowed to visit the United States. Catlett chose to spend the rest of her life in Mexico, carving out a rich artistic, political, and family life in her adopted home.

Catlett's series of fifteen linoleum cuts *The Negro Woman*, produced in Mexico in 1946–47, reflects the influence of Popular Front political and aesthetic ideas. Each of the prints is accompanied by a line of text, creating a simple, powerful narrative reminiscent of Lawrence's *Migration* series. In fact, in a review of Lawrence's work published in Harlem's *People's Voice*, Catlett expressed her admiration, noting "his style of painting with almost elemental color and design is a perfect means for the expression of the fundamental needs of the Negro."[17] Catlett's series highlights the racial and class dimensions of black women's experience and places them in a long, interwoven tradition of feminist, antiracist, and labor activism. Although Melanie Herzog interprets Catlett's *Negro Woman* as "a visually accessible and unavoidable connection between herself and African Americans in the southern United States," I view the series as a migration narrative, moving from southern agricultural labor in the third cut to urban tenements in the thirteenth cut. In fact, Catlett's students in Harlem inspired the project. While working at the Carver school, she realized, "Suddenly I wanted to draw these people, these women, who were to me so strong and so wonderful, and from whom I was learning a lot."[18] Her students were the working poor of Harlem—domestics, janitors, and cooks—who exposed her to the reality of poverty, made her acutely aware of her own privilege, and solidified her commitment to social art that ordinary people could appreciate.

The text begins with a strong assertion of self, "I am the Negro Woman," and proclaims in the following three lines the importance of black female agricultural and domestic labor. Catlett departs from the imagery of migrant motherhood in photo-books like Richard Wright's *12 Million Black Voices* by depicting them not as victims but as freedom fighters. Although Wright astutely recognized the multiple dimensions of capitalist oppression, arguing that black women workers "are triply anchored and restricted in their movements within and without the Black Belts," he depicted them as victims and even barriers to men's revolutionary activities.[19] In contrast,

Catlett invokes Phillis Wheatley, Harriet Tubman, and Sojourner Truth, who "fought for the rights of women as well as Negroes," placing black women in a long protest tradition that combined women's rights and civil rights. She asserts black women's place in the women's movement while insisting on the centrality of racial and class issues—lynching, segregation, poor housing, and underpaid jobs—to this movement toward "a future equality with other Americans."

Reflecting her Left commitments, Catlett uncovers black women's role "in the struggle to organize the unorganized." The ninth panel depicts a black woman in the center of a cluster of male workers, two black and two white (see Figure 11). Typical of Catlett's style, the female figure has a disproportionately large fist, evocative of her strength and the manual labor she performs. Counterbalancing the fist, which is raised toward the upper right corner of the cut, is her rounded breast, at center. This parallel between breast and fist, similar in shape and size and visually aligned, creates a striking symbol of black female militance. This image of interracial, gender-inclusive working-class solidarity not only departs from the hypermasculine iconography of the period but also recognizes black women's participation in labor activism.

Like agricultural workers, domestic workers encountered serious obstacles to their efforts to organize unions: They did not work in a centralized workplace; they often worked part time and on a temporary basis; and they were excluded from New Deal provisions for collective bargaining, minimum wage, minimum hours, unemployment insurance, and Social Security. Nonetheless, many African American women got involved in Left-labor politics. Pauli Murray, the African American woman hobo discussed in Chapter 1, credited her experience with labor organizing in the 1930s for her subsequent leadership in the Civil Rights Movement of the 1960s. "I came into the civil rights struggle by way of the labor struggle for the right to organize in the mid-thirties," she reflected in an interview taken in 1968. "I began then to relate of those methods of struggle, such as picketing, sit-ins, confrontations, to the struggles of civil rights. And this is probably what made me more of a militant than some of my contemporaries at that time because of my exposure to labor and labor struggles."[20] Others like her joined the CIO or the CP, organized boycotts, picketed newspaper offices that published denigrating images, and lobbied on behalf of the National Council of Negro Women.[21] Catlett's Popular Front work taps into the power of the mother as a symbol of black women's radical activism, infusing this image with the particularities of black working women's struggles. In these drawings and sculptures, the multiple aspects of black women's identities

Figure 11. *My role has been important in the struggle to organize the unorganized.* Linocut on paper by Elizabeth Catlett (1947). Courtesy of Pennsylvania Academy of the Fine Arts, Philadelphia. Art by Women Collection, Gift of Linda Lee Alter. Art © Catlett Mora Family Trust/Licensed by VAGA, New York, N.Y.

are as inseparable as the abstraction and representation, African and European elements, and popular and modernist styles.

In asserting black women's historical role in the family, in the economy, and in protest movements, Catlett anticipated the important work of Claudia Jones, considered the foremost Communist organizer of black women and a major Party theorist. Jones published in the Party's theoretical journal *Public Affairs*, wrote a column on women's issues for the *Daily Worker*, and served as secretary of the Women's Commission. According to her biographer Carole Boyce Davies, her 1949 essay "An End to the Neglect of the Negro Woman!" was the most radical expression of black feminism available at the time and served as a foundation for the feminist thought of Angela Davis and the next generation of New Left Civil Rights activists.[22] Like Catlett, Jones vehemently rejects the "mammy" stereotype by recovering black women as pillars of strength and sources of nurturance in their own families. She imbues black mothers with the qualities of a warrior, describing their role in "militantly shielding [the family] from the blows of Jim-Crow insults, of rearing children in an atmosphere of lynch terror, segregation, and police brutality, and of fighting for an education for the children."[23]

Like Catlett, Jones uncovers black women's leadership in social and political organizations, claiming they "are the real active forces—the organizers and workers—in all the institutions and organizations of the Negro people" and "among the most militant trade unionists."[24] Jones's most important contribution to black feminist thought was her theory of the "superexploitation" of black women as mothers and domestic workers. Black women were paid the lowest wages for performing some of the most difficult jobs—sometimes as maids to white women workers, their purported class allies—and they reproduced another generation of cheap workers through unpaid domestic labor at home.[25] More than a decade before Jones's landmark essay, African American leftist Louise Thompson wrote about African American women's "triple exploitation" in an article published in the CP magazine *Woman Today* in 1936.[26] Elizabeth Catlett's *Negro Woman* series contributes to these early articulations of black left feminism by visualizing the intersections of race, gender, and class in black women's experience. These images are alternatives to the icons of migrant motherhood that have come to define the Great Depression.

After World War I, migration offered black women a form of resistance to the exploitative conditions of domestic labor. Northern factory work, as grueling, low paid, and repetitive as it was, seemed like a desirable alternative. As one migrant woman working in a box factory in 1920 exclaimed, "I'll never work in nobody's kitchen but my own anymore. No indeed! That's the one thing that makes me stick to this job."[27] For the majority of black female migrants, however, the North was a disappointment in this respect. "Jane Crow" followed them to Chicago, Detroit, and New York, where racial divisions of labor excluded black women from factory, sales, and clerical work. As white women entered the "pink-collar" sector, domestic service came to be known as black women's work. Moreover, this racial division of labor shored up the whiteness of migrants from Europe and the American South who could gain access to these more desirable jobs. To make matters worse, a system of residential segregation confined black families to the most overcrowded, unsanitary, and dilapidated sections of northern cities, where they were charged the highest rents. Women who had to juggle wage earning and child care worried about the temptations of the street, which offered a host of dangers unknown or harder to access in the South, such as brothels, dance clubs, gangs, gambling establishments, and saloons.[28] Insisting on "living out" so they could maintain a modicum of control over their lives and their families, black women were caught, as Richard Wright put it, "between the kitchenette and the white folks' kitchen." They had to leave their children in squalor, at the mercy of the streets, to travel long distances to work for low pay caring for white families.

A pairing of photographs from Edwin Rosskam and Richard Wright's 12 Million Black Voices highlights the destructive impact of poor housing and women's paid domestic labor on black children (see Figure 12). Captioned "From the kitchenette . . . to the white folk's kitchen," this two-page spread presents mirror images of a black mother and child in a Chicago tenement and a black maid and her white charge in a white suburban home. In both photographs a woman, with bent arm extended, holding a dish, is standing near the edge of the frame, looking down toward a child. However, the gleaming white walls and the shiny kettle of the suburban home contrast starkly with the soiled, peeling background and the blackened kettle of the tenement kitchen. The differences between the two children in the photographs are also striking. The plump white baby with storybook-blonde curls sits with her back facing us, feeding herself. The thin black boy, on the other hand, soberly stares directly at the camera. Both children are enclosed, in a sense, but whereas the white baby is safely ensconced in her high chair, the boy is trapped by the corner of the stove and the half-open door. He is cut off from his mother and the sustenance she offers; half his body is already out the door, claimed by the dangerous street. These photographs provide a pathology of the city that links juvenile delinquency to poor housing and the exploitative conditions of domestic labor. The title of this chapter, "Death on City Pavements," gives a sense of this losing battle between the black urban home and the vice-ridden street, as do the titles of contemporaneous works of African American literature: Marita Bonner's short-story collection Frye Street & Environs and Ann Petry's best-selling novel, The Street.[29]

Two African American women writers, Ann Petry and Marita Bonner, produced fiction in the 1930s and 1940s that probed the "superexploitation" of black women as mothers and domestic workers. The work of Catlett, Petry, and Bonner is linked by maternal imagery as well as their Left commitments. However, their contribution to the literary Left has been by and large overlooked, both at the time and in more recent historiography. Looking at Depression-era culture through the lens of the migration narrative helps us fill this gap, since it was a dominant mode of African American expression that often placed black women at the center.[30] In a recent collection of essays that argues for Petry's place in the literary Left, Alex Lubin describes her as an "ambivalent radical" who refused to identify as a leftist, yet who employed aesthetic strategies that consistently offered a radical, even Marxist critique.[31] Most notably, Petry wrote for Harlem's People's Voice in 1941, which

Figure 12. "From the kitchenette . . . to the white folk's kitchen," from Richard Wright and Edwin Rosskam's photo-book 12 Million Black Voices (1941), 132–33. Original photograph credits: *Corner of kitchen of apartment rented to Negroes, Chicago, Illinois.* Photograph by Russell Lee (April 1941). Courtesy of Library of Congress, Prints & Photographs Division, FSA/OWI Collection, LC-USF34-038777-D. *Negro domestic servant, Atlanta, Georgia.* Photograph by Marion Post Walcott (May 1939). Courtesy of Library of Congress, Prints & Photographs Division, FSA/OWI Collection, LC-USF34-T01-051738-D.

was an important forum for the black Popular Front during the war. She also studied at the Harlem Community Art Center; performed in the American Negro Theater; cofounded the advocacy group Negro Women, Inc.; and taught classes for the Laundry Workers Joint Board—all key institutions of the black Popular Front.[32] Drawing on her experiences in Harlem during the war, Petry wrote her first novel, *The Street*, which sold over 2 million copies when published in 1946. The novel, whose nightmarish plot and naturalist style often invite comparisons to Richard Wright's *Native Son*, centers on a single mother, Lutie Johnson, who struggles to protect her son against the toxic ghetto environment. Placing her faith in the Protestant work ethic, not realizing that its recipe for success does not apply to black women, Lutie struggles to find decent work and a safe, clean apartment. While she struggles to make ends meet, her innocent son is duped into thievery by an unscrupulous building superintendent. In the end, Lutie murders the man who wants to prostitute her, leaving her son to become a ward of the state.[33]

Petry denies her readers a redemptive image of black motherhood, offering instead a class analysis of a maternal crisis that results in a self-destructive, militant act of violence. A subway advertisement symbolizes the compounded nature of black women's domestic labor exploitation, which alienates them from their own families while sustaining white families. The advertisement features a "miracle of a kitchen" with a "sink whose white porcelain surface gleamed under the train lights. The faucets looked like silver. The linoleum floor of the kitchen was a crisp black-and-white pattern that pointed up the sparkle of the room." This kitchen was "almost exactly like the one she had worked in in Connecticut" while her son Bub "had to do without her."[34] That the kitchen appears in an advertisement reinforces its status as a commodity, and the gleaming surfaces remind us of the labor that produced it. Bill Mullen argues that the advertisement depends simultaneously on domestic labor, which produces its gleaming qualities, and on the erasure of this labor, which allows the kitchen to become a commodity seemingly independent of human social relations.[35] Domestic labor produces not products but services, such as cleaning, cooking, and child care, that are so quickly consumed so as to erase the domestic worker's labor.[36] Alienated from her own labor, Lutie fails to see the social relationships that produce this miracle kitchen. Instead, she believes the American myth "that anybody could be rich if he wanted to and worked hard enough" (43). Ironically, Lutie uses "he" as a gender-neutral pronoun (which would have been standard practice in 1946) but fails to see how the myth of the self-made "man" obscures the gender and racial structures of inequality that constrain her upward social mobility. Despite her hard work and thrift, she finds there are only two brutal alternatives available to her: prostitution or working in the "white folks' kitchen." The Street offers a scathing critique of a capitalist system whose racial and gender division of labor reproduces urban black poverty and suburban white affluence.

Another middle-class black woman writer, Marita Bonner, countered the redemptive image of universal motherhood with stories of migrant women whose families were torn asunder by the geographic, class, and racial distances "between the kitchenette and the white folks' kitchen." Yet unlike Wright and Petry, Bonner highlights how migrant women used kinship networks and the sustaining aspects of southern culture to provide for and protect their families. Bonner's work advances, to an extent, Zora Neale Hurston's cultural project of formulating an affirming black culture based in the southern folk experience, yet from an urban perspective. While Bonner's women are not the freedom fighters depicted by Catlett, whose graphic medium and radical politics gave rise to more heroic portrayals of black women's political activism, Bonner's short fiction prefigures some of the black feminist works of a later generation. Not until the postwar period would African American migration narratives begin to adopt this redemptive view of the South.[37]

Between 1925 and 1941, Bonner published essays, three experimental plays, and nearly two dozen short stories in *The Crisis* and *Opportunity*, winning literary prizes for three of these short pieces. She was born to a middle-class family in Boston and was educated at Radcliffe. An anthropology course during her senior year (1921–22) titled Criminal Anthropology and Race Mixture influenced her writing, which explores the themes of juvenile delinquency, interracial sex, and mixed-race identity.[38] A couple of years after graduation, Bonner moved to Washington, D.C., where she worked as a teacher and volunteered for the Southeast Settlement House, the first for people of color in the district.[39] While engaged in these "racial uplift" activities common among middle-class African American women, she also hobnobbed with luminaries of the New Negro Renaissance such as Langston Hughes, Countee Cullen, Alain Locke, and Jessie Fauset at Georgia Douglas Johnson's S Street salon. Bonner married William Almy Occomy in 1930, and the couple moved to Chicago, which became the setting for most of Bonner's stories.[40] Bonner's middle-class values shaped her urban fiction. Her stories point to the social and moral causes of violence and promiscuity—working mothers' absence from the home, the decline in church attendance, and incompetent leadership in the school system. A word of advice Bonner gave to her daughter in 1965 demonstrates her faith-based moral outlook: "Living as we know it creates so many tensions that people turn to smoking, drinking, goofballs, drugs, etc., aspirin etc.—ad infinitum. It is best to turn to God I found for myself. I never wanted a habit."[41]

Like Ann Petry, Bonner fits uneasily into the Popular Front's literary cohort. Yet even though her political commitments were not explicitly radical, her aesthetic strategies advance twin goals of economic and racial justice that characterized Popular Front culture. Situating Bonner within Chicago's black Popular Front is important because it helps us to see the ideological flexibility of this movement as well as the prominence of African American women both as writers and as workers whose "superexploitation" best illustrated the inextricability of gender, race, and class. Black women's experience provided a powerful rejoinder to white Marxists who elevated class over other categories, and Bonner's stories sent this message to a broad liberal-Left readership.

Bonner's vignettes about urban black life and women's domestic labor anticipate the main themes in the African American little magazine *Negro Story*, which was the main outlet for Popular Front literary expression in Chicago in the 1940s.[42] While her depiction of urban life tends to infantilize black migrants, it nonetheless underscores the connection between black children's welfare and the domestic service economy. In many of Bonner's stories, vulnerable children are left to their own devices—and grow up far too fast or die far too young—while their mothers work in domestic labor. In "A Sealed Pod," for example, eighteen-year-old Viollette Davis "entertained a varied assortment of men of every race every night" and eventually gets her throat cut by one of them while her mother works nights as a scrubwoman.[43] In "Light in Dark Places," fourteen-year-old Tina narrowly avoids getting raped while her mother "went to work at six-thirty in the morning and never got home until eight at night" (281). In "Tin Can," the mother works long hours for "her rich white folks," and her son Jimmie Joe accidentally murders a romantic rival and dies a brutal death in the electric chair.[44] Each of these stories warns of the moral dangers—promiscuity, theft, and murder—that threaten children while their mothers perform domestic labor for white families. Bonner emphasizes the exploitative nature of domestic service, with unregulated hours and a decentralized, privatized workplace. "To work as long as that at the distance from the colored section that Ma had to go each day, left little time for jokes" and presumably the other kinds of nurture that adolescents like Viollette, Jimmie Joe, and Tina needed (280).

The first Frye Street stories were published as a trilogy titled "A Possible Triad on Black Notes" in *Opportunity* magazine in August 1933. Nearly a dozen stories with a similar setting followed between 1934 and 1941.[45] First, I will discuss the tension between naturalism and modernism in the "Triad" stories, and then I will examine two additional Frye Street stories—"The Whipping" and "Light in Dark Places"—that dramatize the "superexploitation" of the migrant mother and offer a black feminist vision of resistance. Bonner's aesthetic strategies betray her middle-class perspective yet also work to undermine it. Her Frye Street stories waver between naturalism, a middle-class mode that makes the slum intelligible to the reader, and what Denning calls the "ghetto pastoral," which is episodic, sketchy, and resistant to narrative.[46] The ghetto pastoral struggles to represent the neighborhood, thwarted by the ghetto's shifting geographic, ethnic, and racial boundaries. Elements of the ghetto pastoral can be seen in Bonner's subheading to the Frye Street trilogy: "*From 'The Black Map' (a book entirely unwritten).*" Bonner may simply have been announcing a larger collection unified by the geographic setting of the fictional Frye Street, similar to James Joyce's *Dubliners* or Sherwood Anderson's *Winesburg, Ohio.* Yet the paradoxical syntax of the heading suggests the ghetto pastoral's resistance to narrative: If the book is "*entirely* unwritten" (my emphasis), how does one explain the existence of these three stories? This paradox suggests the limitations of the form in charting the urban, ethnic terrain.

In the "Triad," Bonner's narrator is unsuccessful in her attempt to create a "black map" of Frye Street that makes this ethnic neighborhood navigable for the middle-class reader. Bonner's narrator acts as a kind of tour guide, addressing the reader directly as "you" and orienting one geographically to Frye Street, which *runs from the river to Grand Avenue where the El is* (102, emphasis in original). The narrator urges the reader to experience the urban environment as a living mystery, a "marvel," "puzzle," and "wonder" to be explored through the senses. Yet she ultimately concedes the city's inscrutability, thus undermining this middle-class tourism. The narrator insists on reorienting the reader several times, thus calling into question the utility of the map. By the third orientation, one can detect the narrator's irritation, as she reminds the reader in the course of a single sentence that she is repeating information through the appositive "as you know" and the parenthetical aside "(as I have already told you)" (142). The narrator also struggles to navigate the city's ethnic terrain. In guiding the reader/tourist, the narrator shifts from geographic to phenotypical to linguistic signs: "You have been down on Frye Street. You know how it runs from Grand Avenue and the L to a river; from freckled-faced tow heads to yellow Orientals; from broad Italy to broad Georgia, from hooked nose to square black noses. How it lisps in French, how it babbles in Italian, how it gurgles in German, how it drawls and crawls through Black Belt dialects" (69). This passage ends with the image of Frye Street as "muddy water in a brook"—an unnavigable waterway (69).

While the inefficacy of Bonner's literary tour guide undermines the disciplinary gaze of the naturalist narrator, her representation of working-class characters betrays a middle-class perspective. The southern migrants who inhabit Bonner's Frye Street are unable to successfully navigate the modern city. Farah Griffin argues that Bonner figures African American migration as a movement away from the "mother" and the values she represents.[47] Not only is migration a movement away from the mother, but, I would add, it is also a regression into childhood. The words used to describe the sounds of Frye Street's ethnic languages are telling—who "lisps," "babbles," "gurgles," and "crawls" but a baby? Rather than coming of age, as do the ethnic protagonists in working-class ghetto pastorals, Bonner's migrant characters become more childlike. The grandparents who had been "dragged north to the city" by their children, for example, "believed everything they heard and knew that everything they saw was real," like young innocents

(179). Whereas Reuben and Bessie, "late of Georgia," "did not know much," their city-born son "knew lots of things," like how to transform the light and dripping faucet of his tenement apartment into art and music (70). Bonner's infantilization of working-class migrants reflects middle-class representational traditions found in nineteenth-century sentimentalism and urban realism, as well as the ideology of progressive reform that shaped the settlement house movement and child welfare services in which Bonner was involved.[48]

In the migration tale "The Whipping," the protagonist, Lizabeth, fails to navigate the streets and the civic bureaucracy. Lizabeth's failure to navigate begins with the family's haphazard journey: "They walked—they begged rides—they stopped in towns, worked a little and they rode as far as they could on the train for what they had earned. It took months, but they found Federal Street" (188). Encountering hostile neighbors on Federal Street, the family moves once more, but in the wrong direction, to a place "worse than Federal Street" where "folks fought and cursed and cut and killed" (190). Finally, Lizabeth's desperate search for government relief for her starving family is in part a losing battle with geography. The narrator carefully records her route: She walks fifteen blocks to the relief station, thirty blocks home from jail, and another fifteen blocks back to the relief station (192). After stumbling from hunger at the relief office, Lizabeth is charged with drunkenness and spends the night in jail. When her son repeats the neighbors' accusation that she was out all night with men, she slaps him, and he dies. Distraught, she cannot defend herself in court and is sentenced to life in prison. Thus Lizabeth fails to navigate the state bureaucracy, the legal system, and the racist stereotypes that condition people's responses to her. When facing the relief officer whose "books had told her that colored women carried knives," she cannot effectively represent herself, and she winds up in jail for violent behavior. In court, she "seemed too stupid to defend herself" (194). Denied education and lacking urban experience, Lizabeth is unable to communicate intelligibly with the relief workers, her neighbors, and the court. She knows only the hunger that drives her, and the more sophisticated urban dwellers consistently misread her actions.

Even though Bonner's middle-class sensibilities shape her writing, her stories unfailingly remind us of the economic basis of black women's social struggles. Like many stories in the collection, "Light in Dark Places" features a migrant mother faced with the impossible task of being in two places at once—she must raise her children on her own while commuting to the "white folks' kitchen" to earn their daily bread. The narrator details the mother's long hours ('she went to work at six-thirty in the morning and never got home until eight at night") and the impact of her fourteen-hour day on family life (280). More importantly, the mother's fourteen-hour day makes her daughter more vulnerable to the dangers of the street—in this case a classmate named Luke who tries to rape her.

One reason why African American women on the Left have been overlooked is that the vast majority were relegated to domestic service, which remained outside trade union organizing. Bonner does not offer an improbable vision of domestic workers joining together in a union, but this is not to say that her work falls outside Popular Front politics. Instead, her work challenges us to broaden the scope of the Popular Front to include black feminist perspectives. Bonner's story "Light in Dark Places" offers (as the title suggests) a more hopeful outlook on the plight of black migrant mothers by including what Toni Morrison has called an "ancestor" figure—a source of protection, kindness, and wisdom.[49] Eighty-year-old Aunt Susie offers a living connection to the South and an alternative maternal presence. Suspecting that Tina is in harm's way, Aunt Susie twists off the handle of her cane to reveal "the three-sided blade of an old-fashioned dagger" and scares the rapist away (285). Aunt Susie's role in the story suggests vital survival strategies for urban migrants: the retention of southern cultural values, particularly the authority of female elders and reliance on extended family. One might argue that this strategy relies on individual networks rather than collective action, but defining collective action only in terms of nonfamilial relationships marginalizes black women. "Light in Dark Places" posits a model of migration that emphasizes the continuity of culture and kinship. Without community or cultural ties, the migrant's quest for a new home in the North fails. Bonner attributes this failure to the working conditions of black domestics, thus linking labor issues with black feminist concerns about maternal and child welfare.

Marita Bonner's migrant mothers resemble the mother in Catlett's *Mother and Child*; they strive for the nurturing ideal of the Christian icon, but the forces of racism and poverty threaten their ability to protect their children. In the Frye Street stories, these forces manifest as a variety of features of urban life: street gangs, house parties, loose women, predatory men, and above all, the system of domestic labor. While the fear of the city's vice districts reflects the sensibilities of a black club woman, Bonner ultimately challenges the middle-class strategies of both representation and reform, falling into the orbit of the Popular Front. Several of Bonner's stories, for example, satirize the reform efforts of the black middle class. In "Tin Can," the black school principal, derisively nicknamed "Old Black Bass Drum," had only empty platitudes to offer in the face of social problems, and whatever "character he might have once had, had long been swallowed up in a morass of petty littleness, snobbishness and downright silly conceit" (126). "Stones for Bread" mocks two black social workers more concerned with their wardrobe than for children, and "The Makin's" exposes the absurdity of a teacher's notion that a child might improve his trash-strewn tenement by planting flowers. These satirical pieces suggest that the crisis of the migrant mother cannot be solved by social uplift spearheaded by the black middle class, but by a more radical change in the capitalist service economy.

Working-Class Writers and the Grotesque Migrant Mother

So far we've looked at how middle-class African American women with varying degrees of commitment to Popular Front ideologies and institutions injected black migrant mothers into Left discourses of proletarian struggle. They challenged mainstream liberal strategies to represent and reform the migrant mother, exemplified by FSA photography and the New Deal programs it promoted. Elizabeth Catlett's icons of maternal power and Marita Bonner's abject protagonists defy sentimental representations of maternal suffering and redemption. Moreover, they show how domestic workers help to sustain the capitalist economy yet are denied the protections of the New Deal. Another aesthetic strategy, favored by working-class writers, was the use of grotesque imagery to push beyond Lange's redemptive icon. Countering a vast historiography that dismisses Popular Front culture as sentimental, middle brow, and conservative, Michael Denning characterizes the dominant mode of 1930s writing as a "proletarian grotesque," a modernist aesthetic that responded to the failure of realism to depict communities in crisis.[50] Joseph Entin extends Denning's notion of the proletarian grotesque, arguing for a "countertradition" of "sensational modernism" in the Depression era that used striking images of pain, violence, and prejudice to convey "a new, more urgent understanding of poverty" through "avante-garde aesthetics of astonishment."[51] This sensational style departed from the more palatable modes of naturalism and sentimentalism that middle-class artists had traditionally used to represent the poor.[52] According to Entin, this sensational rhetoric lays bare the power relations embedded in sentimental and documentary forms, which tend to romanticize the poor and invade their privacy.[53] Grotesque imagery pervaded Depression-era literature, photography, film, and popular culture and was deployed by black and white writers alike. Working in different modes, working-class writers such as Richard Wright and Tillie Olsen represented mothers as grotesque symbols of the failure of migration.

Richard Wright's photo-book of African American migration, 12 Million Black Voices, uses visual images of dirt and decay to represent racialized poverty in a shockingly visceral way. The book is the product of an interracial collaboration between Wright and white FSA photographers Edwin Rosskam and Russell Lee. Lee photographed three black families in Chicago in 1940 with the project in mind; Rosskam selected the images and wrote lengthy captions drawn from University of Chicago sociologist Horace Cayton's studies on black urban life. Although Lee took many photographs that depicted the African American families in a positive light, emphasizing their intergenerational bonds and their efforts to create decent homes, Rosskam left many of these images of intact families and fixed-up apartments out of the book. Based on Cayton's files and the photographic materials, Wright wrote the accompanying text.[54] This process of selection, sequencing of photographs, and combination with text shaped 12 Million's grotesque aesthetic.

The third chapter, titled "Death on City Pavements," ruminates on the kitchenette as the primary symbol of failed migration. The centerpiece of this chapter is a fifteen-stanza prose poem driven by rhythms resembling sacred incantations or a blues song.[55] Each line constructs a metaphor in which the kitchenette stands for racialized poverty: "the kitchenette is our prison, our death sentence without trial, the new form of mob violence that assaults not only the lone individual, but all of us, in ceaseless attacks." The middle stanzas (with one exception) follow "the kitchenette" with a verb, figuring the impoverished black home as an agent of violence: "the kitchenette . . . kills our black babies," "scatters death," "injects pressure and tension," "blights," and "jams."[56] Wright's kitchenette piece is accompanied by unmitigated photographs of human suffering and environmental decay, such as a photograph of a revoltingly dirty toilet in a decrepit bathroom. Far from escaping slavery, state-sanctioned execution, lynching, and the annihilation of the body and the self through grinding oppression, the migrants discover these horrors in new forms where they least expect to find them: the home. The images and text of 12 Million Black Voices are disturbingly scatological, depicting the home as a repository of blood and bodily waste.

Lee's photograph captioned "Mother and two children" demonstrates how the editorial acts of selection, sequencing, and word-image combination can transform the stylized Madonna imagery of the FSA into a grotesque

Figure 13. *Mother and two children. Family is on relief. Chicago, Illinois.* Photograph by Russell Lee (April 1941). Courtesy of Library of Congress, Prints & Photographs Division, FSA/OWI Collection, LC-DIG-fsa-8c00713.

(see Figure 13). Photographs—even iconic ones—do not have fixed meanings. Rather, many variables influence their interpretation, such as the caption or text accompanying them, editorial interventions such as cropping or retouching, their placement in a series, and the particular perspective brought to them by the viewer. Interartistic texts like 12 *Million Black Voices* demand close attention to word, image, and their complex interaction. According to Joseph Entin, visual and textual methods of analysis complement each other. While literature helps us to see how photographs tell a story, especially when they are arranged in a series, photographs help us to recognize how narratives are framed.[57] The cropping of Lee's photograph tightens its composition so that it more closely resembles Lange's iconic image.

Moreover, the mother's clear-eyed gaze, slight smile, tilted head, and posture of embrace lend some sentimentality to the image. Like Lange's "Migrant Mother," Lee's "Mother and two children" has the potential to engage a middle-class viewer's sympathies for a marginalized population by referring to the mother-child bond that viewer and subject ostensibly

LEFT Figure 14. *Madonna della Scala* (detail). Bas-relief marble sculpture by Michelangelo Buonarroti (ca. 1489–92). BOTTOM Figure 15. *Pietà* (front view). Marble sculpture by Michelangelo Buonarroti (1498–99).

share. However, when placed in the context of Wright's text and scatological images in 12 Million, other elements in the photograph come to light that resist this hopeful interpretation. For example, the composition is not symmetrical—the older girl sits somewhat apart from her mother and younger brother—and the children face the camera. In doing so, they appear in the photograph as individuals rather than as symbols of dependency. Their faces accentuate their particularities as human beings: The boy's facial features could possibly indicate a disability, and the girl stares at the camera with a look of defiance. The girl's striking facial expression may make viewers wonder whether the hint of a smile on the mother's lips is false; if one covers up her mouth, her eyes appear to stare as defiantly as her child's. Placed amid other migrant mother images, Lee's photograph may fit the stylized iconography of the Madonna and child and its claims to universality. Placed in the context of Wright's raging jeremiad and images of tenement squalor, however, this photograph challenges the FSA's more palatable representation of migrant motherhood that serves a liberal political agenda.

Novelists also relied on grotesque imagery to represent white migrant mothers' bodily experience of poverty amidst economic collapse. Even though Steinbeck's *Grapes of Wrath* relies primarily on middle-class representational strategies, such as sentimentalism and ethnography, it also deploys a grotesque aesthetic that destabilizes this rhetoric of redemptive motherhood. The ending of *Grapes*—which, tellingly, was too controversial to be included in John Ford's popular film version of 1940—features a grotesque tableau as Rose of Sharon bares her breast and urges an old man to take it: "Her hand moved behind his head and supported it. Her fingers moved gently in his hair. She looked up and across the barn, and her lips came together and smiled mysteriously."[58] In her serenity, conjured by her mysterious smile and gently moving fingers, Rose of Sharon resembles Michelangelo's Virgin Mother. While the act of breast-feeding alludes to the Madonna and child motif, as in Michelangelo's *Madonna della Scala*, the prostrate and "gaunt" body of the man, supported by Rose's hand, calls to mind the *Pietà* (see Figures 14 and 15).

In this final tableau, Steinbeck superimposes two opposite Christian icons, that of maternal nurturance and that of maternal despair. The result is a grotesque—an "entity for which there is no appropriate noun" that results when "logical categories are illegitimately jumbled together."[59] Just as the image of Rose of Sharon feeding the dying man is both Madonna and child and pietà, Rose herself is neither Virgin nor Mother. Her redemptive power derives from the experience of motherhood, but ultimately she exists outside the only two roles available to "good" women in the Christian tradition. Therefore, Steinbeck's grotesque mother challenges the categories of motherhood as defined by the Western Christian tradition, even as it relies on the traditional notion of motherhood to craft a redemptive ending. Merging opposing referents into a single image, Steinbeck's migrant mother is a liminal image that contrasts with Lange's icon. Whereas the icon is instantly knowable, the grotesque mystifies in its fusion of familiar parts into a monstrous whole. It destabilizes the categories we use to understand the world. The grotesque migrant mother is a body in flux, challenging the notion of teleological progress embedded in both terms "migration" and "motherhood."[60]

In her novel *Yonnondio*, Tillie Lerner Olsen pushes further than Steinbeck to show how migrant mothers embody the interlinked struggles of migration, wage work, and reproduction. Olsen is a product of the international migration, communist movement, and economic crisis that shaped her novel. Her parents, Samuel and Ida Lerner, fled Russia for the United States after the failure of the revolution in 1905 and settled on a tenant farm in Nebraska. Olsen was born seven years later and moved with her family to Omaha, where her father got a job as a packinghouse worker. She attended school until the eleventh grade but had to drop out upon the onset of the Depression so she could help support her family. Both parents influenced Olsen's political consciousness. Her father was the state secretary of the Nebraska Socialist Party, and her mother encouraged her to become a revolutionary writer. Like her friend Sanora Babb, Olsen imbibed the socialist politics of the Midwest as a child; her parents kept socialist and Marxist journals lying around the house, and she remembers fondly presenting a rose to Eugene Debs after hearing him speak.[61]

Olsen's activist career began in earnest when she joined the Young Communist League at age eighteen in 1931. She worked in a tie factory in Kansas City while attending a Party school and was jailed for passing leaflets to packinghouse workers. She moved to Faribault, Minnesota, in 1932 to recover from pleurisy and bore her first child soon thereafter at age nineteen. Olsen struggled for the next few years, a new mother, poor, and involved in an unstable relationship. She remained committed to the labor movement, however, and was again jailed for her participation in the great San Francisco maritime strike of 1934. As luck would have it, her literary talents were discovered while she was in jail. In a survey of 200 short stories written for the *New Republic*, Robert Cantwell recognized Olsen's story "The Iron Throat," which had been published in April in the *Partisan Review*, as "a work of early genius." Bennett Cerf of Random House offered Olsen a contract and a stipend to finish the novel of which the story was part—a deal similar to one he would make with Sanora Babb a few years later. Comparing Babb's and Olsen's experiences writing their novels sheds light on the unique challenges and perspectives of the writer who must also work for wages. Whereas Babb adapted easily to the literary circles of the Hollywood Left, Olsen felt alienated, as if she were a "curiosity." Olsen's status as a mother also made it harder for her to write. Babb happily immersed herself in her writing; Olsen had to leave her two-year-old daughter with her parents. She eventually broke her contract with Random House and reunited with her daughter, and only then did she produce her best work, albeit slowly.[62]

These economic pressures gave Olsen a different perspective on the relationship between art and activism. Babb—who had time and resources as well as talent and desire—saw writing as the best way to contribute to the movement. In contrast, Olsen gave priority to union organizing, which had a more immediate impact on her family's welfare. Even when Olsen did have time to write, as during her convalescence in 1932, she felt disconnected from the movement. She vowed in her journal to "abolish word victories," insisting that "without action feeling and thought are disease." Yet she also confided that "I don't know what is in me, but I must write too," expressing a tension between art and activism that was a major preoccupation of the literary Left more generally.[63] Moving back and forth between the Midwest and California, Olsen wrote intermittently, frequently deterred by illness, childbirth and child-rearing, labor organizing, and wage work. She eventually abandoned her novel after her second child was born. Like Babb, she would have to wait several decades before her literary labors were delivered. Left unfinished, with no rewriting or added chapters so that it would remain true to the vision of "that long ago young writer," *Yonnondio* was published in 1974.[64]

In an influential essay, Deborah Rosenfelt attributes Olsen's failure to complete the novel to her resistance to the literary prescriptions of Marxist critics, who supposedly called for a dramatic strike and the characters' conversion to class consciousness, that is, an appropriate revolutionary ending.[65] However, this interpretation misrepresents the Left critics, who adamantly resisted the association of radical literature with didacticism and a specific political program. When left-leaning critic Kenneth Burke insisted at the American Writers' Congress in 1935 that the "writer is really a propagandist," he was met with fierce opposition.[66] *New Masses* editor Granville Hicks dismissed as "simplistic" Burke's view that radical literature should "aim at very specific effects" in the reader.[67] Extricated from these critical approaches that are tinged by Cold War anticommunism, *Yonnondio* may be understood not as an "incomplete" strike novel but, rather, as an "uncompleteable" work of urban regionalism. As discussed in greater depth in my analysis of Sanora Babb, regionalism appealed to women writers whose domestic experience was not easily expressed by realism's action-driven plotlines. Moreover, working-class writers often rejected the bourgeois novel, preferring mass cultural forms, nonlinear modernism, and the autobiographical sketch.[68] *Yonnondio* uses grotesque imagery to shock readers with the visceral reality of working-class women's experience of urban poverty. The story remains unfinished because it defies the notion of progress embedded in the novel form and in the myths of migration, progress, and prosperity that provide the ideological foundation for industrial capitalism.

Olsen's *Yonnondio* traces the journey of the Holbrook family from a Wyoming coal mining town to a Nebraska tenant farm to an unnamed midwestern city that is most likely Omaha. Jim Holbrook is a failed farmer and wage worker who takes out his economic frustrations on his wife and family. Anna, the working-class housewife, exists in a continuous cycle of childbearing that strains her body as well as the family's resources. The story is told mainly from the point of view of Mazie, the Holbrooks' eldest daughter, who comes of age as a woman and as a political activist. The Holbrook family reaches a city that is not a destination but, rather, a grotesque slum that overwhelms Mazie. The city is occupied by "skeleton children," "monster trucks" with "blind eyes and shaking body," and "machinery" that "rasps and shrieks" (63, 78). The children see "faces masked in weariness and hate and lust," "faces distorted into laughter" with "teeth bared into a terrible smile," and figures "misshapen" and "hunched over" (91–93). Pervading Omaha is the "vast unmoving stench" of the stockyards merged with "human smells, crotch and underarm sweat" (63). Mikhail Bakhtin helps us to understand these bodily images, as the "main events in the life of the grotesque body" take place in the orifices, which mediate between bodies and the world, facilitating "an interchange and interorientation."[69] In the Omaha slum, there is no security, no safety, no boundaries. Even bodies have no confines, emitting fluids and odors just as they ingest the stinking air around them. For Mazie, who clings to her memories of the Nebraska farm, "these [urban sights] had no reality, only the reality of nightmares, for there had she seen such grotesqueness and crooked vision" (78).[70] The grotesque images—distorted people, monstrous machines, and ghastly sensations—represent the city not as a promised land but as a hideous industrial landscape that infects the bodies of its working-class inhabitants.

Like Wright's kitchenette, the working-class home in *Yonnondio* offers no safe haven from the lusty, stinking streets but is a grotesque structure in its own right. The Holbrooks rent an "ancient battered house" that, like the grotesque body, collapses the boundary between inside and outside. Its second floor is "windowless and roofless," with "paper thin boards" and "dirt which has eaten into and become part of the wall" (65). When Anna first sees the house, she looks "like you're seein a corpse" (66). In "seein a corpse," Anna experiences what Julia Kristeva calls "abjection"—our horrified reaction to the blurring of boundaries between subject and object, between self and other. The corpse is the perfect example of the abject because it places us "at the border of [our] condition as a living being," reminding us of our precarious mortality.[71] Fittingly, Kristeva's metaphor for "the one by whom the abject exists" is a migrant—'an exile who asks, where?" a "*stray*" on a journey with no end.[72] Thus Kristeva's notion of the abject helps us to see the migrant mother as one straddling the border between life and death, trapped in a terrifying liminal space that is the antithesis of women's "proper" sphere—the home. The grotesque breaks down the binary between outside and inside, public and private, wage work and housework, that excluded working-class women from both New Deal reforms and much of Left theory and practice in the 1930s.

Olsen's grotesque rendering of the pregnant and lactating mother, for example, shows how the household economy depends on and exploits women's bodies. In her reproductive cycles, Anna reflects the cyclical nature of the grotesque body, which "swallows the world and is itself swallowed by the world."[73] When pregnant, Anna is a devouring mother, growing "monstrous fat as if she were feeding on [her children]" (53). When lactating, she herself is devoured. As Anna's husband, Jim, puts it, "[The infant] Bess eatin off you don't cost no more" (66). Mazie's view of Anna reveals the darker truth behind Jim's casual observation about the economic benefits of breast-feeding, as she saw "before her a woman with her mother's face grown gaunter, holding a skeleton baby whose stomach was pushed out like a ball" (78). Jim and Mazie "read" Anna's body in two different ways: Whereas Jim sees Anna as a cash-saving source of food, Mazie sees the painful effects of caloric deprivation on a lactating mother.

The image of the pregnant female body also breaks down the distinction between the male realm of the workplace and the female realm of reproduction. At each of the stopping points in their journey—the mine, the farm, and the city—Mazie witnesses a kind of pregnancy. As a young child in a coal mining town, she conflates the mine, a male workplace, with a distorted image of a pregnant woman. Explaining the phrase "bowels of the earth" to her younger brother, Mazie imagines the mine as a man-eating woman: "Bowels of earth. It means the mine. Bowels is the stummy. Earth is a stummy and mebbe she ets the men that come down" (5). Having already witnessed three of her mother's pregnancies, Mazie associates the man-eating "stummy" with the figure of the pregnant mother, thus extending this grotesque by conflating digestive and reproductive processes. Like the mature female body, the mine contains an orifice that mediates between two worlds. By creating images that conflate the female body and the male workplace, Olsen challenges what labor historian Sonya O. Rose calls the "quintessential worker problem," or the tendency in labor history and economic theory to universalize the experience of white male wage workers to stand for the working class.[74]

The grotesque body of the mother reaches its apogee in the miscarriage—the fusion of birth and death—that results from marital rape. In a terrified stream of consciousness, the child Mazie bears witness to her mother's miscarriage:

Oh, Ma, Ma. The blood on the floor, the two lifeless braids of hair framing her face like a corpse, the wall like darkness behind. Be away, Mazie, be away. "Poppa, come in the kitchen, Momma went dead again, Poppa, come on." The drunken breath. (Fear remembered such a breath.) So cruel the way he pushes her away, uncomprehending. "Lemme sleep." "Oh, Poppa," crying now, "Momma's dead again. Please, Poppa, please come."

Running in the kitchen (so ugly, Momma, all the hair, the blood), running back with water, calling "Poppa" again till he somehow comprehends and comes (100).

Anna Holbrook's miscarriage is narrated through fragments: terrifying images of the prostrate mother interspersed with Mazie's unvoiced pleas for escape, her voiced pleas to her father for help, and parenthetical glimpses of her subconscious. Olsen's novel rejects a middle-class sensibility by giving the reader direct access to Mazie's consciousness. As Joseph Entin argues, we view the miscarriage from her fragmented perspective rather than attaining a more complete picture through a distanced narrator.[75] As Mazie's father takes control of the crisis, the fragmented prose relaxes into complete sentences, which narrate events more fluidly. On the subconscious level, Mazie battles against both her traumatic memory of being thrown down the mine shaft by a drunken miner "(Fear remembered such a breath.)" and her repulsion from the mature female body "(so ugly, Momma, all the hair, the blood)." Mazie's impossible statement, "Momma went dead again," and the morbid references to "lifeless braids" and a "face like a corpse" invoke the grotesque body's mediation of life and death. Anna's body transgresses itself, turning the inside out for gory display. In the act of miscarrying, Anna embodies the horror of homelessness, as her failure to shelter the fetus mirrors the family's failure to find a livable home. Olsen thus rewrites the conventional white migration narrative—a tale of regeneration and rebirth, of mobility and progress—as one of miscarriage and dislocation. In fact, Olsen planned to end the novel with Anna's death in a botched abortion attempt. The pregnant woman is figured as a devouring mother and a living corpse. Far from being a symbol of redemption for a people in exile, the migrant mother is a grotesque, her children ever wandering.

Tillie Olsen's Yonnondio and Richard Wright's 12 Million Black Voices render the bodily and psychic suffering induced by grinding poverty through textual and visual images of grotesque migrant mothers. These texts lay bare the class and racial conflicts experienced by labor migrants in the 1930s, as do Elizabeth Catlett's images of militant domestic workers. Likewise, Marita Bonner's migrant mothers are triply bound by race, gender, and class exploitation and thus turn to one another—to the power of their communal, kinship-based culture—for survival. Together, these migrant mothers upend the American mythology of progress, prosperity, and self-making. Rather than eliciting middle-class sympathy for the "Madonnas of the Fields," they provoke a more visceral reaction that matches the communist Left's urgent call for social change.

Unlike single men in some migration stories, however, these migrant mothers do not ally in common cause against poverty, racism, and sexism. In other words, narratives of migrant mothers tend to be about black or white women, but rarely both.[76] This meeting of the black and white migrant mother will happen later, in Harriette Arnow's epic novel of Appalachian migration, The Dollmaker, published in 1954. As in the hobo narratives discussed in Chapter 1, this interracial encounter occurs on a train. Gertie Nevels, an Appalachian migrant to Detroit, encounters a black migrant, Beulah Mae, in the ladies' lounge, where both women sought respite from the crowded, fetid passenger car. The women bond over their shared folk values; both carry "hard-earned bills, worn from saving," and Beulah Mae appreciates Gertie's handiwork. They exchange tokens of friendship, a dollar to be kept for a "good luck piece" so it wouldn't seem like payment, and a wooden doll as a "good luck token."[77] Once the women reach Detroit, however, their migratory paths diverge. Gertie moves into the white company housing, the "only places in Detroit," according to her Irish neighbor, "where they keep u niggers out" (180). Beulah Mae moves on to the black neighborhood ironically called "Paradise Valley," where "since u riots [the police] go mostly in prowl cars, three by threes, sometimes two by twos" (165). Although their husbands might ally in their industrial unions and their sons on boxcar journeys, these migrant mothers remain separated by housing segregation and labor markets segmented by race and gender.

This fundamental divergence in black and white migration narratives points to a persistent stumbling block in American race relations. The civil rights movement that gained new life in the 1930s and evolved into the postwar period made inroads in the public realm by integrating schools, unions, and other public spaces, and African Americans gained legal protections through the judicial process. However, the private, daily realms of the home and neighborhood still remain staunchly resistant to integration. Both African American and white migration narratives in the Depression era entail, at a fundamental level, a mythic quest for "home." However, these homes, as Gertie Nevels found out, are divided by a color line.

CHAPTER 5

WARTIME SHIPYARD

Through stories of freedom-seeking hoboes and militant migrant workers, through images of failed births that give rise to a new collective consciousness, radical writers of the 1930s envisioned southern migrants as the harbingers of change. They insisted that shared class interests transcended differences of race and gender. The mobilization for World War II would dramatically alter economic and political conditions in the United States, as well as writers' strategies for imagining social democracy. While the Roosevelt administration and its Popular Front allies issued an urgent call for unity against fascism, bloody racial conflicts embroiled the American home front. Impoverished dust bowl migrants secured steady jobs in the defense industries. Yet they guarded their precarious social status against new workers—women and African Americans—who also sought financial security after a decade of Depression, who sought full citizenship after generations of servitude. Amidst these wartime conflicts, Steinbeck's image of the Okie as populist hero was no longer tenable, nor was William Attaway's image of black and white southerners shaking hands. Southern migrants continued to play a lead role in the drama of American identity and working-class struggle in the 1940s, but their characterization shifted dramatically. A symbol of democracy's promise in the 1930s, the strained relationship between black and white migrants foretold the perils of homegrown fascism and democracy's limits in the 1940s.

Writers on the Left interpreted the wartime conflicts between black and white migrants in different ways, and these differences show us how a concept that most Americans take for granted—the racial and ethnic inclusiveness of the American liberal creed—was deeply contested in the 1940s. This chapter examines three texts that express a range of views on the impact of migration on American democracy during the war. First, liberal sociologist Katherine Archibald's ethnography *Wartime Shipyard* (1947) views southern white migrants as racial extremists that pose a serious threat to American democracy. Drawing on the emerging discourse of America as a "nation of immigrants," she urges unions and the New Deal state to modernize these newcomers and incorporate them into the democratic fold. Second, Arna Bontemps and Jack Conroy's popular history of African American migration *They Seek a City* (1945) builds on this notion of America as a "nation of immigrants," offering a counternarrative of the Detroit riots and Los Angeles housing crunch with tales of interracial unity and social democracy. The similarities between these two texts reflect a liberal-Left consensus that consolidated into what Gunnar Myrdal called the "American Creed" in the postwar period. Third, I explore a radically different vision of civil rights and American democracy through the writings of African American novelist Chester Himes. Unlike Archibald, Bontemps, and Conroy, Himes viewed the conflicts in the shipyards through an anticolonialist framework that challenged the notion of American universalism—the idea that the nation-state could expand to include all people as free and equal citizens. In Himes's wartime novel and essays, southern white migrants transplant Jim Crow to California and export it abroad, aided and abetted by unions, the police, the legal system, and the military. Developing the hard-boiled style he would become famous for, Himes places sex at the center of his novel *If He Hollers Let Him Go*. By structuring the novel according to the rhetoric of the rape-lynch triangle, Himes offers the transnational yet disturbingly masculinist view that the sexual repression of men of color is not merely a southern phenomenon but an instrument of colonial conquest at home and overseas.

The labor migration during World War II was the largest the nation had ever seen, more extensive than the dust bowl migration of the 1930s and even the African American Great Migration of the preceding decades. Twenty-five million people—more than 20 percent of the population of the United States—migrated to another country or state for military service or employment in the 1940s.[1] With its burgeoning shipbuilding and aviation industries, the West Coast received more migrants than any other region in the United States. This influx of new workers transformed the gender and racial landscapes of war production cities. Women dominated the migration to the West Coast by a ratio of 94:100, and never before had so many married women entered the industrial workforce. In San Francisco, for example, 46 percent of the shipyard workers were married women. While government propaganda, such as the famous "Rosie the Riveter" icon, framed women's industrial work as a temporary patriotic duty, these work experiences caused many women to question the restrictive domestic ideology of white, middle-class society. By the end of the war the vast majority of women wanted to continue welding, riveting, and earning the high wages that compensated these traditionally male occupations.[2] African Americans were also lured to defense production zones by high wages and improved job prospects. In 1941 President Franklin D. Roosevelt opened the flood-gates of African American migration to California when he issued Executive Order 8802, which prohibited racial discrimination in hiring by the government and defense industries. These inexperienced workers—women, African Americans, and also rural whites—were quickly hired by shipyards. These tiny enterprises ballooned into a gigantic industry employing 700,000 workers at the peak of wartime production in 1943. Suffice it to say, wartime migration reconfigured the American working class.

With the black population of California skyrocketing, racial tensions flared in its overcrowded cities. Housing was incredibly scarce. Even though defense workers earned decent wages, many could be found sleeping on benches and in restaurants, theaters, cars, and public buildings.[3] Los Angeles County alone had a deficit of over 11,000 units. African Americans bore the brunt of this shortage, as they were excluded from federal construction programs, from the war guest program, and by restrictive covenants.[4] According to Carey McWilliams, former director of the Division of Housing and Immigration known for his antiracist activism, the Federal Housing Authority codified residential segregation in California by following the practice of "respecting local attitudes" in determining the racial makeup of public housing.[5] When these structural impediments weren't enough, white citizens resorted to violence to defend the color line in urban neighborhoods.

African Americans, Mexicans, white migrants, and longtime residents also vied over physical space on buses, streets, restaurants, and other public venues. In cities like San Francisco and Los Angeles, rumors flew that African Americans formed "bumpers and pushers clubs" to harass white citizens.[6] In turn, Popular Front writers Arna Bontemps and Jack Conroy blamed southern "Lily Whites" for provoking "clashes on streetcars, in shops, in public parks and playgrounds, and in the factories."[7] These competing accusations indicate the importance of public space as a racial battleground in destination cities. Racial mixing on crowded streetcars and in other public places was particularly galling to white southerners unaccustomed to uninvited physical contact with nonwhites. As Archibald noted, "The very crushing together of black and white flesh in the enforced intimacies of public vehicles was an almost unbearable affront to fastidious members of the superior race."[8] This escalation of racial tension in the defense production areas, the director of the

Los Angeles Urban League warned, was no less than the "Southernizing of California."[9]

Racial tensions in Los Angeles and across the United States reached a fever pitch in 1943. With wartime production at its peak, migrants pushed against the limits of crowded neighborhoods and strained city resources. Deadly race riots broke out in Harlem, Detroit, Los Angeles, and other destination cities. While the riot in Harlem was sparked by a rumor of police brutality against a black boy, the violence in Detroit and L.A. was sexually charged. In the sweltering summer of 1943, a brawl erupted on the Belle Isle bridge, a recreational area on the Detroit River. Although the exact origins of the violence are unknown, rumors flew on both sides of the color line: Some said a white crowd threw a black woman and her baby into the river; others reported that a black mob killed a white mother; soon throngs of black men were allegedly tearing the bathing suits of white women and raping them. These sexually charged rumors quickly fueled a full-blown race riot. Gangs of white men roamed through Paradise Valley (the ironic name of the black district), burning cars, attacking pedestrians, and ripping riders from streetcars and beating them. African American men retaliated by looting white-owned stores and attacking hapless white defense workers as they got off shift. Police shot seventeen black people to death but spared white rioters. After three days, thirty-four people lay dead, twenty-five of whom were African American.[10]

In Los Angeles that same June, Mexican American youth were the target of unrestrained racial violence. Over the course of four days, white servicemen on leave in the city viciously attacked Mexican American youth wearing the trendy "zoot suit" of draped trousers, broad-brimmed hats, and oversized, fingertip-length coats. Hundreds if not thousands of zoot suiters— some as young as twelve years old—were stripped and beaten and then carted off to jail for disturbing the peace.[11] As in Detroit, the riot seemed to be caused by sexual tensions. U.S. servicemen claimed that they were defending white women from lascivious Mexican juvenile delinquents, while black and Mexican men aggressively defended women in their communities from predatory sailors. Sexual transgressions may have been the spark that ignited riots in Los Angeles and other American cities during the war, but more broadly speaking, the riots were a response to the disruption of social relations due to the influx of diverse newcomers and the economic boom. Cultural historian Luis Alvarez argues that Mexican youth in their elaborate outfits signified a threat to home front stability; their extravagant clothes and leisure pursuits flouted patriotic calls for austerity and duty, and their highly visible presence on the streets challenged the traditional domain of white men.[12] The zoot suit riots "raised critical questions about what and who was considered a legitimate part or member of U.S. society during World War II."[13] African American, Mexican, and white working-class migrants came to California not only to make a better living but also to assume the responsibilities of citizenship, to claim, as African American writer Chester Himes put it, their "heritage of equal participation in government and equal benefit from natural resources."[14] These migrants asserted their right to belong on city streets, on public transportation, in unions, and in the body politic.

The shipyards were another arena for this contest over cultural citizenship. But rather than facilitating the incorporation of southern migrants and women into the larger social fabric, the shipyard unions obstructed their quest for full participation in the economic, social, and political life of the city. In exchange for a no-strike pledge at the onset of the war, both the AFL and the CIO were granted a closed shop, which meant that the shipyards could only employ union members. This agreement gave the unions tremendous control over the work process, including placement, training, advancement, and discipline. Whereas the CIO used its power to push for more democratic unions, such as the International Union of Marine and Shipbuilding Workers of America on the Atlantic coast, the AFL, which dominated the West Coast shipbuilding industry, shored up its exclusive practices.[15] Faced with a massive inexperienced workforce, shipbuilders de-skilled the production process, replacing skilled tasks with an assembly line process.[16] In response, older skilled workers used the unions to protect their crafts.[17] The AFL's International Brotherhood of Boilermakers, Iron Shipbuilders, and Helpers of America, which represented 65 to 70 percent of shipyard workers, effectively denied African Americans and women the benefits of union membership. African American men and women were required to pay dues for their membership in separate auxiliaries that were absolutely powerless, lacking the voting rights, representation at conventions, grievance procedures, insurance, and other benefits enjoyed by white members.[18] Due to intense labor shortages, the brotherhood finally admitted white women in 1942, but they could not vote or hold office. African American women gained employment in the shipyards after white women and faced the most discrimination, yet war mobilization provided a welcome alternative to domestic service. Two-thirds of black women in the San Francisco Bay area worked in domestic service in 1940; by 1948 this proportion had dropped to 20 percent. African American women filed grievances with the federal government to protest hiring discrimination, but they did not gain access to the better-paid jobs as "helpers" in the shipbuilding industry until the end of the war. Most were relegated to menial positions such as janitorial and food service workers.[19] Although African Americans enjoyed unprecedented economic opportunities during the war, patterns of segregation and discrimination followed them from the Jim Crow South to the shop floors, neighborhoods, and urban spaces of California.

Chester Himes's novel of wartime migration, *If He Hollers Let Him Go*, responds to these conflicts over housing and public space and, in particular, to the discriminatory practices of the shipyard unions. Himes was an educated African American writer who migrated from Ohio to California in 1941. He worked in twenty-three different positions in the defense industries over the course of a few years, often quitting in response to the racial discrimination he experienced. His semiautobiographical novel follows four frenetic days in the life of Bob Jones, a leaderman supervising an all-black crew at Atlas Shipyard in Los Angeles. Bob rankles at the Jim Crow practices that prevent his crew from meeting their production goals. Hank, a white leaderman from Georgia responsible for assigning "tackers" to the crews, makes the black mechanics wait until there is a black tacker available, "and if they got mad about it he gave them a line of his soft Southern jive."[20] Himes suggests that white southerners made these discriminatory practices more entrenched. Bob's boss, for example, uses the racial sensibilities of southern white workers as an excuse to keep black workers in their place. "You know how Southern people talk," he admonishes Bob, "how they feel about working with you coloured boys" (29). The central conflict in the novel between Bob and a southern white woman, Madge, is sparked when Madge refuses to work with Bob and calls him a "nigger." Bob retaliates by calling her a "cracker bitch" and is demoted. When Bob demands that the union steward force Madge to "work with Negroes here or lose her job," the steward replies, "If we tried that, half the workers in the yard would walk out" (113).

Indeed, white rank-and-file workers across the country instigated "hate strikes" to protest the hiring, promotion, and integration of black workers. Electrical workers in Baltimore, transport workers in Philadelphia, shipyard workers in Mobile, autoworkers in Detroit, welders in Michigan, and many other white workers across the country walked off the job, sometimes rioting and attacking black coworkers, to protest the hiring and promotion of African Americans.[21] While often motivated by bald racism, white workers also initiated unofficial "wildcat" strikes in order to gain control over their working conditions in the face of speedups, long hours, fewer breaks, unsafe conditions, and increasingly stringent workplace discipline. As they lost power on the shop floor, many white workers perceived the hiring of African Americans as another example of management's violation of their right to control their working conditions, specifically their "right" to choose with whom they worked.[22] Black workers also initiated wildcat strikes to protest employment discrimination, but their relatively small numbers made these direct action tactics more risky. Many others, such as L.A. shipyard worker Walter Williams, filed grievances through Roosevelt's Fair Employment Practices Commission. These legal strategies had some success in advancing working-class civil rights, but the commission lacked enforcement muscle. Due to the exigencies of the war, unions and the commission gave efficiency of production priority over African American rights by capitulating to white workers' racist demands.[23] Himes's novel indicts white working-class racism but also reveals the patterns of discrimination by unions, employers, and the state that support these practices.

These racial conflicts on the American home front thwarted the efforts of activists, organizers, and writers to build more democratic unions and a broader labor front. Like Himes, many progressive and radical commentators blamed white southerners for this troubling surge of racial hostilities in the defense production zones. Although migration was only one of many factors in this social turmoil, southern migrants became the symbol of the crisis of unions, racial divisions, and the uncertain future of American democracy more broadly. For example, Walter White and Thurgood Marshall, executive officers of the NAACP, charged southern white migrants with instigating the 1943 Packard strike in Detroit, in which 25,000 workers walked out of an automobile plant to protest the promotion of three African Americans. According to White and Marshall, agitators "whipped up [racist] sentiment particularly among the Southern whites" and pulled off the strike despite the fact that a majority of employees initially opposed it, as did the CIO-affiliated union the United Auto Workers.[24] Arna Bontemps and Jack Conroy similarly charged a "loud-mouthed and aggressive minority" for initiating the Philadelphia transport workers' wildcat strike. However, historian James Gregory argues that southern white migrants were not proportionately more active in the Ku Klux Klan and in the Detroit riots than their northern-born peers, but that they were merely more visible. "The white migrant as bigot," Gregory asserts, "became one of the defining stories of the wartime and postwar news media."[25]

In my view, southern migrants took center stage in the social conflicts of the 1940s because they personified the cultural contradictions between the democratic rhetoric of the war and the ongoing—even escalating—demonstrations of white supremacy through segregation, race riots, Japanese internment, and U.S. military occupations in Asia and the Caribbean. Even though white northerners profited from and enforced differential treatment based on race, southern white migrants symbolized the nationalization of Jim Crow. More specifically, the conflicts between black and white migrants in the defense industries posed a troubling contradiction to the national mythology of America as a welcoming "nation of immigrants" that came to the fore in the 1940s. Whereas liberal writers saw wartime race riots and hate strikes as a painful episode in a larger process of modernization, Chester Himes rejected this national narrative. Instead, he pushed his allies on the Left to consider the expansion of Jim Crow as part of a larger imperial project.

Southern Migrants and the Nation of Immigrants

Whereas myths of Anglo-Saxon superiority sustained a racialist strain of American nationalism for centuries, Popular Front writers were instrumental in developing a new narrative of America as a "nation of immigrants" in the 1930s and '40s. According to this civic myth, the United States is exceptional in its liberal access to citizenship and derives its strength and vitality from the incorporation of diverse immigrant groups into the national core. Yet the term "immigrant" was fairly new in the 1940s, emerging in public discourse during the great wave of migration from southern and eastern Europe between 1890 and 1920 to distinguish older, northern European settlers from these "undesirable" Jewish and Catholic newcomers.[26] In response to this perceived social threat, the United States passed the Immigration Act in 1917 and the Johnson-Reed Act of 1924 that closed the American border, established discriminatory quotas based on national origins, and excluded virtually all nonwhite immigrants outside the Western Hemisphere. By the late 1930s and 1940s, a new cultural context called for a new national mythology. According to historian Gary Gerstle, during the New Deal era a more inclusive ideology of "civic nationalism" supplanted the "racial nationalism" that thrived in the 1920s. Rooted in the Declaration of Independence and the Constitution, civic nationalism insists that the nation was founded upon the ideals of liberty, equality, and government by consent. Racial nationalism, in contrast, defines the nation by common ancestry and, as the Johnson-Reed Act attests, posits an exclusive concept of citizenship.[27] Many factors contributed to the ascendency of civic nationalism in the 1930s and '40s. A generation after immigration restriction went into effect, the children of southern and eastern European immigrants had entered the mainstream of U.S. political, social, and economic life. Commemorating the fiftieth anniversary of the Statue of Liberty, President Franklin D. Roosevelt remarked that the children of these new immigrants "more and more realize their common destiny in America."[28] Moreover, anthropologists such as Franz Boas discredited biological explanations of human difference, ushering in a new understanding of culture. Perhaps most importantly, the rise of fascist regimes in Europe finally made eugenics and other biological theories of race untenable in the United States. In 1941 the newly coined tern "ethnicity" entered public discourse to replace "race," which became increasingly associated with the Nazi regime.[29]

Writers associated with California's Popular Front were instrumental in developing new theories of ethnicity in the 1940s that informed the "nation of immigrants" myth. Two key figures, Carey McWilliams and Louis Adamic, founded the journal *Common Ground* in 1940, which brought the term "multiculturalism" into common currency.[30] The editors included stories by European immigrants as well as Asian, Latino, African American, and "Okie" writers, blurring the distinctions between race, region, and national origin within an inclusive concept of ethnicity. Adamic popularized this ideology of American pluralism his book *A Nation of Nations* (1945), a compendium of the country's various immigrant groups. According to this master narrative, the Puritans were the first immigrants, and each successive wave, though experiencing hardship, eventually assimilated and helped the United States to redefine its core values. Aiming to rewrite American history with immigrants (and African Americans) at the center, Adamic reminds readers "that the Negroes' American tradition of fighting for liberty dates from 1526; that a handful of Polish, German and Armenian workers at Jamestown, Virginia, in 1619, staged one of the first rebellions in the New World; that John Peter Zenger, a German printer in the 1730s . . . fathered the American ideal of freedom of the press; that Philip Mazzei, the Italian friend and neighbor of Thomas Jefferson, influenced the Revolution of 1776; that the Irish were the backbone of the political-military movement that won American Independence."[31] During World War II, this narrative of a "nation of immigrants" provided ideological support for America's claim to being a model of freedom and democracy for the rest of the world.

Yet while the "new" European immigrants such as Adamic were being incorporated into the American body politic, black and white migrants from the U.S. South remained civic outsiders, for different reasons. African

Americans and other dark-skinned peoples remained outside the national community through structural discrimination and entrenched racist attitudes. In turn, southern whites remained outside due to their recalcitrant racism, which contradicted these public avowals of American universalism. The conflicts between black and white migrants in the "arsenal of democracy" thus challenged the very premise of the "nation of immigrants" mythology. Stories of the suppression of black rights, publicized in novels, social studies, and the mass media, raised the question of whether African Americans and dark-skinned peoples fit into a narrative that is based on the experience of European immigrants. Meanwhile, the visibility of southern whites in hate strikes, race riots, and military service raised the question of whether the American concept of citizenship was founded on inclusivity or racial exclusion.

In June 1942, sociologist Katherine Archibald began working at the Moore Dry Dock in Richmond, California. While contributing to the war effort by building ships, she also trained her professional eye on the social interactions among her fellow workers. Perhaps never before had such a diverse group been plunged together, as labor-hungry defense industries lured housewives and farmers, teenaged girls and elderly men, African Americans and immigrants, and domestics and drifters with the promise of high wages and steady work. She published her findings in her oft-cited book, *Wartime Shipyard: A Study in Social Disunity*, in 1947. Giving shape to the emerging myth of America as a "nation of immigrants," Archibald likens the shipyard to another Ellis Island, through which "thronged the inhabitants of America's various geographical and social regions, to be subjected to a fleeting but intense process of unification."[32] Whereas William Attaway imagined the steel mill as a crucible in which a united proletariat might be forged, Archibald describes the shipyard as a port of entry that could be a gathering place for citizens who, with the proper discipline, identify themselves on a basis of class or nation rather than common ancestry. Archibald's vision is a conversion narrative of a multiracial democracy without the radical implications of class revolution. She posits, in other words, that African Americans and southern whites could be incorporated, like previous waves of immigrants, into the national fold.

Although Archibald believed that the democratic state had the potential to provide a larger social identity for a diverse working class, she felt that the United States was far from reaching this goal. Her work, subtitled *A Study in Social Disunity*, is far less hopeful than Gunner Myrdal's *An American Dilemma*, which "transformed conditional hopes for racial equality awakened by the war into teleological certainties," according to historian Nikhil Singh.[33] Instead, Archibald struggles to reconcile the "nation of immigrants" framework with the racial hostilities she so carefully documents. In a deeply personal anecdote, Archibald relates the psychological grip of white supremacy on a female defense migrant named Beulah. Archibald describes Beulah as a "classical Okie"—loud, uncouth, uneducated, superstitious—who was frequently the "butt of ridicule and caustic humor" from her more seasoned fellow workers. One morning, a disgruntled passenger on a crowded streetcar told Beulah that the Okies should "go back where they came from." Seizing the opportunity to impart a lesson in democracy, Archibald urged Beulah to see "the similar injustice in her hatred of the Negro. Prejudice is always unfair, I pointed out, whether it be prejudice against the Okie or the man whose skin is black." Beulah's reaction fell far from the mark: "She fairly shrieked in answer to my Christian counsels, 'But I'm no nigger! I'm not black!' And, sobbing in her now immense distress, she ran off to tell whoever would listen that I had said she was 'no better than a nigger wench.'"[34]

This anecdote is a prime example of the intersection of race, gender, class, and sexuality in the social relations of the shipyard. Notably, Archibald refers to prejudice against "the *man* whose skin is black," yet Beulah tells her friends she had been called a "nigger *wench*." Beulah's twisting of words illustrates how, in Matt Wray's terms, race, gender, class, and sexuality are "four deeply related subprocesses of a single, larger process of social differentiation."[35] The term "nigger wench" combines signifiers of all four categories, describing a black woman who is both a common worker and sexually available. The term "wench" became associated with black women in colonial Virginia, where the economic and sexual exploitation of African women made it possible for English women to be domestic "goodwives" in the New World.[36] Beulah's claim to respectable white womanhood was tenuous: She violated middle-class gender norms by working and working-class gender norms by performing male work, and these violations made her sexually suspect. Beulah was already distanced from the white community along these lines of class, gender, and sexuality; Archibald's parallel reinforced the notion that she was "not quite white."[37]

Beulah's story stands in sharp contrast to interracial conversion scenes in radical literature of the 1930s, in which black and white migrants recognize their shared outsider status and gain class consciousness. Instead, coworkers like Beulah tested Archibald's Marxist framework for understanding social inequality. Archibald had recently earned a doctorate in social institutions from the University of California at Berkeley and studied Marxist economic theory with Leo Rogin.[38] She envisioned a better society in Marxist terms, as "the achievement of the ultimate equalitarian ideal, the end of classes and the destruction of all status."[39] Yet Archibald identified herself as "an academician and a liberal," and her political sympathies with the working class aligned with the New Deal establishment rather than the radical Left. Archibald's real-world tale of failed conversion challenges the Marxist theory that capital divides labor along racial lines and, instead, locates the origins of racism in the white worker's psyche. "Hatred of the Negro," she concludes, was "an indispensable constituent of his sense of well-being and the very foundation on which his estimate of his own importance was erected. His conviction that the Negro was inherently inferior carried with it the assurance of the white man's God-given right to the more prominent place in the sun. Thus even the most ignorant white shipyard worker whose post was at the bottom of a thousand higher steps might by virtue of racial heritage alone look arrogantly down upon his black-skinned companions in toil."[40] In asserting that racism has psychological rather than economic origins, Archibald questions the viability of the communist mantra "black and white, unite and fight!" As radical labor and antiracist movements became increasingly incorporated into the New Deal, racial liberals looked to large institutions such as unions, schools, and the American nation-state to modernize racist citizens and extend the fruits of citizenship to racial minorities.

Archibald's analysis signals a major shift in liberal thought in the 1940s from a populist belief in workers as agents of change to the state-centered approach of modern racial liberalism. Archibald entered the shipyards hoping to find a unity of purpose but was shocked and distressed by the bitter racial, ethnic, and gender hostilities she witnessed. Her experience destroyed her populist belief in the power of workers to level social hierarchies. Instead, she developed a view of the shipyard worker as a politically "docile" creature whose "acceptance of the claims of his nation was undoubtedly far more the result of a consciousness of irresistible might before which the rebellion of the individual would be futile than the outcome of a positive sense of loyalty, alliance, or complete agreement."[41] According to Archibald, workers did not support the war because they believed in American democratic ideals; they supported it out of deference to power. Likewise, Archibald sees workers as individualists who jockey for position in the social hierarchy rather than questioning the hierarchy itself. "So far as status within the shipyard hierarchy implied superiority to other groups and involved external advantages," she writes, "status was prized and guarded from disturbance and the whole hierarchical system was protected and sustained."[42] Dismissing workers' kinship-based allegiances as "childlike" and "limited in scope,"[43] Archibald calls on larger institutions such as the trade union, political party, and nation-state to act as "agencies of fusion" that might provide a broader basis for social identification.[44] Thus she understands national identity as a favorable alternative to ethno-racial identity, creating a dichotomy between "race" and "nation" that continues to dominate the political discourse today. According to historian Nikhil Singh, "The prevailing common sense of the post–civil rights era is that race is the provenance of an unjust, irrational ascription and prejudice, while nation is the necessary horizon of our hopes for color-blind justice, equality, and fair play."[45]

While Archibald laments the failure of unions and the state to act as "agencies of fusion," she sustains a hopeful outlook on American ethnic and race relations by placing black and white newcomers in the "nation of immigrants" framework. She understands the Okies to be a kind of primitive subculture undergoing the initial stages of modernization. Whereas writers during the 1930s downplayed differences of race and region to narrate a dramatic change in consciousness, many writers came to realize during the war—particularly after the bloody conflicts of 1943—that migrants preserved their cultural beliefs and traditions. Trained by Robert H. Lowie, a student of Franz Boas,[46] Archibald relies on sociological and anthropological theories to understand this process of acculturation. The family, Archibald explains, was the fundamental social unit of migrants, and they understood their relationship to others through familial logic. While a kinship model of social relations fostered charitable giving and camaraderie among small groups of workers, it also "implied the existence of non-kin, the stranger, for whom there were no provisions in the code of cooperative relationships. Thus his system of society was marked by definite boundaries beyond which friendly contact was summarily discounted; it was, so to speak, a small and compact island around which raged a mighty alien sea."[47] Sexual tensions are at the heart of these social conflicts, and Archibald attributes them to the Okies' "primitive" mindset. Fear of miscegenation and its attendant violence reflects "the ancient fear of despoliation of women of the privileged race by men of inferior blood, which has played so large a part in the establishment and elaboration of caste systems in all societies."[48] Archibald's analysis of the conflicts between the Okies, African Americans, and other groups of shipyard workers accords with Chicago sociologist Robert Park's "race relations cycle," which entails the successive stages of contact, conflict, accommodation, and assimilation. Inhabiting the early phases of this cycle, the Okies demonstrate a primitive mentality to be eradicated through a process of modernization and Americanization. This notion of immigration as a process of modernization originated with the Chicago school of sociology and persisted into the latter half of the twentieth century, entering the popular imagination through John F. Kennedy's *A Nation of Immigrants*, published in 1958.[49]

Using immigration as a model, Archibald understands the racial conflicts in the shipyards as a temporary phase of adjustment. The overall pattern she describes is one of increasing democracy rather than systematic racial exclusion. As in so many migration texts, the Okies symbolize the nation's capacity for change: "For change there obviously was," she writes: "Its variety and degree appear as especially noteworthy when the Okies are considered. Most, if not all, of these people had never used the same toilet facilities or eaten at the same tables or sat in the same streetcar seats with a Negro until they migrated to the shipyards. They would have judged such familiarity unbearable. Yet from their first day in the shipyards they accepted it without open revolt, and after a few months even their protests tended to die away."[50] In this passage, the Okies have reached the stage of "accommodation," and their eventual assimilation heralds a more democratic future. Yet Archibald has little faith that the workers will follow this path toward greater democracy on their own. Although she acknowledges the "malleability of workers' attitudes," she claims that they could just as easily succumb to reactionary influences and activate "pogroms as bloody as have ever afflicted society." She calls upon unions and the state to teach the migrants to identify with one another based on "common needs and goals" rather than shared blood.[51] While this framework insists on an inclusive national identity rooted in economic justice, it fails to confront the ways in which racism grew out of modernity and how slavery and conquest gave rise to the American nation. Instead, Archibald's *Wartime Shipyard* advances the teleological "nation of immigrants" myth that views race and racism as aberrations in America's inevitable march toward universal democracy.

Writers and activists mobilized the patriotic "nation of immigrants" trope not only to counter prejudice against minority groups and generate unity for the war effort but also to advance the rights of workers. As Gerstle notes, the CIO leaders and ordinary workers framed the labor movement as a struggle for national well-being.[52] Even before the United States entered the war, black Communist singer-activist Paul Robeson likewise fused class politics, antiracism, and patriotic rhetoric in his "Ballad for Americans," performed on CBS radio in 1939. The song celebrates the racial, ethnic, and religious diversity of American workers, the "et ceteras and so-forths who do the work," who are "Irish-Negro-Jewish-Italian-French and English, Spanish, Russian, Chinese, Polish, Scotch, Hungarian, Swedish, Finnish, Canadian, Greek and Turk, and Czech and Double Czech American."[53] Robeson's pun— "Czech and Double Czech American"—equates the ethnic worker with the ideal citizen. Even Earl Browder, chairman of the CPUSA, joined in this nationalistic spirit by coining the slogan "communism is twentieth-century Americanism."[54] As critic Barbara Foley argues, Popular Front expressions of unity increasingly resembled mainstream American patriotism.[55] Thus the Left mobilized the popular narrative of "a nation of immigrants" to cast pro-labor, antiracist politics as a patriotic endeavor.

Popular Front writers Arna Bontemps and Jack Conroy created a class-conscious version of the "nation of immigrants" narrative in their history of African American migration, *They Seek a City* (1945). Like Archibald, they place African American migration within a larger narrative of progress that accords with the ideology of American universalism. Their embrace of this liberal creed is worth exploring because unlike Archibald, Bontemps and, even more so, Conroy had radical political commitments and were active in the literary Left of the 1930s. These migrant writers, one black and one white, met in 1940 through the Illinois Federal Writers' Project, which supported their Left politics and provided opportunities for interracial collaboration. *They Seek a City* began as a federally funded study of black migration called "The Negro in Illinois." It was the first of four books they wrote together. With funding from a Guggenheim fellowship, Conroy, a white working-class writer, researched the migrations of rural southerners to northern cities. Having grown up with and labored alongside black migrants in the coal mines of Missouri and, later, in the auto factories of Detroit, Conroy was fascinated by the African American experience and committed to interracial organizing. Bontemps, an African American intellectual, toed the line between middle-class respectability and radical dissent. He was born in Louisiana and migrated to California as a child. He hobnobbed with the Harlem literati in the 1920s, but when times got tough during the Depression, he moved to Alabama to take a job at a junior college in order to support his growing family. Horrified by the trials in nearby Scottsboro and forced by his employers to burn politically objectionable books, he returned to California. He then moved his young family to Chicago in 1936, where he taught, worked for the Illinois Federal Writers' Project, participated in the radical South Side Writers' Group, and pursued a degree in library science.

Bontemps and Conroy refocus the African American migration story—traditionally a South-to-North trajectory—on the West, making it a national story bound up with colonization, westward expansion, and the rise of cities. Thus the structure of *They Seek a City* incorporates stories of fugitive slaves and subsequent black migrations into a broader narrative of the frontier and immigrant success. The first chapter, for example, connects African American migration to the founding of the nation by beginning in the eighteenth century, profiling Jean Baptiste Point Du Sable, a trader who settled at the mouth of the Chicago River in 1779 and now lies buried along with "other pioneers of the Western midlands."[56] Four chapters trace black migration to the West, including the story of a fugitive slave, Jim Beckwourth, who is portrayed as the quintessential western hero; various sketches of nineteenth-century pioneer families to the Pacific Northwest; and tales of twentieth-century migrations that "turned the page on the early settlers and opened a new chapter on Negro migration to the West coast."[57] This language of the frontier places African American history in the center of national experience, affirming the democratic potential of the nation-state and African Americans' claims to citizenship. In contrast, the traditional slave narrative more forcefully confronts America's liberal creed with its practice of racial domination. In emphasizing the *voluntary* migrations and self-fashioning of African Americans, these chapters tell a story of American universalism in which African Americans gain entry to the national community.

Bontemps and Conroy use evidence from the leading voice of Popular Front multiculturalism, the California-based journal *Common Ground*, to support their implicit claim that with proper guidance from unions and the state, migration can be a democratizing process for black and white southerners. For example, in an article about integrated public housing in Marin County, a white migrant from Texas admits, "My Negro neighbors are all right."[58] His colloquial profession of racial tolerance testifies to the power of living and working together to transform racist thinking. In settings where the state mandates integration, the authors submit, "Negroes and Southern whites mingle at social affairs without the least friction. If the whites feel any animosity, they usually conceal it with at least a measure of grace, and its gradual evaporation becomes almost visible as time goes by."[59] This view of racial tensions as a phase of social adjustment resembles Archibald's image of the Okies learning to eat with their African American coworkers.

Moreover, both these texts assume that California is essentially racially liberal—that antiblack sentiment is imported from the South rather than homegrown. "Now out in the West, where the free-and-easy frontier spirit was said to prevail still," write Bontemps and Conroy, "a colored man might be recognized for whatever merit he possessed without anybody sneering at him or taking exception to the shade of his skin. He might have some room to throw out his chest and breathe deeply—even let out a whoop or two."[60] With these hopeful images of the social integration of black and white southerners, Bontemps, Conroy, and Archibald depict wartime migrants as the most recent wave of newcomers in the "nation of immigrants."

Unlike Archibald, Bontemps and Conroy downplay the sexual fears that underpinned white resistance to integrated housing. One could argue that white workers resisted the integration of personal spaces even more vehemently than they did integration in the workplace.[61] Archibald, for example, contends that African Americans made inroads into economic equality more easily than social equality, noting that "men who would have butchered in frenzy and willingly have spent the last breath of their lives, if the sanctity of their homes had been threatened by the trespassing of a minority group, contented themselves with malevolent mutterings and promises of eventual revenge at the sight of the invasion of their jobs."[62] In Bontemps and Conroy's view, the state plays a significant role in eradicating this hostility and facilitating the democratic process. *They Seek a City* opens with a sketch of "Mudtown," a nickname for the Furlough Track neighborhood of Los Angeles now better known as Watts. They describe a lively frontier community that devolves into an urban ghetto, only to be revived by state intervention into mixed-race public housing. Integrated housing projects like Pueblo del Rio were "Mudtown's true promise," transforming a village of shacks into "nearly five hundred units, housing white families along with many shades and varieties of colored."[63] Moreover, the title of their chapter on California, "Freedom's Frontier," refers not to the promise of California for black migrants but to the promise of governmental efforts throughout northern and western cities to alleviate housing problems and racial tensions through integrated public housing projects, the integration of police forces, and what we would now call "diversity training" in public schools. This argument aligns with the liberal creed, articulated most forcefully in Myrdal's *American Dilemma*, that an expanded state apparatus would extend equal citizenship to African Americans and other racial minorities.[64]

Twenty years later, however, amidst the urban riots of the 1960s, Bontemps and Conroy would admit that the housing project Pueblo del Rio—a "stone's throw away" from Watts—merely "postponed" calamity.[65] Voices of the interracial Left, Bontemps and Conroy insisted that the solution to America's race problems required broad economic reforms such as public housing and integrated unions. Yet while the New Deal expanded the role of the state in providing for the common good, it also implemented new structures of inequality. The Social Security Act excluded agricultural and domestic workers, effectively barring African American women and Latino immigrants from this benefit of citizenship; the Wagner Act failed to prohibit racial discrimination in unions; and the Federal Housing Authority blatantly discriminated against people of color.[66] In fact, wartime patterns of housing segregation shaped the postwar landscape. The housing authority's mortgage guarantee program spurred massive white suburbanization and black ghettoization after World War II by systematically refusing loans to people of color and even supporting racial covenants until 1950. Until the late 1940s, the housing authority's underwriting manual prohibited realtors from introducing "incompatible" racial groups into white neighborhoods, and the practice continued into the 1960s.[67] Thus the Watts riot of 1965 was not a new phenomenon but, rather, an extension of the interracial conflict over urban housing and economic inequalities of the 1940s.[68] The revised and updated version of They Seek a City was published in 1966, shortly after the Watts race riots left thirty-four people dead. Bontemps and Conroy changed the title to Anyplace but Here, shifting in tone from opportunity to flight, from hope to despair, from progress to uncertainty. In 1945, however, their vision of social democracy still seemed tenable, positioned in a hopeful window between the implementation of New Deal reforms and the anticommunist crackdown of the late 1940s and '50s, which silenced political dissent, weakened unions, and blocked more radical change.

In the original 1945 version of the book, however, Bontemps and Conroy bolster their vision of an integrated nation in their analysis of one of the most bloody and divisive moments of the decade: the Detroit riots of 1943. Like Archibald and Himes, they challenge the 1930s image of the white male migrant as populist hero, showing how he infects the North and West with a virulent brand of southern racism. "The Southern Negroes who found their way to Detroit were always pursued by the nemesis of the intolerant white Southerner," the authors explain, implicating white migrants in the race riots, hate strikes, and resurgence of the Ku Klux Klan in northern cities. Referring to white migrants as "transplanted white Southerners," they warn that migration sustains group culture, bringing Jim Crow to the nation. Yet they conclude their analysis of the Detroit riots with the observation that

"Negroes and whites who lived together as neighbors had no trouble, nor did fellow workers in the war plants where the United Automobile Workers have a contract."[69] The chapter closes with a vignette about white sailors who rescue a black man from a gang of white rioters. The sailors explain, "'We're doing this for a colored boy in our outfit that saved a couple of white lives over in the Pacific. He lost his own while he was doing it.'"[70] In Bontemps and Conroy's vision of the Double V, a black martyr sacrifices his life for freedom abroad, inspiring his white comrades to fight against racism at home. Recovering rare moments of interracialism from the rubble of race war, Bontemps and Conroy insist that integrated housing and unions—institutions regulated and protected by the government—will give rise to a peaceable, democratic society.

In sounding a note of optimism in their account of the Detroit riots, Bontemps and Conroy not only express faith in the New Deal state but also weigh in on a larger debate over how to balance the competing aims of African American rights and wartime unity. During World War I, Du Bois and other African American leaders urged black people to set aside their grievances for the sake of the war. But in return for their bravery and national loyalty, African American soldiers and civilians were beaten in bloody riots, excluded from unions, turned away from decent jobs, and even lynched for daring to wear a uniform in public. Still feeling this burn, African Americans during World War II were unwilling to abandon their antiracist struggles for the sake of military efficiency. The black press launched its Double V campaign, which insisted that victory over fascism abroad and victory over racism at home were inseparable causes. While many leftists also remained committed to the African American social struggle, the Communist Party put civil rights on the back burner. For example, the CP refused to endorse A. Philip Randolph's March on Washington Movement to protest the segregation of the army and employment discrimination. While many African Americans were increasingly frustrated by the CP's neglect of domestic racial issues, Bontemps and Conroy aimed to strengthen the connection between African Americans and the Left. In particular, their chapter on the Detroit riots sustains the compatibility of the Popular Front rhetoric of wartime unity and African American civil rights.

Bontemps and Conroy's story would have puzzled many African American readers, as the black press aggressively covered racial conflicts in the military.[71] What was most immediately galling, perhaps, was the segregation of the armed forces, which so blatantly contradicted the war's democratic aims. Millions of African Americans rallied behind A. Philip Randolph in the March on Washington Movement, which demanded the desegregation of the military and equal access to employment. Another factor that made this story idiosyncratic was that black soldiers were rarely sent into combat. It would have been even more unusual for a black soldier to see action in the Pacific, since the Marine Corps only accepted its first African American recruit in 1941.[72] A few U.S. sailors served on integrated ships, but not until 1944, a year after the Detroit riots, and these were not combat details. The 480,000 black servicemen who were sent overseas were usually relegated to jobs that required hard labor or food service, and the 12 percent who saw combat were given the most dangerous missions. Moreover, the officer corps were dominated by white southerners who considered black soldiers to be "well-meaning but irresponsible children" and inculcated a white supremacist culture from the top down.[73] Since training centers were located in the South, black recruits were subjected to harassment and denied access to recreational facilities and eating establishments. As Chester Himes pointed out in an essay published in *Common Ground* in 1945, the army sent "unarmed Negro soldiers into a hostile South to be booted and lynched by white civilians."[74]

Bontemps and Conroy's anecdote, whether apocryphal or not, counters the historical experience of the vast majority of U.S. servicemen. Yet it makes a compelling argument for the integration of the military by suggesting its power to transform the racial views of GIs and the broader American public. Cognizant that segregation demoralized black troops and contradicted American ideals, the United States experimented with integration late in the war. In 1945 the First Army in Europe integrated some of its companies so that black and white soldiers fought alongside one another for the first time, but troops remained segregated on the more intimate level of the platoon.[75] Touring the Mediterranean and Europe in 1944, NAACP leader Walter White testified to the power of shared danger to erode racial prejudices. "When German shells and bombs are raining about them," White reported, "they do not worry as much about the race or creed of the man next to them."[76] White was most impressed by the successful integration of the Air Corps' Seventy-Ninth Pursuit Group, which included among its four squadrons the first African American flyers. As in so many texts in the 1930s and '40s, the conversion of white southerners is the ultimate symbol of interracial solidarity. Almost half the personnel came from the South, "but one would never know that," remarked White.[77] "Inside the building and outside, pilots, both white and colored, stood talking and smoking together with apparent complete forgetfulness of race."[78] In his history of American nationalism, Gary Gerstle asks "whether civic nationalism would have enjoyed somewhat more sway in the immediate postwar period had black and white men learned to fight alongside each other in the military, to experience each other as friends and buddies, and to begin the delicate process of imagining each other as neighbors."[79] Writing on the eve of this postwar period, Bontemps and Conroy answer in the affirmative, calling on the U.S. nation-state to make up for its lost opportunity by making racial integration imperative to its postwar economic plan.

Bontemps and Conroy's image of interracial camaraderie not only offers a countervision to the reality of race relations in the military; it also provides a positive image of black soldiers that is lacking in U.S. popular culture. Many Hollywood actors, directors, and screenwriters were also active in the Popular Front and committed to the war and to racial and ethnic equality. Yet they were less successful in advancing an antiracist agenda in their war films. The multiethnic platoon was a stock image in many 1940s war films— a military version of the "nation of immigrants" trope. According to this narrative, the shared hardship of battle dissolves differences of ancestry, religion, region, and class to create a united force of American heroes.[80] Louis Adamic, the leading purveyor of the "nation of immigrants" mythology, believed that the armed services led the way in ethnic tolerance, as "there's nothing like being together in a foxhole, a bomber or a submarine."[81] But the U.S. military couldn't conceive of this degree of intimacy for its soldiers. Due to the segregation of the military, African Americans were excluded from the image of the multicultural platoon, resulting in what Gerstle calls a "racialized melting pot."[82] Bontemps and Conroy's idiosyncratic story may work as an anecdote, but translated into a feature film, it would have tried viewers' willingness to suspend disbelief. Another option for progressive Hollywood filmmakers was to depict African American military experience realistically, racial discrimination necessarily included. For example, Communist screenwriter John Howard Lawson included a scene in the film *Action in the North Atlantic* (1943) in which a black pantryman wonders why he should fight for the Allies, given his discriminatory treatment by the U.S. Merchant Marine. But the Office of War Information (OWI), which screened films for subversive content, forced Lawson to cut the scene. The OWI did not object to strong black characters—from the government's point of view, positive images of African Americans would reinforce its rhetoric of democracy and help to quell the discontent of black servicemen and their allies. The problem was that the OWI protected the nation's public image, making sure that films offered a rose-colored depiction of American society.

Progressive filmmakers who wanted to include black soldiers were faced with either condoning racial segregation and subordination, on one hand, or risking censorship, on the other. The result was that African American soldiers were by and large absent from the silver screen.

Considering the treatment of black soldiers in the military and on film, it is easy to understand the claim made by a character in Himes's novel *If He Hollers Let Him Go* that "'every time a coloured man gets in the Army he's fighting against himself'" (120). Early in the war, African American intellectuals, activists, and journalists argued that black people had little interest in what they perceived as a conflict between European imperial powers. In fact, many African American communists supported the CP's noninterventionist stance after the signing of the Hitler-Stalin pact in 1939.[83] By 1942 the vast majority of African Americans supported the war, but the radicals among them continued to view the conflict through the lens of anticolonialism. They championed African American soldiers as fighters for the freedom of colonized peoples. A writer for the *Chicago Defender* reported that black soldiers in Africa "who more than a century ago came to the United States in the shackles of slave ships, last week went back to African shores aboard an Allied invasion armada, to prevent the threatened re-enslavement of Africa by the goose-stepping slavers of 1942."[84] This anticolonialist perspective does not come through Bontemps and Conroy's vignette of the African American war hero. Even though Bontemps's historical novel of the Haitian revolution, *Drums at Dusk* (1939), located the roots of black radicalism in an anticolonial uprising, his migration history lacks this global scope. Rather, it expresses faith in the notion that the U.S. "nation of immigrants" can expand to include African Americans.

Jim Crow, International

In *Black Is a Country*, Nikhil Singh posits, "If there was a great divide in the modern black freedom movement, it was between those who gravitated toward an identification with the U.S. state and social policy as the answer to black mass discontent, and those who eyed rhetorical professions of American universality and inclusiveness from the more exacting and worldly standpoint of subjection to racializing power."[85] This notion of black activists' divergent views of American civic nationalism helps to explain the stark differences between Bontemps and Conroy's depiction of white servicemen and those of Chester Himes. Whereas Bontemps and Conroy depicted white sailors as defenders of black freedom in the Detroit riots, Himes blamed the

Los Angeles zoot suit riots on the large number of servicemen—particularly southern white servicemen—on leave in the city. The specter of the white migrant looms large in Himes's wartime novel and essays, acting as a kind of fifth column infecting the United States with fascism from within and exporting it abroad. In his article "Zoot Riots Are Race Riots" published in the *Crisis* in 1943, Himes begins, "I suppose you have been reading about the birth of storm troopers in Los Angeles, the reincarnation, or rather should I say, the *continuation* of the vigilantes, the uniformed Klansman," combining southern and German white supremacy in the figure of the U.S. serviceman. He describes the zoot suit riot as a kind of domestic colonial conquest, "wherein the combined forces of the United States navy, army, and marine corps, contacted and defeated a handful of youths with darker skins."[86] Challenging the characterization of American patriots as lovers of freedom and democracy, he asks, "What could make the white people more happy than to see their uniformed sons sapping up some dark skinned people?"[87] Himes thus extends the politics of the Double V to include not only antifascism and antiracism but also anticolonialism, which was central to African American radical politics in this period.[88] As Singh argues, black writers such as Richard Wright, W. E. B. Du Bois, Ralph Ellison, and Chester Himes—and I would add black female radicals such as Claudia Jones, Louise Thompson, and Elizabeth Catlett—increasingly linked their struggles to those of colonized peoples around the world.[89] They revealed the failure of the "nation of immigrants" myth to account for slavery, Jim Crow, Japanese internment, and other structural patterns of racial exclusion. Thus, black radical writers like Himes challenged the prevailing optimism about America's role as a world leader and the liberal consensus that racial problems could be solved by internal reforms alone.

Through his engagement with the Left, Himes developed an anticolonial consciousness that connected racial struggles at home with national liberation movements worldwide. In his autobiography, Himes downplays his Left commitments, as do his biographers. Yet in an interview with Marxist critic Earl Conrad published in the *Chicago Defender* in 1946, he recalls being swept up in the "terrific movement of people" while working for the Ohio WPA in 1936.[90] After spending the previous eight years in the Ohio State Penitentiary serving a sentence for armed robbery, he started out as a laborer, worked his way up to the library staff, and eventually was assigned to the Ohio Writers' Project. He also wrote and edited articles for the CIO newspaper *Cleveland Union Leader* and the *Yearbook of the Cleveland Industrial Council*.[91] Like his peers in the Illinois Federal Writers' Project, including Bontemps and Conroy, he experienced cross-racial exchanges that changed his out-look on race and class. "I developed a hatred of the ruling class of whites," he reported to Conrad. "I identified myself with labor, worked for the CIO in Cleveland." He believed the CIO expanded African Americans' political horizons: "Negroes made contact with new outlooks, came to understand things about segments of society from which they had been excluded, and with whom they had no means of contact." Their involvement with the labor movement propelled them away from the timeworn accommodationist at-titude and allowed them to become "a part of new ideas and of democracy itself."[92] In my view, Himes's life and writings complicate the standard argu-ment that African Americans became disillusioned with the Left during the Popular Front period, as well as the revisionist history that claims that these ties remained strong but were later repudiated under the pressure of the an-ticommunist purges of the 1950s. I follow Nikhil Singh in seeing the black-Left alliance as both productive and conflicted. Although radicals such as Himes deplored the CP's policies on domestic racial issues, they built upon the Marxist tradition of anticolonialism to place African American struggles in a global context.[93] Popular Front intellectual networks and anticapital-ist ideologies continued to nurture Himes into the late 1940s, making him an imperfect exemplar of black disillusionment with the Left. But his work challenged his leftist allies to see the colonized people of the world as the vanguard of the working class.

After he moved to Los Angeles in 1941, Himes attended CP meetings, par-ties, and lectures; joined the League of American Writers and took classes at its Hollywood school; attended a conference at the University of Califor-nia at Los Angeles sponsored by the Hollywood Writers' Mobilization; and collected used clothing for veterans of the Spanish Civil War.[94] Most strik-ingly, Himes celebrated the Soviet Union in his 1946 interview with Conrad, despite the accumulating evidence of Stalin's atrocities. Himes saw com-munist revolution as a possible route for black liberation and believed that Russia came closest to the goal of universal freedom: "Today you have a nation that represents a new ideology in which the masses of people have more freedom. The fact is, it is a new way of life which would be better for the people, and, in Russia, has passed from theory to practicality." This interview offers a glimpse of Himes not as a bitter anticommunist but as a politically engaged writer who sees black liberation, anticolonialism, and class struggle as coterminous projects.

In an article published in *People's World*, a West Coast communist newspa-per, Himes extended the logic of the African American Double V campaign to India, supporting its struggle for independence against Great Britain, a U.S. military ally. Moreover, Himes wrote a remarkable series of articles between 1942 and 1945 that forcefully connects the oppression of minority groups at home to the spread of fascism abroad and warns of the high cost of neglecting domestic racial issues for the sake of the war. In "Now Is the Time! Here Is the Place!" published in *Opportunity* in 1942, Himes embraces the Popular Front call for unity, declaring, "At this time, we 13,000,000 Negro Americans are united with all Americans of all races, colors, and creeds . . . in a war to defeat and destroy nazism, fascism, and imperialism originating in Germany, Italy, and Japan."[95] Yet he emphatically insists that the United States "*is the place for us to open a second front for freedom.*"[96] To Himes, the argument that the fascist threat looms larger than domestic racism holds no water. "But to us Negro Americans," he asks his readers, "is not victory abroad without victory at home a sham, empty, and with no meaning, leaving us no more free than before?"[97]

Himes's wartime novel, *If He Hollers Let Him Go*, is an extended rumination on this very question. The novel dramatizes the conflict between the Popular Front's patriotic calls for unity and the Double V campaign in an argument between the protagonist Bob Jones, a shipyard worker, and the union steward, a Jewish Communist named Herbie Frieberger. When Frieberger asks Bob to soften his approach toward racist white workers for the sake of unity, Bob responds with a tirade that points out how blacks and whites make disproportionate compromises: "'Get these crackers to unite with me. I'm willing. I'll work with 'em, fight with 'em, die with 'em, goddamnit. But I ain't gonna even try to do any uniting without anybody to unite with. Do you understand that?' I put my finger on his chest. 'What the hell do I care about unity, or the war either, for that matter, as long as I'm kicked around by every white person who comes along? Let the white people get some goddamned unity'" (115). In his wartime writings, Himes challenged the Popular Front's concept of unity with a more expansive concept of freedom, insisting that the fight against fascism extend to the liberation of oppressed minorities in the United States and the Third World.

In particular, Himes's wartime essays and novel reveal the global reach of sexual myths of white supremacy. The rape-lynch complex not only enforced segregation in the South but also justified violence in California and beyond America's shores. In fact, the U.S. government used this image of the dark-skinned rapist who imperiled white womanhood in its anti-Japanese propaganda campaign. A series of posters with the slogan "This Is the Enemy" featured animalistic Japanese soldiers with slanted eyes, garish skin

Figure 16. *This Is the Enemy*. Poster by C. V. Lewis (1942). This poster was submitted to a contest sponsored by Artists for Victory, a federation of twenty-six arts organizations, and the Council for Democracy. It was published in *Life* magazine's 21 December 1942 issue and displayed at the Museum of Modern Art.

tones, hunched backs, and apelike arms threatening white women.[98] In one particularly obscene example, a naked woman is slung over the man's back in a seductive pose, her legs spread and nipples erect (see Figure 16). Lithe female figures hang by their necks in the background, silhouetted by fire. This image not only reflects the racist beliefs that were held by ordinary Americans and sanctioned by the state; it also indicates how fears of female promiscuity amplified them.

Himes's article on the zoot suit riots reports sailors deploying this discourse of white supremacy in the service of colonialism. Himes relates an incident he witnessed on a city bus in which white soldiers with thick southern accents attempt to attract a Mexican American woman and humiliate her date. They brag about their physical and sexual conquests overseas in the language of racial imperialism: "'Ah'm tellin' yuh, Ah fought lak a white man! Din Ah fight lak a white man, boy?' . . . 'Boy, did those native gals go fuh us. Boy, uh white man can git any gal he wants. Can't he, boy, can't he git 'em if he wants 'em?'"[99] By representing the sailor's speech in heavy dialect punctuated by the racially pejorative term "boy," Himes suggests that southern racism is not an exception to American liberal democracy but, rather, fundamental to American global power. The final line of the essay puts it plainly: "The outcome is simply that the South has won Los Angeles."[100] Himes warns readers that Jim Crow is not a southern peculiarity but a national predicament with global implications.

Recently, critics have called our attention to the importance of Japanese internment, the zoot suit riots, and anticolonial movements abroad to Himes's wartime writings.[101] During the 1940s, black radicals articulated a global vision that located the origins of racial oppression in the expansion of Western empires and their hunger for cheap labor.[102] In Himes's novel, for example, Bob Jones traces the origins of his racial fear to the internment of the Japanese: "I was the same colour as the Japanese and I couldn't tell the difference. 'A yeller-bellied Jap' coulda meant me too" (4). Jones also notes the similarity between his skin tone and that of Mexican youths, who "were both brown-skinned, about my colour" (203). By drawing parallels between people of Japanese, Mexican, and African descent, Himes links the challenges facing the African American community in Los Angeles to a broader pattern of colonialism. In one revealing scene, a white woman in a bar makes sexual advances toward a couple of black men, compelling her white male companions to step up to defend her. Feeling the racial tensions escalate, Bob fears a race riot: "If the boy got hurt, or if there was any kind of rumpus with the white chick in it, there wouldn't be any way at all to stop a riot—the white GIs would swarm into Little Tokyo like they did into the Mexican districts during the zoot suit riots" (77). As critic Lynn Itagaki argues, the novel represents conflicts between white authorities and minority communities as a kind of domestic warfare, as "Bob superimposes the image of white GIs penetrating the boundaries of the community in order to discipline the unruly racialized body."[103] By placing the oppression of African Americans in a global context, Himes gives expression to the transnational vision of the black Popular Front.[104]

Yet the context of southern migration is also crucial to Himes's anticolonial critique. If African Americans and other racial minorities are akin to enemy combatants within the United States, then southern migrants are the foot soldiers of U.S. racial dominance. In other words, southern migrants are not another immigrant group to be shorn of parochial attachments and incorporated into the democratic fabric but, rather, America's racist heart. In Itagaki's analysis of the bar scene, she neglects to mention that the "drunken white prostitute" who provokes the racial tension is also a southern white migrant, "an Arkansas slick chick, a rife, loose, teenage fluff, with a broad face and small eyes and a hard mouth and straggly uncombed hair, dressed in a dirty white waist open at the throat and a dirty blue skirt, barelegged and muddy-shoed. She looked like she had just got off an S.P. freight—but she was white" (74). In my view, this scene reenacts the southern rape-lynch drama. Although "Arky Jill" is from Arkansas, not from Alabama, the suggestion that she is a promiscuous hobo calls to the southern white women who falsely accused nine black boys of rape in the Scottsboro case. In fact, Scottsboro seems to be on Bob's mind when he muses, "She could take those two black chumps flirting with her outside and get them thirty years apiece in San Quentin; in Alabama she could get them hung" (76). This scene not only imagines domestic racial conflicts as a kind of warfare but also positions American servicemen as southern vigilantes. It suggests that U.S. military power enforces racial dominance, envisioning the United States as a colonial power rather than a beacon of democracy. Similarly, black intellectuals in the 1940s likened the American South to other colonized regions of the world. Even though the vast majority of black intellectuals supported the Allied cause, they saw the crisis of European empires as a liberating force for people of color. For example, Langston Hughes assured readers of the *Chicago Defender* that the fall of the British empire "will shake Dixie's teeth loose too, and crack the joints of Jim Crow South Africa."[105] Himes's novel connects southern U.S. racism and American and European colonialism, showing them to be cut from the same cloth.

Just as this scene reenacts the southern rape-lynch drama, so does the novel as a whole. The triangular lynch myth gives shape to the central conflict. A southern white woman, Madge, pretends to be afraid of Bob, secretly playing out a rape fantasy. A socially marginalized figure, she uses the rape-lynch drama to bolster her claim to white femininity. Meanwhile, Bob is also psychologically trapped in this drama, as he attempts to assert his manhood by sexually dominating Madge and retaliating against white men. Although Bob never rapes Madge, she frames him, and he is beaten by coworkers, jailed, and forced by his bosses and a judge to fight in a Jim Crow army. Thus, the "white male defender" in this lynch triangle manifests as an alliance between white male workers, the legal system, capitalist employers, and the U.S. military. This narrative structure denies the assumption made by Archibald, Bontemps, and Conroy that California is more racially progressive than the Jim Crow South. In Himes's novel, in fact, Bob Jones fails to anticipate his demise because he clings so tenaciously to this illusion. When a white driver cut in front of Bob's car, for example, Bob "leaned out of the window and shouted, 'This ain't Alabama, you peckerwood son of a bitch'" (13). Even at the end of the novel, after four harrowing days in which he is called a nigger, barred from a restaurant, fired, falsely accused of rape, and beaten, he reassures himself that "she couldn't get away with that. This wasn't Georgia" (184). The novel's ultimate message, however, is that the South *is* America, that racial domination is its true civic religion. By the end of the novel, Bob realizes "the inexorability of one conclusion—that I was guilty. In that one brief flash I could see myself trying to prove my innocence and nobody believing it. . . . The whole structure of American thought was against me; American tradition had convicted me a hundred years before" (187).

Although Himes's rhetorical lynching triangle provides a crucial antiracist critique of Popular Front and mainstream patriotism, it also denigrates all women and denies the active role black and Mexican women played in the social struggles of the period. Himes's negative treatment of women in his essays and fiction stems in part from his personal history of abusive relationships. Himes was jealous of the success of his African American wife, Jean, who was codirector of women's activities for the USO and for the Pueblo del Rio housing project in Los Angeles. "It hurt me for my wife to have a better job than I did and be respected and included by her white co-workers," he remembers in his autobiography. He goes on to implicitly blame her for the failure of their marriage, likening her professional success to prostitution: "That was the beginning of the dissolution of our marriage. I found that I was no longer a husband to my wife; I was her pimp. She didn't mind, and that hurt all the more."[106] Offering a "black male feminist criticism" of *If He Hollers*, David Ikard argues that the perspectives of black women, particularly that of Ella Mae, Bob's neighbor, are undermined in the novel. Moreover, Bob's resistance to white supremacy relies on the domination of both black and white women, which reinforces white patriarchy.[107] Himes's misogyny took on monstrous proportions in his violent affairs with white women. "In New York at the time there were many white women who wanted to give me their bodies and I took them," he writes in his autobiography, as if his lovers' bodies were commodities to be possessed. He established a pattern in which he would fall in love with a vulnerable white woman, beat her—sometimes to the point where she required hospitalization—and then rescue her. According to Himes's biographers, Ralph Ellison "thought Himes a cad for exploiting white women while hating them for being white."[108] Himes himself remarked in his autobiography, "The final answer of any black to a white woman with whom he lives in a white society is violence."[109] According to Himes, white women sabotaged the reception of the novel. Although the role of white women is unclear, there is some factual basis to the accusation that Doubleday had second thoughts. Apparently due to the outrage of a white female secretary, the publisher attempted to excise a misogynistic scene in which Madge and Bob enact a rape fantasy, but Himes successfully protested the censorship. Adding fuel to Himes's theory, Doubleday awarded the prestigious George Washington Carver prize for best book on Negro life to a white woman, Fannie Cook, for her novel about a domestic worker, *Mrs. Palmer's Honey*, even after insiders had assured Himes that he would win.[110]

The form of the novel—its psychologically intense noir style—conveys the inexorability of white supremacy. Like the hard-boiled protagonists Himes would perfect in his later crime fiction, Bob Jones is on a path of self-destruction, and there is no exit. In the dream sequence that opens the novel, Bob imagines a dog with "heavy stiff wire twisted about its neck," foreshadowing his own inevitable lynching (albeit figurative). Just as the narrative structure of the rape-lynching drama seems to seal Bob's fate, the other characters cannot escape their prescribed roles. In one dream sequence, the "hard cultured voice" of the shipyard president commands a couple of white workers to beat Bob even though they want to stop (69). This scene illuminates the psychic destructiveness of whiteness, which conveys material privileges but degrades the humanity of white workers, undermines their class interests, and closes off avenues for real social change. It suggests a kind of "compulsory whiteness" that coerces white workers to do the bidding of the white ruling elite. Even though Himes believed that race "was a problem more psychological than economic," he suggests that antiblack violence serves those in positions of power.[111] Just as the white workers in Bob's dream lack agency, the characters in Himes's novel, black and white, seem to follow the script of the rape-lynching drama. The performative nature of their behavior—and its inevitability—suggests that America's national story is not one of freedom and ever increasing inclusiveness but one of coercion, segregation, and racial hierarchy enforced by violence. In other words, Himes suggests that the rape-lynch drama is not just a southern story but the nation's origin myth. This national narrative runs so deep in the characters' psyches that they cannot deviate from it, even when it contradicts their economic interests, the national interest, California's promise of freedom and opportunity, and the democratic rhetoric of the war.

To highlight the fictional quality and power of the rape-lynch myth, he represents the sexual dynamics of the shipyards as a finely tuned drama that has a psychological stranglehold on its actors. Each time Bob encounters

Madge aboard the ship they are building, she launches into an overstated performance of the white female victim in the rape-lynch drama. When Bob first meets her within the time frame of the novel, "she deliberately put on a frightened, wide-eyed look and backed away from me as if she was scared stiff, as if she was a naked virgin and I was King Kong." Bob makes clear to the reader that this behavior is a well-practiced routine: "It wasn't the first time she had done that. I'd run into her on board a half-dozen times during the past couple of weeks and each time she'd put on that scared-to-death act" (19). The repetition of this scene throughout the novel emphasizes its ritualistic, performative nature.

In fact, Madge is able to go off script when it suits her purposes. When Bob greets Madge and her sister-in-law, Elsie, during a lunch break, she surprises him with her friendliness: "After all that tremendous anxiety I had gone through; after all that murderous build-up, that hard hollow scare; after all the crazy, wild-eyed, frightened acts she had put on, the white armour plate she'd wrapped herself up in, the insurmountable barriers she'd raised between us, here she was breaking it down, wiping it all out, with a smile; treating me as casually as an old acquaintance" (130). Madge's friendliness is manipulative, catching Bob off guard so as to diffuse his resistance, then luring him back into sexual pursuit. This scene highlights the absurdity of black male and white female relations: Madge may be attracted to Bob and has the capacity to interact with him normally but nevertheless resorts to the role of the imperiled white woman. This role bolsters her status at Bob's expense but also reflects her utter lack of options. According to Archibald, "No white woman, even if she wanted to, could establish normal friendly relations with a Negro man, or even talk with him at length on any topic. Contact of this type, no matter what its actual substance, was immediately translated by the on-looker into sexual terms."[112] Both Himes and Archibald suggest that sexual tensions in the shipyard stem, in part, from the lack of available roles, as "white workers would admit no halfway point between the Negro's allotted role of servile, silent distance from the white women and the intimacies of sexual union."[113]

Bob's description of Madge calls attention to her bleached hair and garish makeup, suggesting the artificiality of her physical features, the constructedness of her race and gender identity: "She was a peroxide blonde with a large-featured, overly made-up face, and she had a large, bright-painted, fleshy mouth, kidney-shaped, thinner in the middle than at the ends. Her big blue babyish eyes were mascaraed like a burlesque queen's and there were tiny wrinkles in their corners and about the flare of her nostrils. . . . She looked thirty and well sexed, rife but not quite rotten. She looked as if she might have worked half those years in a cat house, and if she hadn't she must have given a lot of it away" (19). Made up like a burlesque queen, Madge is an erotic performer, acting out her youth, whiteness, and femininity through displays of sexuality. Yet like the wrinkles that betray her age, Madge's low social status penetrates this veneer. Bob sees her as low class, artificial, aging, and sexually disreputable—characteristics that threaten her claim to the whiteness. In order to secure her precarious social position in the shipyard, Madge plays the part of the vulnerable white woman in the rape-lynch drama, cuing white men to defend her: "So it wasn't that Madge was white; it was the way she used it. She had a sign up in front of her as big as Civic Centre—KEEP AWAY NIGGERS, I'M WHITE! And without having to say one word she could keep all the white men in the world feeling they had to protect her from black rapists. That made her doubly dangerous." (125). By shifting the term "white" from an adjective to the antecedent of the pronoun "it" ("it wasn't that Madge was white; it was the way she used it"), Himes presents race not as a biological or even cultural characteristic but as a tool for shaping power relations, a kind of technology. Like the hobo "Arky Jill," Madge relies on black male lust to reinforce her status and her own sense of self-worth: "She wanted them to run after her. She expected it, demanded it as her due" (125). The farther Madge falls down the social ladder, the more aggressively must she advertise her allure for—and unavailability to—black men. This sexist image of the promiscuous, low-class white woman builds on an antilynching trope found in Ida B. Wells's widely read tract *Southern Horrors* of 1892 and replicated in the Scottsboro literature. As it did for the Scottsboro accusers Ruby Bates and Victoria Price, southern rape-lynch drama allows Madge to exchange the stigma of poor white trash for the ideal of pure white womanhood—at the expense of black men's lives.

By depicting Madge as a prostitute, Himes not only "embodies his own misogyny," as Eileen Boris puts it, but also draws upon the negative stereotypes of women war workers and the national hysteria about prostitution in the shipyards.[114] For many female migrants, the shipyards provided economic independence and freedom from familial supervision, and they took advantage of this mixed-gendered space by pursuing intimate relationships.[115] Archibald describes "young and adventuresome girls, their normal boy-centered lives rent asunder by war, who turned to the shipyards primarily for excited roving among droves of draft-exempt men," and married women "fleeing the housewife's routine" and using the shipyard to "satisfy vague personal hungers."[116] Young Mexican American women also broke from parental control in this period, sporting the zoot suit along with their male peers and flouting both ethnic and mainstream American standards of femininity.[117] Moreover, women's entry into male-dominated occupations unleashed a widespread fear of female sexuality. Resentful male workers created a hostile environment by exchanging sexual jokes, stories, and banter. According to Archibald, the ship was abuzz with rumors about illicit sexual liaisons in its nooks and crannies. "The end result of such talk," she concludes, "was to deny the possibility of the establishment of businesslike relationships between men and women on the job and to discredit women as effective workers." Employers also betrayed a "restless, sexually interpreted distrust of women as shipyard workers" by requiring a strict dress code for female manual laborers but not for women who performed traditionally feminine jobs, such as secretaries.[118] The fear that the expansion of women's economic function would give rise to transgressive sexuality circulated in the mass media as well. An article published in *Business Week* in 1942 brought the "problem" of prostitution in the defense areas to national attention, warning that "the world's newest industries are at grips with the world's oldest profession." In their attempts to rid shipyards of prostitutes, unions in Portland, Oregon, fired fifty women who "were discovered plying their trade in the holds of new Liberty ships; others because, with date books in hand, they spent their working hours in the shops soliciting patrons for their leisure hours."[119] Bob Jones voices this sexist myth in remarking, "The white guys treated some of those white women like they were bitches in heat. A lot of 'em were prostitutes anyway; they were always firing some of 'em for tricking on the job" (124).

Anxieties about female sexual autonomy and race mixing fed off one another, even in politically divergent ways. In Himes's article on the zoot suit riots, for example, he describes a young Mexican American woman who refuses to move away from a lascivious sailor who is harassing her on a streetcar. Himes interprets her action not as antiracist resistance but as a form of ethnic betrayal. "Perhaps the girl realized that she had attracted the sailors' attention, and perhaps it flattered her," Himes remarked, noting that all women "are hero worshipers."[120] Similarly, in his novel, Himes represents the sexual autonomy of Madge and "Arky Jill" as a means to bait black men and encourage sexual rivalry. Thus, Himes blames women—white and Mexican—for using sex to instigate racial conflicts between men. While Himes linked female sexual and economic autonomy to the subordination of men of color, the *Business Week* article about prostitution in the shipyards expressed the fear that female promiscuity would embolden black men and imperil decent white women. The article reported the Portland police department's concern that "prostitutes may consort with negroes, who then may try to take liberties with other white women—and that this might lead to serious race complications." While Himes depicted the promiscuous white women as a tripwire for lynching, the writer from *Business Week* saw them as a threat to the moral and racial integrity of the white community.

This stereotype of the promiscuous woman worker also conditions the interactions between Bob, Madge, and their coworkers in Himes's novel. Her theatrics do not deceive her white male companions, who see her through this lens. In one instance, Bob says "'Get a load of this'" to a supervisor as Madge performs her racial fear, while the mechanic she is working with "gruffly" urges her to get back to work (117–18). Yet even though these white men seem to be aware of the disingenuousness of her fear, they can't seem to abandon their designated role in the rape-lynch drama but, rather, respond on cue. After Bob calls her a "cracker bitch" for refusing to work with him, Madge goads a white coworker, "'You gonna let a nigger talk tuh me like that?'" and he "started up tentatively, a bar in his hand" to defend her (27). Similarly, in the bar scene discussed above, the white soldiers attempt to leave "the little tramp" in the bar but "got defiant" once the racial conflict escalated (76). These scenes depict the compulsory whiteness that divides black and white workers.

Even Bob is ensnared by the rape-lynch drama, unable to break out of his prescribed role. Upon Madge's display of fear, "lust shook me like an electric shock" (19), and when he runs into her later, "I knew the instant I recognized her that she was going to perform then—we would both perform" (27). Bob's volitional performance of the role of black rapist reveals the absurd paradox of African American experience in a white world. The only way he can prove he is equal to white men is by dominating a white woman, which also verifies the racist stereotype that justifies black subordination in the first place. When Bob's supervisor humiliates him by forcing him to listen to a racist joke, Bob goes after Madge "to make her as low as a white whore in a Negro slum" (123). For Bob, Madge personified racist America, and "all I could see was her standing there between me and my manhood" (123). Like his white coworkers, Bob is caught up in the rape-lynch drama, even though he rejects its premise of black male lust for white women. Like actors playing a well-rehearsed scene, "we kept looking at each other and I knew she expected me to say something. I knew she wanted me to. I knew she knew what I'd say" (124).

Himes's rendition of the rape-lynch triangle answers back to southern anticommunists who insisted that black men were interested in the CP because it gave them sexual access to white women. Instead, Himes argues, the sexual myths of white supremacy incite black male lust by equating manhood with the domination of white women. Himes also parodies the communist antilynch triangle that celebrates male interracial bonding at the expense of white female accusers. In an act of solidarity, a white comrade gives Bob Madge's home address so he can "'take some of the stinking prejudice out of her.'" (118). This offer leaves Bob at a loss for words: "I wanted to tell him I didn't want to go to bed with her, I wanted to black her eyes; but just the idea of her being a white woman stopped me" (119). Even though Don invites Bob to rape Madge, sexual taboos inhibit an honest dialogue between the two men: "I couldn't tell him I didn't want her because she was a white woman and he was a white man, and something somewhere way back in my mind said that would be an insult. And I couldn't tell him that I did want her, because the same thing said that that would be an insult too" (119). In the noir spirit of the novel, Bob is caught in a paradox, an absurd racial conundrum. Don's invitation, made in a spirit of male interracial alliance, is actually an indictment of black male sexuality, making Bob feel like a criminal, "flustered, caught, guilty" (119). Although Don tries to reverse the logic of the rape-lynch triangle by acting as the black man's ally rather than the white woman's defender, he fails to change the terms of this racial discourse. Madge is still the object of illicit black male desire, and Bob is the Negro lusting for white flesh. In order for black and white men to have an honest dialogue, Bob muses, "both would have to reject the theory of white supremacy and condemn all its institutions, including loyalty and patriotism in time of war" (120). The psychological grip of the rape-lynch complex on the minds of Himes's characters suggests that the rejection of white supremacy is social and sexual as well as political. The nation's racialized sexual taboos give the lie to its claims to universal citizenship.

In a synopsis of the novel submitted with his application for a Julius Rosenwald Fund fellowship, Himes expressed the hope that the migration of black southerners would "roll the Negro problem in front of them, big and vicious and explosive, so that it will either have to be settled or chopped down."[121] By dramatizing the racial conflicts in destination cities, Himes hoped to catalyze a radical change in social relations. Whereas the mainstream media scapegoated southern white migrants for urban violence, Himes fictionalized this racial discord to bring about a reckoning, for both the Left and the broader American public. The interactions between black and white migrants, once a symbol of promise, had become a symbol of creative destruction. The nation would have to confront its deeply entrenched ideologies and institutions of racism by recognizing the southerner within.

Returning to the question that Himes posed to readers of *Opportunity* in 1942, we can see the animating spirit behind *If He Hollers Let Him Go* : "But to us Negro Americans, is not victory abroad without victory at home a sham, empty, and with no meaning, leaving us no more free than before?"[122] This question points to the vexed relationship between African American citizens and the nation, and between African American radicals and the Left. The segregation of troops, internment of the Japanese, discrimination in unions, and violence in the streets in the 1940s gave African Americans reason to question who, exactly, they were fighting for. While some young black men eagerly enlisted to serve their country, others rankled at the similarities between Hitler's regime and Jim Crow. "I hope Hitler wins," a black student told Walter White, chairman of the NAACP. "Things can't be any worse than they are for Negroes in the South right now. The army Jim-Crows us. The Navy lets us serve only as messmen. The Red Cross refused our blood. Employers and labor unions shut us out. Lynchings continue. We are disfranchised, Jim-Crowed, spat upon. What more could Hitler do than that?"[123] African American radicals also favored different strategies for black freedom. Whereas Arna Bontemps envisioned social democracy through the expansion of the New Deal state, Himes questioned the very premise of the American liberal creed. As Bob Jones learns, his exclusion from the American Dream is not a correctable anomaly within an essentially inclusive concept of citizenship but, rather, the logical extension of a history of conquest and domination of people of color both within and outside U.S. borders. In their representations of black and white migrants, writers on the 1940s Left engaged in a contest over the meaning of American nationhood, whether, at its core, America was an inclusive "nation of immigrants" or a bastion of white imperialism.

CONCLUSION

In the poem "I Heard a Black Man Sing," Earl Conrad pairs iconic images of white and black migrants to celebrate interracial unity:

> The peat bog soldier in the camp,
> The Joads out seeking food,
> The black man breaking from his chains:
> He sang in fighting mood![1]

Conrad, a white Communist, originally wrote the poem in 1941 and dedicated it to Paul Robeson, the radical black singer famous for his anthem of cultural pluralism, "Ballad for Americans." Republished in the Popular Front journal *Negro Story* in 1944, Conrad's poem serves as a counterpoint to Himes's withering depiction of racist Okies in *If He Hollers Let Him Go*. The pairing of Steinbeck's fictional Joad family, the populist heroes of *The Grapes of Wrath*, with the fugitive slave "breaking from his chains" testifies to the continuing power of the migration story as a narrative vehicle for the Left's interracial social movement, despite the outbreaks of racial violence and the CP's backsliding on civil rights during the war. Throughout the 1930s and 1940s, writers and artists on the interracial Left turned to the themes and forms of the migration narrative to advance a broad-based struggle for democracy. Stories of hoboes, migrant workers, and dispossessed families unmoored from traditional sources of stability allowed these writers and artists to imagine the transformation of capitalist economic, racial, and gender hierarchies. The durability of these Popular Front migration narratives into the postwar period challenges a lingering historiographical understanding of the black-Left alliance as one of white co-optation and black disillusionment that splintered with the onset of World War II. Yet while civil rights unionism still seemed possible in 1944, Cold War anticommunist repression eviscerated class-based social movements in the United States, narrowed the range of the African American freedom struggle, and altered the trajectories of black and white migration narratives.

As postwar political repression destroyed the possibility for a union-led civil rights movement, the migration narrative lost its salience as a vehicle for revolutionary social change. It took a vicious, protracted, state-sponsored crusade against communism to sever the alliance between African Americans, trade unions, and the communist Left. Radical activists such as W. E. B. Du Bois, Claudia Jones, Shirley Graham, Paul Robeson, Elizabeth Catlett, and Lorraine Hansberry continued to rail against capitalism, imperialism, and racial hierarchies in the Cold War era, but they relied less on the domestic trade union movement and the white Left, turning instead to Third World liberation movements for alliance and inspiration. As historian Robin Kelley argues, "A vision of global class revolution led by oppressed people of color was not an outgrowth of the civil rights movement's failure but existed alongside, sometimes in tension with, the movement's main ideas."[2] In other words, Kelley argues for international black radicalism as a countertradition to—not a successor of—the racial liberalism of the 1950s. In this global context, stories of internal migration no longer adequately conveyed the vision of an interracial class struggle. Moreover, narratives that imagined alliances between African American and southern white workers withered amidst anticommunist purges and escalating racial hostilities in the South.

The fracturing of the interracial Left resists sharp periodization, in part because it continued to shape postwar social struggles, although it was increasingly embattled. At first, a surge of strikes immediately following the war attested to the new power of American labor and its potential role in reshaping the American economy.[3] In both the South and the North, trade unions were on the vanguard of a vigorous civil rights movement in the immediate postwar period. In Winston-Salem, North Carolina, for example, the CIO's Food, Tobacco, Agricultural and Allied Industries attacked Jim Crow by organizing voter registration drives, challenging voter qualification tests, and encouraging black citizens to participate in electoral politics.[4] In 1946, when CIO president Philip Murray launched an effort to organize southern industrial workers called "Operation Dixie," he referred to the campaign as a "civil rights crusade."[5]

A civil rights movement based on equal access to employment and housing flourished in northern cities as well, built upon the foundations of the black Popular Front. In New York City, for example, African American leaders from four CIO unions organized the Negro Labor Victory Committee that placed over 15,000 black workers in defense jobs. Communist activists continued to shape urban politics after the war, joining union leaders, city councilmen, and members of the NAACP to fight for fair employment, access to housing, and an end to police brutality. Voters in Harlem reelected Communist Benjamin Davis to New York's City Council in 1943 and 1945, where he remained until expelled and eventually imprisoned under the Smith Act.[6] As historians begin to uncover the untold story of the civil rights movement in the North, they reveal, in the words of Thomas Sugrue, a "multifaceted battle that at its broadest included fights for prohibition against discrimination in the workplace, the opening of housing markets, the provision of quality education, the economic development of impoverished communities, and untrammeled access to the consumer marketplace."[7] The legacy of the 1930s interracial Left is evident in these postwar urban struggles as well as in the southern drive to dismantle Jim Crow.

However, the escalation of the Cold War curtailed the social-democratic demands of the labor movement, doomed Operation Dixie, and drastically narrowed the range of African American civil rights in both the South and the North. Several factors, including antilabor legislation, Henry Wallace's divisive third-party campaign, and the purge of Left-led unions from the CIO, led to the weakening of unions in the postwar period and their retreat from their commitment to black civil rights. Animating all these factors was McCarthyism, the federally sponsored crusade that left no facet of American life untouched. Anticommunist assaults on the labor movement helped to usher in the Labor-Management Relations Act of 1947, better known as the Taft-Hartley Act. This conservative legislation tamed the postwar strike wave by repealing many of the gains of the landmark Wagner Act of 1935. By prohibiting wildcat strikes, sympathy strikes, closed shops, mass picketing, and secondary boycotts, Taft-Hartley took the teeth out of unions. Moreover, section 9(h) of the act, which required union leaders to sign affidavits swearing they were not members of the Communist Party, undermined the labor movement, particularly its commitment to civil rights. For example, when members of the radical Food, Tobacco, Agricultural and Allied Industries moved to desegregate bathroom facilities in the union hall, conservatives accused them of using black workers as a ploy to advance a communist agenda.[8] Finally, the third-party presidential campaign of Henry Wallace, who opposed Taft-Hartley and supported civil rights, sharpened divisions within the CIO. Wallace's campaign impelled southern white workers to support Republican segregationist Strom Thurmond and fostered a racially polarized atmosphere that thwarted attempts at interracial organizing.[9] Wallace's defeat in 1948 justified the dismantling of the CIO's radical unions that supported him. In 1949–50, the CIO expelled eleven Left-led unions encompassing over 1 million members.[10] When the CIO merged with the AFL in 1955, there was little to distinguish it from its more conservative rival, as it had to narrow its demands and reinstate exclusionary practices in the face of overwhelming political pressures.[11] As the South became more racially polarized and white workers increasingly defined their politics in opposition to Civil Rights, stories of migration and conversion to class consciousness lost their prophetic power.

The red scare also drastically altered the trajectory of the postwar Civil Rights Movement. In some ways, the Cold War imperative for the United States to shine as a beacon of democracy gave leverage to racial progressives. Racism became a national security threat as images of police attacking peaceful protesters with vicious dogs and powerful fire hoses tarnished America's image abroad and discredited U.S. claims to moral superiority over the Union of Soviet Socialist Republics. Yet the Cold War ultimately limited the extent to which the Civil Rights Movement could change social relations, particularly in terms of economic justice. Cold War anticommunism undermined the class component of the movement, cast suspicion on interracial alliances, and ensured that the federal government would emphasize the national image rather than making deeper structural reforms.[12] As Nancy MacLean's history of affirmative action attests, the African American struggle for justice always entailed a struggle for jobs. However, the anticommunist purges in the CIO and the overarching atmosphere of anticommunism forced activists to change their tactics, focusing on legal protections, individual rights, consumer boycotts, and job training to make inroads into American economic life.[13]

McCarthyism not only hobbled Left economic and political institutions, but it also eroded the cultural networks that gave rise to migration narratives. According to historian Ellen Schrecker, the combination of direct governmental pressure along with private-sector attacks routed the CP from all areas of American life, from unions to higher education to mass culture.[14] In 1947 President Harry Truman established the Internal Security Division of the Department of Justice that created a formal list of "subversive" groups subject to federal investigation. This witch hunt basically equated communism and antiracist activism and targeted Poplar Front cultural organizations such as the George Washington Carver School in New York City.[15] The Carver School's working-class students had been the inspiration for Elizabeth Catlett's arresting visual narrative of black migration, *The Negro Woman*. In Chicago, the SSCAC, which was the cradle of radical art and politics in the 1940s, shored itself up against anticommunist attacks by ridding its board of radical leftists. In 1953, secretary of the board Margaret Burroughs went on sabbatical in Mexico, joining her friend Elizabeth Catlett at the Taller de Gráfica Popular. When Burroughs returned to the SSCAC, she found her membership had been revoked. In California, writers and artists reeled from the blacklisting of the "Hollywood Ten" in 1947. Sanora Babb was married to James Wong Howe, a successful cinematographer, and feared that her communist affiliation would put his career at risk. Like Elizabeth Catlett, William Attaway, and a host of other American writers and artists, she sought exile in Mexico for most of the 1950s.[16] Forced to choose between their leftist political commitments and their careers, many writers and artists either repudiated their communist sympathies or left the country. Richard Wright and Chester Himes sought a more hospitable political climate in Paris, while Arna Bontemps retreated to the relative safety of a college campus, where "a measure of isolation, a degree of security seemed possible. If a refuge for the harassed Negro could be found anywhere in those days, it had to be in such a setting."[17] Bontemps, his coauthor Jack Conroy, and William Attaway not only relocated but also turned to safer narrative forms, embedding their subversive ideas in children's literature and television scripts. Ironically, considering their large and impressionable audiences, these media were less subject to surveillance due to their perceived apolitical nature.[18] The eradication of communist influence from American life spelled the end of the migration narrative as a social weapon.

Both black and white migration narratives changed amidst these social upheavals. In 1952, Ralph Ellison published *Invisible Man*, what Lawrence Rodgers calls the "climactic fictional expression of the African-American Great Migration novel form."[19] A modernist masterpiece, Ellison's novel changed the course of American and African American literature. It also dramatized the rupture between African American writers and the communist Left. Yet as Barbara Foley convincingly argues, "Ellison's masterwork emerged only after a protracted and tortuous, wrestling down of his former political radicalism."[20] In other words, Ellison's narrative of black-Left rupture does not accurately reflect the nature of these interracial alliances in the 1930s and '40s but, rather, the anticommunist political climate in which the novel was finally published. In constructing a powerful myth of communist betrayal in *Invisible Man*, Ellison revises not only the migration narratives explored in this study but also his own positive critical responses to communist writers such as Sanora Babb.

While attentive to the crisis of housing and poverty in urban black neighborhoods, *Invisible Man* staunchly rejects the communist call for interracial unionism that had stirred the imaginations of so many writers—black and white—during the previous two decades. Thinly veiled as the "Brotherhood" in the novel, the Communist Party is depicted as doctrinaire, racist, egotistical, and utterly dismissive of the "man in the street."[21] The key to transcendence for the narrator is not working-class solidarity or populist producerism but, rather, recognition of the sustaining elements of African American culture, which manifest in cultural forms such as food, music, and speech and in human form through the characters of Mary Rambo, Brother Tarp, the narrator's grandfather, and even a portrait of Frederick Douglass. This embrace of African American culture entails reclaiming the American South as a cultural homeland. It imagines migration as a process of cultural hybridity—a fusion of north and south—that is lacking in much of the migration literature of the 1930s. Not surprisingly, in his 1942 review of William Attaway's *Blood on the Forge*, Ellison criticized the young writer for failing to understand this hybrid process: "The writer did not see that while the folk individual was being liquidated in the crucible of steel, he was also undergoing a fusion of new elements. Nor did Attaway see that the individual which emerged, blended of old and new, was better fitted for the problems of the industrial environment."[22] In contrast to Attaway's Moss brothers, Ellison's narrator finds his selfhood by melding the richness of African American southern culture into new patterns in the urban North.

African American migration literature in the late 1940s through the 1950s shifted away from the naturalistic, urban, masculine paradigm of Richard Wright to articulate a more communal, often female-centered vision that began to view the American South in a more positive light.[23] Dorothy West's *The Living Is Easy*, published in 1947, reflects this shift in its early stages. Born to a middle-class black family in Boston and educated at the prestigious Boston Latin Girls' School, West had socioeconomic, educational, and geographic origins that differed starkly from Wright's poor southern background. West moved to Harlem as a teenager, where she became the darling of the black literati.[24] In 1932 she accompanied Langston Hughes and twenty other American artists to Russia to work on "Black and White," a film (which was never made) about the oppression of African Americans in the United States. In a letter to her cousins back home, West gushes about living in "quite bourgeois style ever since we arrived. In our many trips we have had a whole car on a train to ourselves, with our own samovar, and sometimes our own diner. We have stopped in the finest hotels. I've eaten delicacies I'd never heard of before."[25] West's letters from her travels in Russia sparkle with her enthusiasm for new places, sensations, and the Russian people, but this trip did not convert her to a Marxist way of thinking.

When West and Wright founded the *Challenge* magazine together in 1934, their differing political sensibilities caused conflict between them. Whereas West aimed for high aesthetic quality regardless of political orientation, Wright had a more radical political agenda that shaped his editorial vision. Faced with dwindling submissions of mediocre quality, West agreed to refashion the magazine as *New Challenge* and to include more politically motivated writing, but this iteration of the journal only survived one issue.[26] West's first novel, *The Living Is Easy*, departs definitively from Wright's protest paradigm, offering a satire of Boston's black bourgeoisie.

Unlike in the migration narratives of the 1930s, the poor and working-class migrants are merely a shadow presence in *The Living Is Easy*. They are the "raucous," ill-mannered "cotton-belters" who are too loud, too southern, and too black. Anxious about their own precarious social status, the "nicer colored people" flee to the suburbs in order to "escape this plague of their own locusts."[27] Cleo Judson, the protagonist of *The Living Is Easy*, is also a poor migrant from South Carolina, but she launches herself into black Boston's high society through her marriage to Bart Judson, an entrepreneur who made a fortune importing bananas. Although Cleo repudiates her humble origins and works to excise any trace of it through diligent attention to her speech, dress, and manners, she secretly craves the sensuality of the southern childhood she left behind. The part of Cleo that aspired to the puritan pretensions of the black bourgeoisie "was continually at war with the part of her that preferred the salt flavor of lusty laughter."[28] Cleo attempts to reconcile this divided self by importing the South to Boston in the guise of her three sisters. Luring them north through lies and half-truths, Cleo manages to tear them away from their happy marriages, causing the tragic downfall of each of them. Although Cleo ultimately fails to recreate the ideal southern sorority in her Boston brownstone, *The Living Is Easy* offers a positive image of the South through Cleo's memory, which her sisters embody. The migrant mother in *The Living Is Easy* is the link between southern folk culture, coded as producerist, authentic, communal, and female, and northern urban culture, coded as consumerist, artificial, individualistic, and male. In comparing the South favorably to the North, *The Living Is Easy* revises the Wright school of migration narratives. Likewise, the great African American migration novels of the 1950s—Ellison's *Invisible Man* and James Baldwin's *Go Tell It on the Mountain*—portray the black family, the black community, and southern black culture in a more sympathetic light.

The Living Is Easy also differs from the migration narratives of the Depression era—as well as from Baldwin's and Ellison's work—in its satirical form, its focus on the black elite, and its concern with women's circumscribed roles in an affluent society. The gender critique of The Living Is Easy may be characterized as an early, African American version of the "feminine mystique." Rather than celebrating the figures of the populist producer or the Marxist worker, West's novel satirizes bourgeois archetypes. Bart Judson is an entrepreneur in the tradition of a Horatio Alger hero, born in slavery and lifting himself up to a position of great fortune through a combination of "luck and pluck." Cleo, on the other hand, is a tragic figure in that she possesses a capitalist instinct that surpasses even Bart's genius, but gender constraints prevent her from bringing her ambitions to fruition. In the novel, there are only three roles available to black women: the housewife, the whore, or the mammy figure working in the "white folks' kitchen." In the beginning of the novel, Cleo is offered each option. The wild, gender-neutral freedom of her childhood comes to an end in adolescence, when she has to work with "sullen anger" in the "white folks' kitchen."[29] After moving north, she marries hurriedly to escape her mistress's lascivious nephew. Relegated to the safe but unsatisfying role of wealthy housewife, Cleo can exercise her talents only through consumption. Making a striking foil to Depression-era migrant women like Ma Joad, Cleo spends more than she has, her credit books "showing various aliases and unfinished payments, and her pawnshop tickets, the expiration dates of which had mostly come and gone."[30] Unlike Depression-era novels that are infused with images of household and wage labor, The Living Is Easy employs the language of consumption, exploring the tensions between spending and saving, the temptations of credit, the link between personal identity and material possessions, and the erosion of women's domestic productivity and the eclipse of cultural authenticity in a consumer-oriented society.

In satirizing the black middle class through a parody of female spending, West contributes to an emerging liberal discourse in the postwar period that linked maternal consumption to the health of the nation. By the late 1950s, films, scholarly work, political debates, and other outlets of liberal ideology expressed fears about the negative effects of consumer culture on American society. West's satire of Boston's black elite anticipates E. Franklin Frazier's sociological study The Black Bourgeoisie, published ten years later in 1957. In advance of Frazier's landmark book, The Living Is Easy highlights the black bourgeoisie's imitative behavior, its precarious economic foundations, and its conspicuous consumption in place of a more authentic appreciation of high art or African American folk traditions.[31] Yet whereas Frazier depicts elite black women as self-hating, West suggests that Cleo's desire for upward social mobility has more to do with her resistance to constraining gender roles than with race envy. The Living Is Easy marks a shift in liberal discourse away from the problems of the poor and toward the social ills stemming from America's newfound abundance: conformity, the lack of authentic cultural expression, and racial self-hatred.[32]

Southern white migration narratives have followed a much different trajectory in the postwar period. In 1954, Harriette Arnow published The Dollmaker, a novel of the white Appalachian migration to Detroit that rivals Steinbeck's Grapes of Wrath in its epic proportions, its populist ethos, and its tragic pathos. Yet The Dollmaker is an elegy for the producerist values and working-class militancy that invigorated 1930s fiction. Gertie Nevels, the protagonist, is an emblem of populist producerism. In the Kentucky portion of the novel, she grows her own food, makes her own clothes, and pours her creative energy into whittling useful things. Even the money she earns has concrete significance for Gertie, each dollar bill corresponding to real work. As she counts her precious savings, Gertie remembers, "'That was eggs at Samuel's two years ago last July,' and to a five, 'That was the walnut-kernel money winter before last,' and to another one, 'That was the big dominecker that wouldn't lay atall; she'd bring close to two dollars now.'"[33] In contrast, Gertie's husband, Clovis, disdains farming and is enchanted by modern technology. While he flourishes in Detroit, buying goods on credit and filling his home with labor-saving appliances, Gertie withers amidst the consumer paraphernalia that alienates her from her work. By the end of the novel, even Gertie's creativity is crushed by the logic of mass production. She destroys an unfinished sculpture of Christ—the symbol of her guilt and her hope for redemption—and uses the wood to produce machine-made wooden dolls. The Dollmaker narrates the defeat of the producerist vision that was at the heart of 1930s populism and casts a critical glance upon the culture of consumption that replaced it.

However, The Dollmaker offers a full articulation of Appalachian identity as ethnicity and, in doing so, suggests cultural pluralism among white ethnic groups as an alternative source of community solidarity and individual identity. It is Gertie's Italian and Irish Catholic neighbors who appreciate her woodworking skills, commissioning her to carve finely detailed crucifixes. Significantly, Gertie's whittling catalyzes the only scene of interracial bonding in the novel. On the train bound for Detroit, Gertie bonds with a black migrant mother from the South over their shared folk values. Both carry "hard-earned bills, worn from saving," and the black woman appreciates Gertie's hand-carved basket.[34] Once in the alien world of the Detroit housing project, Gertie seeks comfort from the Japanese vegetable peddler, asking, "'I mean—I wondered—I jist got here. Did it take you long to—well, to kinda learn to like it, this country? I figger it's so differ'nt frum mine—it must ha been worse fer you.'"[35] Despite Gertie's inclination to build bridges across cultural lines, the ethnic mix of the factory housing generates more hostility than it does solidarity. Playing in the alley, Gertie's children learn words such as "'wop' and 'kike' and 'shine' and 'limey.'"[36] Mrs. Daly, the fiery-haired Irish woman next door, is a walking tirade against any race, ethnic group, religion, or political persuasion that differs from her own. Nevertheless, the neighbors dispense with their ethnocentric mindsets during hard times by lending one another economic and emotional support. In the final tragic image of the novel, when Gertie destroys her faceless sculpture, she admits that she could have found the face of Christ for it in the faces of "some of my neighbors down in the alley—they would ha done."[37] With this concluding scene, the novel turns the page on the interracial producerism of Depression-era reform and begins a new chapter on cultural pluralism among white ethnic peoples. The reader is left wondering, however, how the African American woman Gertie befriended on the train fits into this new national narrative of a "nation of immigrants."

As southern white and white ethnic workers became the rank and file of a new working-class conservatism, the white migration story no longer provided a usable past for the liberal-Left writers and intellectuals. It is a little known fact, for instance, that Ken Kesey, the radical writer of the 1960s counterculture whose *One Flew over the Cuckoo's Nest* protested rigid bourgeois values through a story of interracial friendship, considered himself an "Oakie." In an unpublished piece, Kesey described "what being an Oakie means":

> Being an Oakie means being the first of your whole family to finish
> high school let alone go on to college . . .
> Being an Oakie means getting rooted out of an area and
> having to hustle for a toehold in some new area . . .
> Being an Oakie means running the risk of striving out
> from under a layer of heartless sonsabitches only to discover
> You have become a redneck of bitterness worse than those
> you strive against . . .
> Being an Oakie is a low rent, aggravating drag, but it does

learn you some essentials . . . essentials like it isn't a new car
   That pulls over to help you when you are broke down with the
      senile carburetor; it is somebody who knows what it is
   to be broke down with a hurt machine.[38]

Kesey's references to lack of educational opportunities, dispossession, and the generosity of the poor echo the populist sentiments of Woody Guthrie, as does his rambling vernacular voice. By the 1960s, Guthrie had been revived as a founding hero by the leftist folk revival, much to the credit of his number one fan and imitator, Bob Dylan. Yet Kesey's reference to "a redneck of bitterness" hints at the crucial tension between the white working class and the New Left. This phrase suggests that the struggle of white migrant workers to resist socioeconomic forms of prejudice and discrimination often resulted in bitterness that manifested as racism. Without the political infrastructure briefly afforded to them by unions, the CIO, and even the Communist Party in the 1930s, white people who were economically marginalized misdirected their grievances toward the people of color who they erroneously believed were the main beneficiaries of federal assistance.

Abandoned by the Left, white migration narratives continued to flourish in country music—the voice of the white working class. Merle Haggard's 1969 hit "Okie from Muskogee" revived the lore of the dust bowl migration for a new generation, yet it countered the leftist politics of Woody Guthrie.[39] Haggard's patriotic song lambastes the counterculture, specifically addressing the antiwar movement, flag burning, drug use, and styles of dress and appearance that expressed the youth movement's interest in androgyny, environmentalism, and pacifism. Haggard's opposition to Civil Rights may be implied as well, but southern white migrants living in the North were no more likely to oppose these reforms than their white northern-born neighbors.[40] Yet, increasingly, the white working class followed the lead of politicians in scapegoating the urban black poor as a depraved underclass that is (paradoxically) overindulged by federal welfare.[41] It is important, however, to recognize the larger political and economic forces—the constriction of organized labor and the defeat of a radical social-democratic vision in the postwar period—that steered many blue-collar workers into the neoconservative movement, rather than adopting the historically static view that the white working-class is inherently racist.

Postwar politics and culture seem to fulfill Chester Himes's prophecy: The South has won America. Indeed, Jim Crow came North in the guise of residential segregation, discriminatory federal housing policy, race riots, and white resistance to the integration of schools. Country music, barbe-cue, and car racing are no longer regional pastimes—they are hallmarks of American national identity.[42] More importantly, conservative politics (hos-tility to unions, civil rights, and social welfare) is no longer the province of southern Dixiecrats but, rather, a dominant force in national politics. When President Lyndon Johnson signed the Civil Rights Act of 1965, he sealed the deal between African Americans and the Democratic Party and trans-formed the South into a Republican stronghold—political realignments that remain today.[43] In their efforts to explain the fracturing of the Left and the rise of working-class conservatism, many analysts look to the limits of populism in regard to race and social issues. Today, in their course syllabi and research, scholars trace the trajectory of American populism from the democratic movements of the 1880s and 1930s to the popular campaigns of George Wallace, Richard Nixon, and Ronald Reagan.[44] They compare the class-based politics of the Old Left unfavorably with the race-based politics of the New Left.

Ain't Got No Home is an alternative account of the relationship between American populism and civil rights. Looking through the lens of migration narratives—stories of the quintessential populist hero—we see how strug-gles against injustice and poverty can expand to include African Americans and women into a broad notion of "the people." While American populism is protean in its ability to serve multiple political agendas, this radical tradi-tion should not be dismissed or forgotten. As social and economic inequal-ity widens in the United States and globally, as labor migrations create an increasingly dynamic and multicultural world, this vision of ordinary peo-ple's collective action has renewed relevance, urgency, and power.

NOTES

Introduction

1. Bradley preface, xii.

2. Kinnamon and Fabre, *Conversations with Richard Wright*, 32.

3. Wright's response is unknown, but apparently he convinced Steinbeck to take back his words. See DeMott, *Steinbeck's Reading*, 187; Webb, *Richard Wright*, 187; Rowley, *Richard Wright*, 205–6; "Steinbeck, John," 361; and "Wright, Richard."

4. Denning, *Cultural Front*, 265. Sarah Wald makes a similar point when she argues that the Okies define themselves in contradistinction to African American, Native American, and foreign-born people. See Wald, "'We Ain't Foreign,'" 484–86.

5. While critic Michael Denning recognizes how figures like Woody Guthrie blended southwestern populism and Popular Front multiracialism, he dismisses Guthrie as exceptional, claiming that this populist tradition was "more often tinged with the Klan." See Denning, *Cultural Front*, 36.

6. With this periodization, I contend that the Popular Front had a deeper and more lasting impact on American culture than many scholars allow. For other articulations of this view, see Denning, *Cultural Front*; Mullen, *Popular Fronts*; and Wald, *Exiles from a Future Time*.

7. More work needs to be done to uncover black women's engagement with Left politics and aesthetics. Promising new studies include Boyce Davies, *Left of Karl Marx*; Gore, *Radicalism at the Crossroads*; Higashida, *Black Internationalist Feminism*; and McDuffie, *Sojourning for Freedom*.

8. Hall, "Long Civil Rights Movement"; Honey, *Southern Labor*; Biondi, *To Stand and Fight*; Sugrue, *Sweet Land of Liberty*. I follow Sugrue in using the terms "civil rights" interchangeably with the "struggles" for "freedom," "democracy," "justice," etc. The proper noun "Civil Rights" distinguishes the organized movement of the 1950s and 1960s from its Depression-era precursor.

9. Young, *Black Writers of the Thirties*, 253, quoted in Maxwell, *New Negro, Old Left*, 3. See also Cruse, *Crisis of the Negro Intellectual*, for the seminal expression of this view.

10. For example, in an essay published in the *Cambridge Companion to the African American Novel* in 2004, Jerry Ward acknowledges that the novels of Steinbeck and Wright "invite comparison," but that they "did not stem from the same political tradition." See Ward, "Everybody's Protest Novel," 177. Particularly relevant to my study, Farah Griffin's 1995 book on the African American Great Migration narrative, *"Who Set You Flowin'?,"* gives little attention to the Left commitments of the writers and artists she examines.

11. Singh, "Retracing the Black-Red Thread," 832.

12. Foley, *Wrestling with the Left*.

13. See Singh, "Retracing the Black-Red Thread," for a useful analysis of this paradigm shift.

14. Wald, *Exiles from a Future Time*, 295.

15. McElvaine, *The Depression and New Deal*, 28.

16. Lange and Taylor, *American Exodus*, 38.

17. Although the theme of migration captured the public imagination in the 1930s, the actual rate of out-migration from the American South decreased by 50 percent due to the lack of jobs in destination cities. Migration peaked during and after the two world wars as northern and western industries demanded a domestic labor supply. Between 1916 and 1919, nearly 500,000 African Americans migrated to northern cities; the term "Great Migration" usually refers to this peak period. Heavy migration continued through the 1920s with more than 800,000 black migrants heading north, totaling 1.3 million between 1910 and 1930. Roughly the same number of white southerners migrated in this period. As the economic crisis gave way to abundance in the 1940s and 1950s, the flow of migrants out of the South surged once again. This second wave was even larger, reaching more than 5 million migrants, roughly evenly divided between black and white. Recent figures tabulated by James Gregory, which account for rates of mortality and return migration, estimate that, in all, 20 million white people and 8 million black people left the South in the twentieth century. See Grossman, *Land of Hope*, 19; Fligstein, *Going North*, 17; Kirby, *Rural Worlds Lost*, 320; Jones, *The Dispossessed*, 219, 224; Trotter, *Great Migration in Historical Perspective*, 10; and Gregory, *Southern Diaspora*, 14.

18. DePastino, *Citizen Hobo*, 200–201.

19. Ransdell, "Report on the Scottsboro, Ala., Case," 13.

20. DePastino, *Citizen Hobo*, 202.

21. "I Ain't Got No Home in This World Anymore," *Songs of Woody Guthrie*, original songbook, undated, box 2, Woody Guthrie Manuscript Collection. Courtesy Woody Guthrie Publications, Inc.

22. McElvaine, *Great Depression*, 225; Denning, *Cultural Front*, 22.

23. Korstad and Lichtenstein, "Opportunities Found and Lost," 792–93; Honey, *Southern Labor*, 118; Zieger, *The CIO*, 255–56; Kelley, *Hammer and Hoe*, 52.

24. Edmund Wilson, *Shores of Light*, quoted in McElvaine, *Great Depression*, 130.

25. Denning, *Cultural Front*, xviii. Popular Front writers and activists drew ideas, resources, and inspiration from the CP; but they were not necessarily beholden to it, and many of them were highly critical of Stalin. I use the term "Left" as an umbrella term describing a broad political spectrum from liberal New Dealers to Communists who advocated for the rights of workers. "Radical" refers to anticapitalists left of the New Deal. Capitalized "Communist" designates official members of the CP, while lowercase "communist" refers to a more general political orientation.

26. Solomon, *Cry Was Unity*, 304.

27. I treat CP theory on the Negro Question and its antiracist organizing in greater length in Chapters 1 and 3.

28. Naison, *Communists in Harlem*, 21–23; Solomon, *Cry Was Unity*, 111.

29. Solomon, *Cry Was Unity*, 148.

30. Quoted in ibid., 149–50.

31. One of the major contributions of Maxwell's *New Negro, Old Left* is the idea that African Americans were active agents in their relationship with the CP, and that they shaped Marxist theory, proletarian literature, and the "black nation" thesis that promoted African American self-determination in the South. This argument overturns the assumption made by many scholars that "the meeting of black and white Reds remade only the black." See Maxwell, *New Negro, Old Left*, 5.

32. Aaron, *Writers on the Left*, 221. This statement was announced in the "Program of Action" of the Second World Plenum of the International Bureau of Revolutionary Literature in Kharkov in November 1930.

33. Wright, *Black Boy*, 373.

34. Morgan, *Rethinking Social Realism*, 13, 17; Smethurst, *New Red Negro*, 20.

35. Walker, *Richard Wright*, 78.

36. According to Larry Ceplair, the term "art is a weapon" was coined by German Communist playwright Friedrich Wolf in 1928 and adopted by the League of Workers' Theaters in New York. Although it was never an official CP slogan, it became a rallying cry for radical artists. See Ceplair, "Albert Maltz."

37. Eddy, "Ballad of a Slightly Addled Culture Worker," 19; Nekola and Rabinowitz, *Writing Red*, 4.

38. Seaver, "Proletarian Novel," 101; Foley, *Radical Representations*, 118–20.

39. Union records and other archival sources may indicate how workers responded to radical art and literature, suggesting a fascinating research project that is beyond the scope of this study.

40. Hegeman, *Patterns for America*, 5. The "spatial turn" in American studies has helped me to theorize the role of the migration narrative in national identity formation. Works that have influenced my thinking include Bramen, *Uses of Variety*; Fetterley and Pryse, *Writing out of Place*; Franklin and Steiner, *Mapping American Culture*; Halttunen, "Groundwork"; Hsu, "Literature and Regional Production"; and Lefebvre, *Production of Space*.

41. Stange, *Symbols of Ideal Life*, 129.

42. On the national obsession with movement during the 1930s, see Casey, "Introduction," ix–x; Denning, *Cultural Front*, 264; Dickstein, "Depression Culture"; and Dickstein, *Dancing in the Dark*, 357–407.

43. Susman, *Culture as History*, 164; Denning, *Cultural Front*, xvi.

44. As Smethurst points out, much of this debate hinges on regional differences, as Robin Kelley's study of southern sharecroppers revealed a decrease in CP membership after 1935, while Mark Naison's study of Harlem portrays a vibrant Popular Front hub. I follow Bill Mullen in my findings that African American engagement with the literary Left came into fruition in the late 1930s and '40s. See Smethurst, *New Red Negro*, 20–22; Kelley, *Hammer and Hoe*; Naison, *Communists in Harlem*; and Mullen, *Popular Fronts*.

45. Burke, "Revolutionary Symbolism in America," 90.

46. Hart, *American Writers' Congress*, 167–69.

47. See Battat, "Okie Outlaws and Dust Bowl Fugitives," for an analysis of the discourses of race and ethnicity implicit in *The Grapes of Wrath*.

Chapter 1

1. Wright, "My Two Sons Face the Electric Chair," 182. For more on the role of the Scottsboro mothers, see Miller, Pennybacker, and Rosenhaft, "Mother Ada Wright."

2. Solomon, *Cry Was Unity*, 197, 205.

3. Ibid., 300; Kelley, *Hammer and Hoe*, 90.

4. Hill, *Men, Mobs, and the Law*, 2.

5. Solomon, *Cry Was Unity*, 229.

6. Du Bois, "The Negro and Communism," 315.

7. Miller, *Remembering Scottsboro*, 11.

8. Wright, "My Two Sons Face the Electric Chair"; Solomon, *Cry Was Unity*, 187.

9. For an excellent cultural history of the hobo, see DePastino, *Citizen Hobo*.

10. Lenin, "Three Sources and Three Component Parts of Marxism," 39–40.

11. Rauty introduction, 4. During the 1920s and '30s, as the economic basis of "hobohemia" began to change, it became less a radical proletarian subculture and more an alternative lifestyle for the urban avant-garde. After World War I, the building of western railroads and infrastructure slowed, agriculture mechanized, and railroads cracked down on vagrants, causing a decline in the population of single, white, male transient workers—the backbone of hobohemia. However, cultural radicals maintained an interest in the liberated world of the hobo jungles and urban lodging houses. Ben Reitman, for example, established a "hobo college" in Chicago featuring lectures and social gatherings that brought together hoboes, urban bohemians, and sociologists. See DePastino, *Citizen Hobo*, 190.

12. DePastino, *Citizen Hobo*, 95–97.

13. Quoted in Kornbluh, *Rebel Voices*, 66–67.

14. DePastino, *Citizen Hobo*, 192–93, quote on 97.

15. Milburn, *Hobo's Hornbook*, 249.

16. Wilkins, "Bonuseers Ban Jim Crow."

17. Guthrie, *Bound for Glory*, 1.

18. "Slip Brings Halt to Tour of Two Girls: Hitch-Hikers Garbed in Boy Scout Outfits Run Afoul in Bridgeport," 25 March (hand-dated 1931), box 4, folder 83v (oversized), Pauli Murray Papers.

19. Letter from Nancy Cunard to Pauli Murray, 12 April and 15 January (no year), box 4, folder 84, Pauli Murray Papers.

20. Murray, "Three Thousand Miles," 67–70.

21. McWilliams, *Factories in the Field*, 26.

22. Reitman, *Sister of the Road*, 255, my emphasis. According to DePastino, correspondence between Reitman and his editor confirms that Bertha is Reitman's fictional alter ego, not a real person. See DePastino, *Citizen Hobo*, 90.

23. DePastino, *Citizen Hobo*, 202–6.

24. Reckless, "Why Women Become Hoboes," 179.

25. Springer, "Men Off the Road," 420; DePastino, *Citizen Hobo*, 201.

26. Miller suggests that Wellman's film refashions the Scottsboro case by inverting the heroes and the villains, making the rapist white and the avengers black, but he does not place the film in the context of the hobo narrative. DePastino does not analyze the

film in depth but mentions that it sensationalized the problem of transient youth. See Miller, *Remembering Scottsboro*, 116; DePastino, *Citizen Hobo*, 203.

27. Bulosan, *America Is in the Heart*, 113.

28. Goodman, *Stories of Scottsboro*, 25–26.

29. Marcy, "'Save Us' Negro Boys Write Folks in Chattanooga."

30. Paul Peters, "From Darkest America," *Labor Defender*, February 1932, 31, quoted in Miller, *Remembering Scottsboro*, 22.

31. "Scottsboro Boys Write from Kilby Death Cells," *Labor Defender*, May 1932, 92, quoted in Miller, *Remembering Scottsboro*, 23.

32. "Girl Hobo Loses Both Legs under Wheels of Freight," *Tatler*, 11 August 1932; "Girl Hobo in Hospital; Fell off Penn. Train," n.d.; Ivy Grant Morton, "A Bride in a Boxcar," *Scribner's Magazine*, n.d.; "Girl 22 Years Old Dresses as Boy," n.d, all from section in scrapbook titled "Vagabondia," box 4, folder 83v (oversized), Pauli Murray Papers.

33. Vorse, "How Scottsboro Happened," 357.

34. Ibid., 356–58, my emphasis.

35. Ibid., 356.

36. Hughes, *Scottsboro Limited*, n.p.

37. Ibid.

38. Miller, *Remembering Scottsboro*, 115.

39. Steinbeck, *Of Mice and Men*, 12. All future references will be cited parenthetically and are to this edition.

40. Attaway, *Let Me Breathe Thunder* (repr. as *Tough Kid*), 29. All future references will be cited parenthetically and are to this edition.

41. Sociologists and hobo writers mentioned homosexual relationships among hoboes, referring to the older predator as a "jocker" and the vulnerable youth as the "punk." Even into the early twentieth century, manhood was not defined through heterosexual relations but through dominance in all-male environments, so these "jockers" were not considered deviant or "queer." See DePastino, *Citizen Hobo*, 90. By the 1930s, however, the increasingly managerial workplace no longer served as an adequate "proving ground" for manhood, and the massive unemployment rates threw American men into a gender crisis. The fear of homosexuality and "effeminate" boys escalated. See Kimmel, *Manhood in America*, 192–217, and Chauncey, *Gay New York*, 331–53.

42. According to Laura Browder, the "Living Newspaper" plays of the Federal Theater Project provided a collective radicalizing experience for audiences. See Browder, *Rousing the Nation*, 11–12.

43. Hughes, *Scottsboro Limited*, n.p.

44. Steinbeck quoted in Shillinglaw introduction, xv–xvi.

45. Garren, "William Attaway."

46. Untitled review of *Let Me Breathe Thunder*.

47. Weiler, "'Man's Castle.'"

48. Melzer, "William Attaway."

49. Young, "Tough and Tender."

50. Page, "Some Americana"; W. N., "Boys of Road" (quotes).

51. Marsh, untitled review of *Let Me Breathe Thunder*.

52. Ward, "Everybody's Protest Novel," 177. In his survey of African American novels, Bernard Bell briefly mentions Attaway's first novel, noting Steinbeck's influence, yet reserves his extended analysis for Attaway's second book, *Blood on the Forge*, and its debt to Richard Wright. See Bell, *Afro-American Novel and Its Tradition*, 168.

53. Kazin, *Populist Persuasion*, 18.

54. While William Goldhurst deems the incorporation of Crooks into the workers' fraternity as the peak of hopefulness in the novella, few others even mention his presence in the story. In her explication of the novel geared for college teachers and students, for example, Charlotte Hadella describes the "brotherhood of George, Lennie, and Candy as they plan for their escape from the ranch to the dream farm," omitting Crooks from this fraternity. Most critics refer to Lennie and George's dream, sometimes including Candy and rarely including Crooks. In a brief sociopolitical reading of the novella within a larger article about fascism, Louis Owens claims that Crooks connects capitalism to the slaveholding economy but does not examine his character more fully. See Goldhurst, "*Of Mice and Men*," 54; Hadella, "Steinbeck's *Of Mice and Men*," 149; and Owens, "Deadly Kids," 325.

55. Maxwell, *New Negro, Old Left*, 131.

56. Meltzer, "William Attaway," 7

57. Ibid.; Pinckney introduction, viii.

58. Killens foreword, 7.

59. William Attaway to Richard Wright, 2 September 1941, box 94, folder 19, Richard Wright Papers.

60. Meltzer, "William Attaway," 7.

61. Lee, "On the Road," 283.

62. Smethurst, *New Red Negro*, 9–10, 66.

63. Ngai, *Impossible Subjects*, 73.

64. Steven Hahn argues that the Populist movement of the nineteenth century excluded black farmers, and that lynching and other forms of racial violence escalated during these agrarian revolts. Moreover, some populists defined "producers" in contradistinction to not only elite landowners and merchants but also poor black people whom they saw as dependents. Similarly, Charles Postel argues that the Populists' logic of progress mandated the exclusion of Chinese immigrants and the codification of Jim Crow. Yet the Populist era was one of the few moments in southern history in which black and white farmers organized together. The Knights of Labor organized black and white workers extensively in the South during the 1880s and 1890s and successfully protested the segregation of theaters and hotels in Richmond during its annual convention in 1886. See Hahn, *Nation under Our Feet*, 427–32; Postel, *Populist Vision*, 19; and Goldfield, "Race and the CIO: The Possibilities for Racial Egalitarianism," 4.

65. Maxwell, *New Negro, Old Left*, 127.

66. Naison, *Communists in Harlem*, 46.

67. "Why We Can't Hate 'Reds.'"

68. Quoted in Kelley, *Hammer and Hoe*, 79.

69. Ibid., emphasis in original.

70. Solomon, *Cry Was Unity*, 149.

71. Gerstle, "Working-Class Racism," 36.

72. Peddie, "Poles Apart?," 124.

73. Quoted in ibid., 128.

74. Ellison, *Invisible Man*, 418.

75. Maxwell, *New Negro, Old Left*, 128.

76. McKay quoted in ibid., 126.

77. Naison, *Communists in Harlem*, 137; Maxwell, *New Negro, Old Left*, 127.

78. Marx and Engels, *Manifesto of the Communist Party*, 29.

79. Rideout, *Radical Novel in the United States*, 185.

80. Algren, *Somebody in Boots*, 122.

81. Maxwell, *New Negro, Old Left*, 200.

82. Steinbeck, "The Vigilante."

83. Ibid., 135.

84. Swing, *Forerunners of American Fascism*, 13.

85. Warren, *Liberals and Communism*, 90.

86. McWilliams, *Factories in the Field*, 231–38, quote on 231. See also Geary, "Carey McWilliams and Antifascism."

87. Payne, *History of Fascism*, 455.

Chapter 2

1. Babb, Babb, and Wixson, *On the Dirty Plate Trail*, 19.

2. Stott, *Documentary Expression and Thirties America*, 58.

3. Entin, *Sensational Modernism*; Kaufman, *Woody Guthrie*; Jackson, *Prophet Singer*.

4. Neither Anne Loftis nor Charles Shindo mention Babb in their studies of the imagery of California migrant workers in the 1930s. Denning mentions her several times in passing as a proletarian regionalist who belonged to the Los Angeles John Reed Club; he also notes how she inspired Bulosan. See Loftis, *Witnesses to the Struggle*; Shindo, *Dust Bowl Migrants*; and Denning, *Cultural Front*, 133, 208, 273, 519 n. 33.

5. Wixson notes that to many midwestern literary radicals, communist theories seemed doctrinaire and out of touch, so they blended them with the "indigenous critiques of capitalism" that made more sense to them. See Babb, Babb, and Wixson, *On the Dirty Plate Trail*, 41–42.

6. Daniel, *Bitter Harvest*, 151–58, 184; Loftis, *Witnesses to the Struggle*, 24; Weber, *Dark Sweat, White Gold*, 190.

7. Daniel, *Bitter Harvest*, 198–201; Loftis, *Witnesses to the Struggle*, 25.

8. Although Congress included agricultural workers in the original drafts of the act, it succumbed to pressure from the Associated Farmers and industrialists, who feared that higher food prices would incite factory workers to demand wage increases. This landmark protective legislation thus created a permanent, predominately nonwhite agricultural underclass in California whose interests were divided from those of industrial workers and outside the purview of the federal government. It set a precedent for agricultural workers' exclusion from other social programs such as Social Security and unemployment insurance, and from federal support more generally. Domestic workers— one of the few jobs available to black women—were also excluded from the act. See Weber, *Dark Sweat, White Gold*, 126.

9. Ibid., 261, 252–54.

10. Guerin-Gonzalez, *Mexican Workers and the American Dream*, 112. Weber cites a higher proportion of 90 percent, noting that Mexican workers were edged out of the labor market by racist repatriation schemes, deportation, and job competition with these new arrivals who would work for next to nothing. See Weber, *Dark Sweat, White Gold*, 138.

11. Weber, *Dark Sweat, White Gold*, 180.

12. McWilliams, *Factories in the Field*, 306; Steinbeck, *Harvest Gypsies*, 23. Though Steinbeck's comments border on the chauvinistic, they highlight the vulnerability of immigrant workers, who "could be treated as so much scrap when it was not needed" and "deported to Mexico at Government expense." See Steinbeck, *Harvest Gypsies*, 54.

13. Steinbeck, *Harvest Gypsies*, 22. McWilliams echoed this prediction, announcing in *Factories in the Field* that "with the arrival of the dust-bowl refugees, a cycle of exploitation had been brought to a close" (306).

14. Taylor, "Again the Covered Wagon," 368.

15. Weber, *Dark Sweat, White Gold*, 161. Weber notes that while Mexican workers saw themselves as members of an agricultural proletariat and worked for decades to change the system, the general pattern is for immigrant families to enter the labor force temporarily, providing enough of a financial base for the second generation to move on to better jobs. See ibid., 264 n. 123.

16. Ibid., 132.

17. Taylor, "Again the Covered Wagon," 351.

18. Quoted in Loftis, *Witnesses to the Struggle*, 128.

19. Jackson, *Prophet Singer*, 130.

20. Quoted in Klein, *Woody Guthrie*, 95; Kaufman, *Woody Guthrie*, 150.

21. Kaufman, *Woody Guthrie*, 150.

22. Guggenheim Application, box 19, folder 5, Sanora Babb Collection.

23. For the most detailed account of the affair, see Rampersad, *Ralph Ellison*, 147–51.

24. Sanora Babb to James Wong Howe, 29 August 1936, box 46, folder 6, Sanora Babb Collection.

25. Ibid.

26. Sanora Babb to James Wong Howe, 19 August 1936, box 46, folder 6, Sanora Babb Collection.

27. Sanora Babb to James Wong Howe, 29 August 1936, box 46, folder 6, Sanora Babb Collection.

28. Coiner, *Better Red*, 41–42.

29. Aaron, *Writers on the Left*, 154.

30. Babb, Babb, and Wixson, *On the Dirty Plate Trail*, 33.

31. Ibid.

32. "SRA Form 101: California State Relief Administration Transmittal," box 18, folder 7, Sanora Babb Collection.

33. D. F. Tom, "The Power and the Strength," box 18, folder 9, Sanora Babb Collection.

34. Babb, Babb, and Wixson, *On the Dirty Plate Trail*, 91. The essay is reprinted in full. In his headnotes, Wixson surmises that Babb wrote the essay for a CP unit, which is

corroborated by phrases such as "our own tactics." Written in first person, the essay has a the direct and personal tone of a letter.

35. Ibid., 96.

36. Ibid., 101, 98.

37. Ibid., 102.

38. Tom Collins to Sanora Babb, ca. 1938–39, box 18, folder 8, Sanora Babb Collection.

39. Ralph Ellison to Sanora Babb, ca. 1943, box 43, folder 3, Sanora Babb Collection.

40. Walter Babb to Sanora Babb, 24 September 1937, and Jennie Babb to Sanora Babb, n.d., box 18, folder 5, Sanora Babb Collection.

41. Riley Dixon to Sanora Babb, 9 November 1936, box 18, folder 6, Sanora Babb Collection.

42. Henry V. Selb to Sanora Babb, 5 November 1938, box 18, folder 6, Sanora Babb Collection. The letters from Dixon and Selb are reprinted in Babb, Babb, and Wixson, *On the Dirty Plate Trail*, 156–58.

43. Rodgers foreword, x.

44. Reader BB, manuscript report on *Whose Names Are Unknown* by Sanora Babb, Random House, Inc., copy in possession of the author, capitalization in the original.

45. Babb, *Whose Names Are Unknown*, 213. All future references will be cited parenthetically and are to this edition. This story matches Steinbeck's account in a letter to Elizabeth Otis, 7 March 1938: "And we found a boy in jail for a felony because he stole two old radiators because his mother was starving to death and in stealing them he broke a little padlock on a shed. We'll either spring him or the district attorney will do the rest of his life explaining." See Steinbeck and Wallsten, *Steinbeck*, 161.

46. Letter from Charles A. Pearce to Kyle Crichton, 21 December 1939, copy in possession of the author, capitalization in the original; Reader BB, manuscript report on *Whose Names Are Unknown* by Sanora Babb, Random House, Inc., copy in possession of the author, emphasis in original.

47. Ralph Ellison to Sanora Babb, 10 April 1942, box 43, folder 3, Sanora Babb Collection, emphasis in original.

48. Due to this tragic publication history, there is virtually no scholarship on the novel, with the notable exceptions of helpful introductions by Lawrence Rodgers in *Whose Names Are Unknown* and by Alan Wald in *Cry of the Tinamou*, a collection of Babb's short stories. See Babb, *Cry of the Tinamou*.

49. Unlike Mexican workers who had well-developed social networks, Anglo migrants came to California sick, starving, homeless, and uprooted; they were willing to work for much less than the Mexicans and did not have the resources to endure a strike. And unlike their industrial counterparts, agricultural workers in general lacked a geographic base, worked seasonally for different growers, and faced a highly organized industry that was a political powerhouse on state and national levels. Considering these issues of political economy, James Gregory, the leading expert on the Okie subculture, contends UCAPAWA would have faced insurmountable odds even with the widespread commitment of Anglo migrants. See Weber, *Dark Sweat, White Gold*, 148; Gregory, *American Exodus*, 164; and Daniel, *Bitter Harvest*, 280–85. In his assessment of cultural factors, Gregory challenges the notion, established by contemporary

observers and replicated by the next generation of historians, that white American migrants were too individualistic to join unions. Given their willingness to organize in other industries, both in oil and mining in Oklahoma and in the California defense industries in the 1940s, Gregory attributes Okies' reluctance to join UCAPAWA mainly to their identities as farmers, which compelled them to sympathize with their employers and to distance themselves from farmworkers, communist organizers, and middle-class sympathizers. See Gregory, *American Exodus*, 164. Historian Devra Weber concurs with Gregory but places greater emphasis on the Populist political tradition the Anglo migrants brought with them, which favored electoral politics over labor organizing as a tool for advancing their economic interests. Okies used the ballot rather than the strike to change conditions, trusting in a political system that did little to alter the class relations between farmworkers and growers. See Weber, *Dark Sweat, White Gold*, 156, 161.

50. Weber, *Dark Sweat, White Gold*, 148–51; Gregory, *American Exodus*, 158–64.

51. Weber, *Dark Sweat, White Gold*, 152; Gregory, *American Exodus*, 160.

52. Gregory, *American Exodus*, 164. This argument contributes to a larger historiography that attempts to locate the origins of white working-class conservatism in the populisms of the 1930s. For an alternative perspective that attributes postwar white backlash on the Left to foreign policy and liberal economic policy rather than white working-class racism, see Stein, *Running Steel*.

53. Babb, Babb, and Wixson, *On the Dirty Plate Trail*, 5.

54. Kazin, *Populist Persuasion*, 1; Postel, *Populist Vision*, 5–6; McMath, *American Populism*.

55. Kazin, *Populist Persuasion*, 14.

56. McMath, *American Populism*, 52.

57. Kazin, *Populist Persuasion*, 14. The CIO advocated for a family wage standard, indicating its masculine bias and emphasis on factory rather than agricultural labor. See Denning, *Cultural Front*, 32.

58. Richard Brodhead has called regionalism "a literary expression of the Populist Movement" of the 1880s and 1890s, but this connection has not been considered in depth. See Brodhead, "American Literary Field," 58.

59. Babb, Babb, and Wixson, *On the Dirty Plate Trail*, 3.

60. Sanora Babb to Tom Collins, n.d., box 18, folder 8, Sanora Babb Collection.

61. For a discussion of twentieth-century texts that incorporate regionalist aesthetics, see Hsu, "Literature and Regional Production," 37, and Campbell, *Resisting Regionalism*, 47.

62. See Brodhead, *Cultures of Letters*, and Kaplan, "Nation, Region, Empire." Eric Sundquist qualifies this argument that regionalism was the tool of the dominant culture, noting that works by white men are often categorized as "realist," while the writings of women and African Americans are considered "regionalist." Similarly, Bramen challenges the view of regionalism as a conservative form, arguing that "local color is neither the authentic voice of the subaltern nor the mouthpiece of the metropolitan elite, but a locus for a variety of ideological positions that articulate the relation between city and country for a local and/or a national audience." See Sundquist, "Realism and Regionalism," 503, and Bramen, *Uses of Variety*, 125.

63. Susman, *Culture as History*, 172.

64. Coats and Farooq, "Regionalism in the Era of the New Deal," 86.

65. Letter from Charles A. Pearce to Kyle Crichton, 21 December 1939, copy in possession of the author, capitalization in the original.

66. Gregory, *American Exodus*, 111.

67. Ralph Ellison to Sanora Babb, 19 November 1942, box 43, folder 3, Sanora Babb Collection.

68. My notion of regionalism as a strategy of resistance is indebted to Judith Fetterley and Marjorie Pryse, *Writing out of Place*. Although few scholars have made the connection between populism and regionalism, the historiographical debates over American populism and the literary critical debates over American regionalism divide into strikingly similar camps. On one hand, the dominant scholarly view criticizes populist politics and regionalist literature as essentially conservative forms, using the same negatively charged buzzwords to describe both traditions: nostalgic, sentimental, nativist, antimodern. For example, Richard Brodhead argues that regionalism is a form of colonization in which urbanites fulfill their desire for a more primitive, simple life by figuratively "touring" rural places. Moreover, during a time when the cultural power of the Anglo-Saxon bourgeoisie was seriously threatened by immigration and its resultant ethnic diversity, regionalism offered a more palatable "other" in the guise of the "rural folk." A rival cadre of scholars is more sympathetic to populism and regionalism, viewing these movements/modes as fundamentally democratic, opposing the dominant capitalistic culture and its urban and coastal centers of power. Such scholars include historians Lawrence Goodwyn, Christopher Lasch, and Robert D. Johnston, and cultural critics Judith Fetterley, Marjorie Pryse, and Richard Slotkin. Feminist critics in particular have championed regionalism as a vehicle for resistance, noting the disproportionately high number of women and writers of color who write in this mode. On regionalism, see Cox, "Regionalism"; Fetterley and Pryse, *Writing out of Place*; Brodhead, "American Literary Field"; Brodhead, *Cultures of Letters*; Kaplan, "Nation, Region, Empire"; Sundquist, "Realism and Regionalism"; and Hegeman, *Patterns for America*. On populism, see Lasch, *True and Only Heaven*; Goodwyn, *Populist Moment*; Kazin, *Populist Persuasion*; Slotkin, *Gunfighter Nation*; and Denning, *Cultural Front*.

69. Hsu, "Literature and Regional Production," 37.

70. Journal re: dust storms, box 18, folder 5, Sanora Babb Collection.

71. Guthrie, *Dust Bowl Ballads*, track 1.

72. Jackson, *Prophet Singer*, 60.

73. Guthrie, *Dust Bowl Ballads*, track 13.

74. Ibid., tracks 4 and 11.

75. Foley, *Radical Representations*, 228.

76. Coiner, *Better Red*, 38; Foley, *Radical Representations*, 224–26.

77. Quoted in Coiner, *Better Red*, 46.

78. Babb, Babb, and Wixson, *On the Dirty Plate Trail*, 110–15.

79. Hicks et al., *Proletarian Literature in the United States*, 211, quoted in Maxwell, *New Negro, Old Left*, 145.

80. Babb, Babb, and Wixson, *On the Dirty Plate Trail*, 114–15.

81. Ibid., 76.

82. Entin, "Monstrous Modernism," 61–62.

83. Rabinowitz, *Labor and Desire*, 2.

84. Ralph Ellison to Sanora Babb, ca. 1943, box 43, folder 3, Sanora Babb Collection, misspellings in original.

85. Gift #12091.2, box 7A, folder marked "Key letter/journal on dust storm; SB's mss. on dust bowl refugees," Sanora Babb Collection.

86. Quoted in Wixson, *Worker-Writer*, 377.

87. Babb, *Owl on Every Post*, 5.

88. Bulosan, *America Is in the Heart*, 235, quoted in Denning, *Cultural Front*, 276. Denning identifies the Babb sisters as the source of the Odell sisters in *Cultural Front*, 519 n. 33.

89. Carlos Bulosan to Sanora Babb, 11 March 1936, Gift #12091, box 2, folder marked "Bulosan, Carlos to SB—1936," Sanora Babb Collection.

90. Carlos Bulosan to Sanora Babb, 22 November 1935 and 7 December 1935, Gift #12091, box 2, folder marked "Buloson, Carlos to SB—1935," Sanora Babb Collection.

91. Critics of whiteness studies such as Eric Arnesen lament that "whiteness" is defined too loosely. I use the term as shorthand for the complicated matrix of racial identity (the perception of belonging to a particular racial group), racism (whether explicitly avowed or internalized), and white privilege (the material benefits of differential treatment based on race). See Arnesen, "Whiteness and the Historians' Imagination," 9. For a definition of whiteness that emphasizes economic structures of privilege, see Lipsitz, *Possessive Investment in Whiteness*, vii.

92. Babb, Babb, and Wixson, *On the Dirty Plate Trail*, 59, quote on 98.

93. Weber, *Dark Sweat, White Gold*, 149.

94. Gregory, *American Exodus*, 166–68.

95. In a forum in *International Labor and Working-Class History* on the historiographical usefulness of whiteness studies to labor history, Eric Arnesen asserts that historians do not dispute the fact that white workers benefited from racial hierarchies, and that labor historians have long rejected the idea of common working-class interests. Thus he argues that the search for an explanation of the failure of working-class solidarity reflects a kind of misguided "Marxism lite" still lingering in cultural studies. In my view, Arnesen's denial of the notion of shared working-class interests fails to account for the vitality of the interracial Left in the 1930s. I follow the more nuanced view of Eric Foner, who asserts that "men and women who take for granted their identity as 'white' have certainly clung to their privileges in our history. They have also, in various times and places, walked picket lines with nonwhites, voted to accord them the rights of citizens, and united with them against common foes." In other words, neither race nor class determines behavior, but rather, either combines with a variety of other factors to shape attitudes and actions. The field of whiteness studies brings into broad relief the tension between race and class, which are often treated as competing rather than intersecting social categories. According to Peter Kolchin, many scholars of whiteness, including pioneers of the field David Roediger and Matthew Frye Jacobson, tend to reify race as a deterministic, transhistorical force and downplay the role of economic interests in the construction of racial hierarchies. Recently, Matt Wray has dispensed with the attempt to disentangle race, class, gender, and sexuality and, instead, uses "boundary theory" to conceptualize these categories as "four deeply related subprocesses of a single, larger process of social

differentiation." See Arnesen, "Whiteness and the Historians' Imagination," 12; Foner, "Response to Eric Arnesen," 58; Kolchin, "Whiteness Studies," 165; Roediger, *Wages of Whiteness*; Jacobson, *Whiteness of a Different Color*; and Wray, *Not Quite White*, 5.

96. MacLean review of Brattain's *Politics of Whiteness*.

97. Babb, Babb, and Wixson, *On the Dirty Plate Trail*, 144. This quote comes from an excerpt of the novel published in *Kansas Magazine* in 1941. The 2004 version of the novel reads, "County hospitals won't take our women 'less we been in the state a year" (42).

98. Babb, Babb, and Wixson, *On the Dirty Plate Trail*, 99.

99. Ibid., 60.

100. Ibid., 66.

101. Ibid., 164, emphasis in original.

102. Roediger, "Guineas, Wiggers, and the Dramas of Racialized Culture," 659. "White nigger" appears in Mary Henderson Eastman's 1852 proslavery response to Harriet Beecher Stowe's *Uncle Tom's Cabin*, titled *Aunt Phillis's Cabin*. In this story, a northern industrialist says to a southern traveler of his white workers, "They're noting but white niggers after all, these Irish." See Eastman, *Aunt Phillis's Cabin; or, Southern Life as It Is*, 73, quoted in Castronovo, "Incidents in the Life of a White Woman," 248.

103. Wray, *Not Quite White*, 139. The term "hillbilly," applied to poor, white Appalachian migrants, is also a boundary term that signifies a "white other." According to Anthony Harkins, the term "hillbilly" is "a construction, both within and beyond the confines of American 'whiteness,'" that "has also been at the heart of struggles over American racial identity and hierarchy." See Harkins, *Hillbilly*, 4.

104. In the original manuscript, "white nigger" is emphasized, and "I'm no better . . ." is not. See Gift #12496, carton 1, Sanora Babb Collection.

105. Research notes, box 18, folder 6, Sanora Babb Collection. Babb transcribed this quote in dialect.

106. Gift #12091.2, box 7A, folder marked "FSA materials," Sanora Babb Collection.

107. Harris-Lacewell, "Of the Meaning of Progress." In her lecture, Professor Harris-Lacewell differentiated between African Americans' claims to citizenship based on rights vs. responsibility.

108. Ralph Ellison to Sanora Babb, ca. 1943, box 43, folder 3, Sanora Babb Collection.

109. Ibid., misspellings in original.

110. Ibid., emphasis in original.

111. Foley, *Radical Representations*, 135, 156. Foley notes that Marxist critics routinely censured the "didactic sins" of an intrusive narrator, conversion plot, and editorializing through political speeches.

112. Quoted in ibid., 15–16.

113. Seaver, "Sterile Writers and Proletarian Religions," 22.

114. Foley, *Radical Representations*, 132. See also Murphy, *Proletarian Moment*.

115. Gold, "Change the World!," *Daily Worker*, 9 February 1934, 5, quoted in Foley, *Radical Representations*, 137.

116. Riley Dixon to Sanora Babb, 9 November 1939, box 18, folder 6, Sanora Babb Collection. Both letters are reprinted in Babb, Babb, and Wixson, *On the Dirty Plate Trail*, 156–58.

117. Ralph Ellison to Sanora Babb, ca. 1943, box 43, folder 3, Sanora Babb Collection.

118. For scholars who see the Popular Front period (1935–39, 1941–45) as the high point of the black-Left alliance and CP effectiveness more generally, see Naison, *Communists in Harlem*; Denning, *Cultural Front*; and Mullen, *Popular Fronts*. For those who see the Third Period (1928–35) as the high point, see Kelley, *Hammer and Hoe*, and Foley, *Radical Representations*. James Smethurst makes the insightful point that a scholar's position in this debate depends a lot on the location he or she studies. The Popular Front was more effective in Harlem (the subject of Naison's book) than in Alabama (the subject of Kelley's book), for example. I tend to agree that the Popular Front period nurtured a black-Left alliance, as indicated by the proliferation of migration narratives in this period.

Chapter 3

1. Deutsch, "Great Depression"; Cohen, *Making a New Deal*, 223.

2. Motley, "Negro Art in Chicago," 21.

3. Quoted in Bone, "Richard Wright and the Chicago Renaissance," 447.

4. For a complete list of African American writers at the Illinois Federal Writers' Project, see Bone and Courage, *Muse in Bronzeville*, 237.

5. Motley, "Negro Art in Chicago," 21, 22.

6. Mullen, *Popular Fronts*, 46–47, 56.

7. Bone and Courage, *Muse in Bronzeville*, 164–65.

8. Meltzer, "William Attaway," 7. See also Chapter 1.

9. Bone and Courage, *Muse in Bronzeville*, 161–65.

10. Walker, *This Is My Century*, 6, 7.

11. Bone, *Negro Novel in America*, 132; Margolies introduction, viii.

12. Morgan, *Rethinking Social Realism*, 46, 244.

13. Hills, *Painting Harlem Modern*, 131.

14. Ibid., 17, 35.

15. Ibid., 23.

16. Ibid., 112.

17. Attaway, *Blood on the Forge*, 53. All future references will be cited parenthetically and are to this edition.

18. Hills, *Painting Harlem Modern*, 130–31.

19. Phillips, *AlabamaNorth*, 106; Nelson, *Divided We Stand*, 166.

20. Quoted in Nelson, *Divided We Stand*, 167.

21. Cayton and Mitchell, *Black Workers and the New Unions*, 79–80.

22. Nelson, *Divided We Stand*, 167.

23. Gottlieb claims that the mills depended on huge numbers of unskilled workers; Cayton and Mitchell and Nelson claim they depended on white skilled men to run understaffed plants. See Gottlieb, *Making Their Own Way*, 157–58; Cayton and Mitchell, *Black Workers and the New Unions*, 79; Nelson, *Divided We Stand*, 166. "Niggers did it" is quoted in Gottlieb, *Making Their Own Way*, 162, and Cayton and Mitchell, *Black Workers and the New Unions*, 79.

24. Quoted in Wald, *Trinity of Passion*, 64.

25. The United Mine Workers made civil rights part of its organizing strategy in the South by conducting voter registration drives, protesting the poll tax, condemning the

Ku Klux Klan, and integrating meeting and social activities. See Goldfield, "Race and the CIO: The Possibilities for Racial Egalitarianism," 8.

26. Dickerson, *Out of the Crucible*, 146.

27. Lewis, "Negro Women in Steel," 277.

28. Schuyler, "Negro Workers Lead in Great Lakes Steel Drive," 58. See also "Virginia and Maryland Negroes Flock to Unions," "Schuyler Finds Philadelphia Negroes are Rallying to 'New Deal' Call," and "Harlem Boasts 42,000 Negro Labor Unionists."

29. Wald, *Exiles from a Future Time*, 294; Bone, *Negro Novel in America*, 139; Foley, "Race and Class," 312, 316.

30. Although both Foley and Morgan acknowledge that Attaway experiments with a multiprotagonist format, they focus on Big Mat's conversion scene, thus reinforcing the primacy of Big Mat's character. In contrast, my reading emphasizes Melody's role and the ways in which Attaway redefines proletarian literature. See Morgan, *Rethinking Social Realism*, 207, and Foley, *Radical Representations*, 372.

31. Morgan, *Rethinking Social Realism*, 293. The term *antibildungsroman* comes from Foley, *Radical Representations*, 328.

32. Dunbar, *Sport of the Gods*, 86.

33. Smethurst, *New Red Negro*, 60–92.

34. Lenin, *Preliminary Draft of Theses on the National and Colonial Questions*, 316.

35. For a woman of any age, class, or color, William Attaway's novels are a very dangerous place. They feature the gang rape of a ten-year-old, incest, the date rape of fourteen-year-old Anna in *Let Me Breathe Thunder*, the forced prostitution and concubinage of Anna (also fourteen) in *Blood on the Forge*, and the prostitution of Zanski's granddaughter, Rosie. The only grown female characters in the stories are Mat's wife, Hattie, whom he abandons, and Mag, a former prostitute who winds up in jail.

36. Lenin, *Preliminary Draft of Theses on the National and Colonial Questions*, 316.

37. See Maxwell, *New Negro, Old Left*, 63–93.

38. McKay, *Negroes in America*, 4, quoted in Maxwell, *New Negro, Old Left*, 81; Kelley, *Freedom Dreams*, 48.

39. Communist International, "1928 Resolution on the Negro Question," 3.

40. Solomon, *Cry Was Unity*, 87. Scholars vary in their assessment of the black nation thesis. Robin Kelley, a historian of black radical thought, hails the black nation thesis for validating the nationalist identities of black proletarians and their need for self-determination, independent black institutions, and pan-African culture. Similarly, James Smethurst does not see the black nation thesis and the call for proletarian unity as contradictory. Conversely, Barbara Foley and Anthony Dawahare emphasize the contradictions between the black nation thesis and the goal of working-class unity. Dawahare denounces nationalism as a liberation strategy and argues that the strongest black writers were those who rejected nationalism in favor of an international Left. Thus, the black nation thesis "represents some of the CPUSA's weakest theoretical work." For discussions of the impact of the "black belt thesis" on African American literature, see Foley, "Race and Class"; Foley, *Radical Representations*, 173–83; Morgan, *Rethinking Social Realism*, 276–79; Smethurst, *New Red Negro*, 9–10, 22–26; Dawahare, *Nationalism, Marxism, and African American Literature between the Wars*, 77–81, quote on 81; Maxwell, *New Negro, Old Left*, 7, 92–93; and Kelley, *Freedom Dreams*, 46–50.

41. Smethurst, *New Red Negro*, 43.

42. Wright, "Blueprint for Negro Writing," 101.

43. I would like to thank Jack Phillips for his help with this analysis.

44. Smethurst, *New Red Negro*, 28.

45. Ibid.

46. Morgan, *Rethinking Social Realism*, 294.

47. Sollors, *Beyond Ethnicity*, 23.

48. Ibid., 29; Sollors, "Theories of American Ethnicity," xi.

49. Bearden, "Negro in 'Little Steel,'" 101.

50. Drake and Cayton, *Black Metropolis*, 331.

51. Schuyler, "Firestone Plant Like Heaven Now"; Cayton and Mitchell, *Black Workers and the New Unions*, 219.

52. Many of these historians follow the lead of David Roediger, who argues that the working class created its own racial views, practices, and identities; see Roediger, *Wages of Whiteness*, 9–13. See also, for example, Nelson, *Divided We Stand*; Foley, *White Scourge*; Hartigan, *Racial Situations*; and Sugrue, *Origins of the Urban Crisis*.

53. Goldfield, "Race and the CIO: The Possibilities for Racial Egalitarianism," 3, 10–11; Phillips, *AlabamaNorth*, 126.

54. Cayton and Mitchell, *Black Workers and the New Unions*, 221.

55. Attaway, *Hear America Singing*, 14–15.

56. Attaway, *Calypso Song Book*, 10; Attaway, *Hear American Singing*, 13.

57. Park, "Human Migration," 892.

58. Mullen, "Breaking the Signifying Chain," 146.

59. The reception history of the novel is complicated because the process of writing, publication, and review occurred during a period of rapid political change. In 1939, Stalin signed the Non-Aggression Pact with Hitler. Until then, the CP had called for a Popular Front against fascism and criticized the failure of the United States to intervene in the war. The Non-Aggression Pact reversed this policy, resulting in the cessation of the Popular Front in favor of a neutral stance in the war. Attaway wrote the novel during this neutral period, and its final image of two blind veterans on a train headed toward the urban ghetto reflects the CP's critique of the war as an imperialist venture. However, by the time the novel was published and reviewed, the political context had changed dramatically. After Hitler invaded Russia in 1941, the CP resumed its Popular Front policy, which called for unity in the war against fascism.

60. Warner, "'Blood on the Forge' Is Story of Negro Brothers," 7.

61. Ralph Ellison to Sanora Babb, 10 April 1942, box 43, folder 3, Sanora Babb Collection, emphasis in original.

62. Ibid.

63. Ellison, "Transition," 90–91.

64. Wright, "Blueprint for Negro Writing," 102–3.

Chapter 4

1. According to Paula Rabinowitz, maternal rhetoric bridged Communists and liberals during the Popular Front era, as cultural imagery of "revolutionary girls" gave way to "partisan mothers." See Rabinowitz, *Labor and Desire*, 55.

2. I borrow from Vicki Goldberg's definition of an icon as an archetypal image that stands for a system of belief that is easily recognized by viewers. See Goldberg, *Power of Photography*, 135.

3. Hariman and Lucaites, *No Caption Needed*, 58.

4. Kozol, "Madonnas of the Fields," 2–3.

5. Goldberg, *Power of Photography*, 137.

6. My reading of Lange's photograph is informed by Stange, *Symbols of Ideal Life*, 129; Curtis, "Dorothea Lange"; Fleischhauer, Brannan, Levine, and Trachtenberg, *Documenting America*, 7–8; Hariman and Lucaites, *No Caption Needed*, 56–60; Goldberg, *Power of Photography*, 135–37; and Stott, *Documentary Expression and Thirties America*.

7. The following analysis of militant and grotesque migrant mothers challenges Paula Rabinowitz's claim that the "celebration of motherhood" marks the CP's rightward shift in the Popular Front period. See Rabinowitz, "Women and U.S. Literary Radicalism," 11.

8. Nadell, *Enter the New Negroes*, 7. The term was originally coined by Steiner in *Colors of Rhetoric*, xi.

9. Browder, *Rousing the Nation*, 9–12; Foley, *Radical Representations*, 106.

10. Quoted in Herzog, *Elizabeth Catlett*, 22, 21.

11. Ibid., 33.

12. Ibid., 31.

13. Ibid., 42.

14. Powell, "Face to Face," 49.

15. Herzog, *Elizabeth Catlett*, 52.

16. Quoted in ibid., 22.

17. Quoted in Hills, "Jacob Lawrence's *Migration Series*," 141.

18. Herzog, *Elizabeth Catlett*, 47.

19. Wright and Rosskam, *12 Million Black Voices*, 131.

20. "A Transcript of a Tape-Recorded Interview with Pauli Murray," Robert Martin, interviewer, 15 and 17 August 1968, Civil Rights Documentation Project, box 1, folder 8, Pauli Murray Papers.

21. Activists like Claudia Jones urged the inclusion of domestic workers into trade unions and labor legislation as well, but to little avail. For example, the New York Domestic Workers Union, founded in 1934, only recruited 1,000 members out of a pool of 100,000 and had little impact on the regulation of hours and wages. See Jones, *Labor of Love, Labor of Sorrow*, 171–74.

22. Boyce Davies, *Left of Karl Marx*, 33–37.

23. Jones, "End to the Neglect of the Negro Woman!," 108.

24. Ibid., 114.

25. Boyce Davies, *Left of Karl Marx*, 42–43.

26. McDuffie, *Sojourning for Freedom*, 112.

27. Quoted in Jones, *Labor of Love, Labor of Sorrow*, 133.

28. Ibid., 154.

29. Although Bonner's editors gave this title to her collected writings, she referred to the first three stories as the "Frye Street Trilogy," and "Frye Street" is the motif that links all the stories in the collection. See Bonner, *Frye Street*, xx.

30. In their literary histories of radical women writers, both Barbara Foley and Paula Rabinowitz acknowledge the absence of African American women. See Foley, *Radical Representations*, 213 n. 1, and Rabinowitz, *Labor and Desire*, 183 n. 1. Scholarship that has begun to address this gap includes McDuffie, *Sojourning for Freedom*; Boyce Davies, *Left of Karl Marx*; Higashida, *Black Internationalist Feminism*; Gore, *Radicalism at the Crossroads*; Maxwell, *New Negro, Old Left*; Harris, "Running with the Reds"; and Washington, "Alice Childress, Lorraine Hansberry, and Claudia Jones."

31. Lubin introduction, 8.

32. Rubin and Smethurst, "Ann Petry's 'New Mirror,'" 25–26.

33. In conceiving of Lutie as a migrant mother figure, I follow Lawrence Rodgers in defining the migration narrative as one in which "a real . . . journey from south to north, occurring either in the novel or figuring prominently in the narrative's recent past, strongly informs the protagonist's psychological constitution and his or her responses to the external environment." Both Rodgers and Farah Jasmine Griffin consider urban novels such as Petry's *The Street* and Wright's *Native Son* to be migration narratives, as they deal centrally with the processes of urbanization, modernization, and cultural transformation from rural "folk" to urban proletariat. See Rodgers, *Canaan Bound*, 3, and Griffin, "*Who Set You Flowin'?*"

34. Petry, *The Street*, 28, 29. All future references will be cited parenthetically and are to this edition.

35. Mullen, "Object Lessons," 44.

36. Peterson, "Invisible Hands," 73.

37. Griffin, "*Who Set You Flowin'?*," 10–11; Rodgers, *Canaan Bound*, 133.

38. List of courses, 1918–1922, box 1, folder 2, Marita Bonner Papers.

39. Radcliffe alumnae information survey for the 1934 directory, box 1, folder 2, Marita Bonner Papers.

40. Bonner, *Frye Street*, xiii.

41. Marita Bonner Occomy to Joyce Occomy Stricklin, 20 July 1965, box 1, folder 3, Marita Bonner Papers.

42. Mullen, *Popular Fronts*, 114.

43. Bonner, *Frye Street*, 142. Subsequent references will be cited parenthetically and are to this edition.

44. "Tin Can" was originally published in two parts in the July and August 1934 issues of *Opportunity*. Considering the numerous similarities in theme, character, and plot, it is likely that this story inspired Richard Wright's *Native Son*, which was published six years later.

45. The exact number ranges between six and thirteen, depending on how liberally one defines the category. Three stories in addition to the "Triad" are explicitly set on Frye Street ("Nothing New," "A Sealed Pod," and "Reap It As You Sow It"). Six more stories take place in an unnamed urban, working-class neighborhood that resembles Frye Street. Another story identifies its working-class neighborhood as "Federal Street."

46. Denning, *Cultural Front*, 243.

47. Griffin, "*Who Set You Flowin'?*," 112.

48. Lang, "Class and the Strategies of Sympathy," 137; Muncy, *Creating a Female Dominion*, xv.

49. Morrison, "Rootedness," 343. This story supports Farah Griffin's assertion that migrants are more successful, better able to negotiate the urban environment, when an ancestor is present in the text. See Griffin, *"Who Set You Flowin'?,"* 5.

50. Denning, *Cultural Front,* 117–23.

51. Entin, *Sensational Modernism,* 2.

52. Entin has coined the term "sensational modernism" to describe the countertradition of Depression-era modernism that blends sensual bodily imagery and formal innovation to challenge the established modes of sentimentalism, realism, naturalism, documentary, and high modernism. Depression-era writers and photographers engaged in an "aesthetics of astonishment" to destabilize established narrative and photographic modes. See ibid., 3, 17.

53. Ibid., 20.

54. On the Wright/Rosskam collaboration, see Rowley, *Richard Wright,* 249–50. On Lee's positive portrayals of black families and Rosskam's manipulation of the Chicago photographs for propagandistic purposes, see Natanson, *Black Image in the New Deal,* 161–63, 249–53. Martha Nadell argues that the photographs sometimes resist Wright and Rosskam's pathological approach. The images of family life offer multiple interpretations: They can represent individuals broken by the American racial system, as the text implies, or "dignity despite harsh reality." See Nadell, *Enter the New Negroes,* 132–34.

55. Reilly, "Richard Wright Preaches the Nation," 118.

56. Wright and Rosskam, *12 Million Black Voices,* 106–11.

57. Entin, *Sensational Modernism,* 28.

58. Steinbeck, *Grapes of Wrath,* 453.

59. Harpham, *On the Grotesque,* xxi.

60. The term "grotesque" was coined during the Renaissance to describe an "estranged world," and this sense of "estrangement" is at the heart of migration myths from the biblical Exodus to black and white Great Migrations of the twentieth century. Critics identify the grotesque by "its lack of fixity, its unpredictability and its instability." Kenneth Burke, a 1930s critic, extolled the grotesque as a revolutionary form that could make sense of the transitory, discordant nature of the Depression. See Kayser, *The Grotesque in Art and Literature,* 184; Connelly, *Modern Art and the Grotesque,* 4–6; Gingras, "Travel," 1293; and Harpham, *On the Grotesque,* 15. Burke's point is noted in Entin, *Sensational Modernism,* 12, and Denning, *Cultural Front,* 122.

61. Coiner, *Better Red,* 143–44.

62. Ibid., 142–47.

63. Quoted in ibid., 154.

64. Olsen, "A Note about This Book," in *Yonnondio,* viii. All future references will be cited parenthetically and are to this edition.

65. Rosenfelt, "From the Thirties," 72.

66. Burke, "Revolutionary Symbolism in America," 88–89.

67. Foley, *Radical Representations,* 158.

68. Denning, *Cultural Front,* 251.

69. Bakhtin and Iswolsky, *Rabelais and His World,* 317. Harpham elaborates: Human excrescences both belong to the body and are radically opposed to it; they mediate

between the "self" and the "non-self," eluding categorization. See Harpham, *On the Grotesque*, 4.

70. Olsen repeats this exact sentence twice, on p. 78 and p. 96.

71. Kristeva, *Powers of Horror*, 1–3.

72. Ibid., 8, emphasis in original.

73. Bakhtin and Iswolsky, *Rabelais and His World*, 317.

74. Rose, "Class Formation and the Quintessential Worker," 139.

75. Entin, *Sensational Modernism*, 162. According to Entin, *Yonnondio* resists narratives that objectify the poor and classical aesthetics that minimize the horror of poverty.

76. Notable exceptions are the "Gastonia" novels dramatizing the North Carolina textile strikes of 1929. In Grace Lumpkin's *To Make My Bread* (1932), the white female protagonist, Bonnie McClure, becomes friends with an African American woman, Mary Allen, who helps her to organize black workers. To some extent, this relationship replicates the mammy trope.

77. Arnow, *Dollmaker*, 155. All future references will be cited parenthetically and are to this edition.

Chapter 5

1. Johnson, *Second Gold Rush*, 6.

2. Lipsitz, *Rainbow at Midnight*, 50.

3. Johnson, *Second Gold Rush*, 84–85.

4. Lotchin, *Bad City in the Good War*, 125.

5. Johnson, *Second Gold Rush*, 105.

6. Boris, "'You Wouldn't Want One of 'Em Dancing With Your Wife,'" 77.

7. Bontemps and Conroy, *They Seek a City*, 218.

8. Archibald, *Wartime Shipyard*, 77.

9. Sides, "Battle on the Home Front," 253.

10. Bontemps and Conroy, *They Seek a City*, 226–27; Sugrue, *Origins of the Urban Crisis*, 26.

11. Alvarez, *Power of the Zoot*, 169.

12. Ibid., 182.

13. Ibid.

14. Himes, "Now Is the Time!," 271.

15. The CIO actively recruited black leaders in California during the war, such as Philip "Slim" Connelly, who was the secretary-treasurer of the Los Angeles CIO Council, and Walter Williams, who worked as an organizer. Both Connelly and Williams made civil rights central to the labor movement, enlisting Roosevelt's Fair Employment Practices Commission to curb discriminatory practices. See Arnesen and Lichtenstein, "All Kinds of People," xxx–xxxi, and Sides, *L.A. City Limits*, 64–65.

16. Lipsitz, *Rainbow at Midnight*, 20.

17. Johnson, *Second Gold Rush*, 60–61.

18. Ibid., 71–72; Kersten, *Labor's Home Front*, 79.

19. Lemke-Santangelo, *Abiding Courage*, 107, 123, 113.

20. Himes, *If He Hollers Let Him Go*, 24. All future references will be cited parenthetically and are to this edition.

21. Isserman, *Which Side Were You On?*, 143; Boris, "'You Wouldn't Want One of 'Em Dancing With Your Wife,'" 94; Lipsitz, *Rainbow at Midnight*, 77.

22. Lipsitz, *Rainbow at Midnight*, 76; Quam-Wickham, "Who Controls the Hiring Hall?," 48.

23. Boris, "'You Wouldn't Want One of 'Em Dancing With Your Wife,'" 83.

24. White and Marshall, *What Caused the Detroit Riot?*, 8; For more on southern white migrants' influence on northern racist organizations and activities, see Gregory, *Southern Diaspora*, 294–302.

25. Gregory, *Southern Diaspora*, 291, 298–300.

26. Ngai, "Short History."

27. Gerstle, *American Crucible*, 4–5.

28. Ibid., 139.

29. Sollors, *Beyond Ethnicity*, 23.

30. Denning, *Cultural Front*, 448.

31. Adamic, *Nation of Nations*, 1–2.

32. Archibald, *Wartime Shipyard*, 12.

33. Singh, *Black Is a Country*, 108.

34. Archibald, *Wartime Shipyard*, 63–64.

35. Wray, *Not Quite White*, 5; Higginbotham, *Righteous Discontent*, 255.

36. Brown, *Good Wives, Nasty Wenches, and Anxious Patriarchs*, 7, 116.

37. I borrow the phrase from Wray, *Not Quite White*.

38. Arnesen and Lichtenstein, "All Kinds of People," xi–xii.

39. Archibald, *Wartime Shipyard*, 151.

40. Ibid., 65. Archibald's analysis of the psychological benefits of whiteness, what Du Bois called a "psychological wage," anticipates "whiteness studies" by nearly fifty years. Historian Eric Arnesen offers a sharp critique of this body of scholarship, arguing that it reflects a "Marxism lite" that presumes that workers share common interests under capitalism. Like most labor historians, Arnesen contends that members of the working class have few shared interests because white workers benefit from differential treatment and access to resources and power. In other words, one should assume multiple divisions within the working class and not spend so much energy trying to explain their failure to unite, as do Archibald and subsequent historians of whiteness. See Arnesen, "Whiteness and the Historians' Imagination," 11–12.

41. Archibald, *Wartime Shipyard*, 202.

42. Ibid., 125.

43. Ibid., 227, 228.

44. Ibid., 232.

45. Singh, *Black Is a Country*, 11.

46. Arnesen and Lichtenstein, "All Kinds of People," xi–xii.

47. Archibald, *Wartime Shipyard*, 225–26.

48. Ibid., 71.

49. Ngai, "'Nation of Immigrants,'" 4.

50. Archibald, *Wartime Shipyard*, 94.

51. Ibid., 236, 227.

52. Gerstle, *American Crucible*, 141.

53. Denning, *Cultural Front*, 432.

54. Gerstle, *American Crucible*, 146.

55. Foley, *Radical Representations*, 192.

56. Bontemps and Conroy, *They Seek a City*, 8.

57. Ibid., 205.

58. Ibid., 241.

59. Ibid.

60. Ibid., 239.

61. While Gary Gerstle asserts that racial conflicts in the workplace paled in comparison with the neighborhood riots of the 1940s, Michael Goldfield insists that racism has economic rather than cultural origins. Cultural factors, such as fear of miscegenation, must be situated in a specific historical context and tied to broader social forces, such as the prohibition of slavery or the power shifts in the Democratic Party. See Gerstle, "Working-Class Racism," 36, and Goldfield, "Race and the CIO: Reply to Critics," 148–49.

62. Bontemps and Conroy, *They Seek a City*, 118.

63. Ibid., xvi.

64. Singh, *Black Is a Country*, 107–8.

65. Bontemps and Conroy, *Anyplace but Here*, 9.

66. Singh, *Black Is a Country*, 6–8.

67. Freund, "Marketing the Free Market," 16.

68. Singh, *Black Is a Country*, 6.

69. Bontemps and Conroy, *They Seek a City*, 231.

70. Ibid.

71. Gerstle, *American Crucible*, 211.

72. Ibid., 207.

73. Ibid., 214.

74. Himes, "Democracy Is for the Unafraid," 54.

75. Gerstle, *American Crucible*, 218.

76. Ibid., 228.

77. Ibid., 229.

78. Ibid., 230.

79. Ibid., 235.

80. Ibid., 205–6.

81. Adamic, *Nation of Nations*, 6

82. Gerstle, *American Crucible*, 220.

83. On the other hand, the Hitler-Stalin Non-Aggression Pact outraged many black radicals as well. Activists like Pauli Murray were dedicated to the Popular Front *because* it led the war against fascism; the comparison between European fascism and American Jim Crow was an invaluable tool for combating racism at home. When the CP declared its opposition to the war, Murray immediately resigned from the Negro People's Committee, a CP organization that aided victims of fascism. A. Philip Randolph ignited controversy at the National Negro Congress when he attacked Russia and Germany for their totalitarianism and rang a nationalist note, concluding that "the Negro and other darker races must look to themselves for freedom." See Gilmore, *Defying Dixie*, 310.

84. Von Eschen, *Race against Empire*, 35.

85. Singh, *Black Is a Country*, 109.

86. Himes, "Zoot Riots Are Race Riots," 200.

87. Ibid., 201.

88. See Von Eschen, *Race against Empire*.

89. Singh, *Black Is a Country*, 113–14, 142.

90. Conrad, "Blues School of Literature."

91. Dolinar, *Black Cultural Front*, 132.

92. Conrad, "Blues School of Literature."

93. Singh, "Retracing the Black-Red Thread," 836.

94. Margolies and Fabre, *Several Lives of Chester Himes*, 48; Dolinar, *Black Cultural Front*, 134.

95. Himes, "Now Is the Time!," 271.

96. Ibid.

97. Ibid., 272.

98. "War Posters," 55–56.

99. Himes, "Zoot Riots Are Race Riots," 200.

100. Ibid., 222.

101. Itagaki, "Transgressing Race and Community"; Singh, *Black Is a Country*; Nieland, "Everybody's Noir Humanism."

102. Von Eschen, *Race against Empire*, 2.

103. Itagaki, "Transgressing Race and Community," 69.

104. Von Eschen, *Race against Empire*, 2.

105. Ibid., 34.

106. Himes, *Quality of Hurt*, 75

107. Ikard, "Love Jones," 299.

108. Margolies and Fabre, *Several Lives of Chester Himes*, 95.

109. Himes, *Quality of Hurt*, 137.

110. Margolies and Fabre, *Several Lives of Chester Himes*, 55–57.

111. Conrad, "Blues School of Literature."

112. Archibald, *Wartime Shipyard*, 72–73.

113. Ibid., 73.

114. Boris, "'Arm and Arm,'" 17.

115. Lichtenstein and Arnesen, "Labor and the Problem of Social Unity," 128.

116. Archibald, *Wartime Shipyard*, 32.

117. Ramirez, *Women in the Zoot Suit*.

118. Archibald, *Wartime Shipyard*, 19, 20.

119. "New Headache," 46.

120. Himes, "Zoot Riots Are Race Riots," 200–201, quote on 200.

121. Dolinar, *Black Cultural Front*, 139.

122. Himes, "Now Is the Time!," 272.

123. Singh, *Black Is a Country*, 101.

Conclusion

1. Conrad, "I Heard a Black Man Sing," 63.

2. Kelley, *Freedom Dreams*, 62.

3. Zieger, *The CIO*, 214.

4. Korstad and Lichtenstein, "Opportunities Found and Lost," 792–93.

5. Honey, *Southern Labor*, 216.

6. Biondi, *To Stand and Fight*, 6–9.

7. Sugrue, *Sweet Land of Liberty*, xvi. See also Biondi, *To Stand and Fight*; Gilmore, *Defying Dixie*; Self, *American Babylon*; and Kurashige, *Shifting Grounds of Race*.

8. Honey, *Southern Labor*, 256.

9. Ibid., 251–52; Freeman, "Labor during the American Century," 196; Biondi, *To Stand and Fight*, 142.

10. Stepan-Norris and Zeitlin, *Left Out*, 264; Zieger, *The CIO*, 253; Biondi, *To Stand and Fight*, 147.

11. Stepan-Norris and Zeitlin, *Left Out*, 264–65. Historians vigorously debate whether the labor movement was a progressive force for civil rights or a defender of white privilege. Herbert Hill leads the charge against the labor movement as fundamentally exclusionary. See Hill, "Importance of Race in American Labor History," and Nelson, *Divided We Stand*. I share the view of other labor historians who locate the origins of civil rights in the trade union movement. See Honey, *Southern Labor*; Korstad and Lichtenstein, "Opportunities Found and Lost"; Korstad, *Civil Rights Unionism*; Gilmore, *Defying Dixie*; and Hall, "Long Civil Rights Movement."

12. Dudziak, *Cold War Civil Rights*, 13; Gilmore, *Defying Dixie*, 7.

13. MacLean, *Freedom Is Not Enough*, 39–42.

14. Schrecker, "McCarthyism and the Labor Movement," 157. For a comprehensive study of McCarthyism in America, see Schrecker, *Many Are the Crimes*.

15. Biondi, *To Stand and Fight*, 139–40.

16. Mullen, *Popular Fronts*, 191. For a fine study of American artist networks in Mexico, see Schreiber, *Cold War Exiles in Mexico*.

17. Bontemps, *Old South*, 19.

18. See Mickenberg, *Learning from the Left*, and Wald, *Writing from the Left*, 100–104.

19. Rodgers, *Canaan Bound*, 157.

20. Foley, *Wrestling with the Left*, 2.

21. Ellison, *Invisible Man*, 473.

22. Ellison, "Transition," 90–91.

23. For an examination of this shift in African American literary history, see Griffin, "*Who Set You Flowin'?*," and Rodgers, *Canaan Bound*.

24. Several of the key figures of the Harlem Renaissance refer to West in infantilizing terms, reflecting her endearing personality and, perhaps, their unwillingness to accept her as a serious artist. In a 1927 letter to West, Hurston referred to her as "juvenile," while four years later Countee Cullen called her a "fascinating and loveable child." In 1934, after the twenty-six-year-old West had founded the journal *Challenge* to stimulate young African American writers, Wallace Thurman called her "naïve as ever," criticizing her journal for lacking "personality" and for being "too highschoolish." Arna Bontemps wrote a letter in support of West's *Challenge* magazine but contested her claim that a new generation of African American writers were replacing the older generation of the Harlem Renaissance. See Zora Neale Hurston to Dorothy West, 24 March 1927, box 1, folder 1; Countee Cullen to Dorothy West, 16 April 1931, box 1, folder

2a; Wallace Thurman to Dorothy West, 12 September 1934, box 1, folder 1; and Arna Bontemps to Dorothy West, n.d., Huntsville, Ala., box 1, folder 1, all in Dorothy West Papers.

25. Dorothy West to Grace and Marie Turner, 22 November 1932, box 1, folder 5, Dorothy West Papers.

26. Rodgers, *Canaan Bound*, 147.

27. West, *Living Is Easy*, 5.

28. Ibid., 44.

29. Ibid., 24.

30. Ibid., 3–4.

31. Feldstein, *Motherhood in Black and White*, 117.

32. Ibid., 111–17.

33. Arnow, *Dollmaker*, 40–41.

34. Ibid., 155.

35. Ibid., 219–20.

36. Ibid., 479.

37. Ibid., 599.

38. Kesey, "The B/tr Wrap Up," quoted in Gregory, *American Exodus*, 248.

39. Haggard's music also stimulated an Okie revival, which was part of the larger ethnic revival of the 1970s. According to Gregory, musicians in Bakersfield, California, began creating "Okie pride songs," Gerald Haslam and James Houston cultivated the literature of second-generation Okie authors, newspapers published feature articles on dust bowl migrants, and high schools and colleges dedicated curricula to the study of the Okie experience. See Jacobson, *Roots Too*, and Gregory, *American Exodus*, 244–45. For Okie revival literature, see Haslam, *Okies*, and McDaniel, *Last Dust Storm*.

40. Gregory, *Southern Diaspora*, 285.

41. Singh, *Black Is a Country*, 9.

42. Gregory, "Southernizing the American Working Class," 137.

43. King, "American Political Culture since 1945," 156.

44. See Kazin, *Populist Persuasion*, and Postel, *Populist Vision*.

BIBLIOGRAPHY

Archival Sources

Austin, Texas
    University of Texas Harry Ransom Center
        Sanora Babb Collection
Boston, Massachusetts
    Boston University Howard Gottlieb Archival Research Center
        Dorothy West Papers
Cambridge, Massachusetts
    Harvard University Radcliffe Institute for Advanced Study
        Schlesinger Library
            Marita Bonner Papers
            Pauli Murray Papers
New Haven, Connecticut
    Yale University Beinecke Library
        Richard Wright Papers
Washington, D.C.
    Library of Congress
        American Folklife Center
            Woody Guthrie Manuscript Collection
            Alan Lomax CBS Radio Series Collection
        Prints & Photographs Division
        FSA/OWI Collection

Other Primary Sources

Aaron, Daniel. "Cincinnati, 1818–1838: A Study of Attitudes in the Urban West." Ph.D. diss., Harvard University, 1943.

Adamic, Louis. A Nation of Nations. New York: Harper and Brothers, 1945.

Algren, Nelson. Somebody in Boots: A Novel. New York: Vanguard, 1935.

Archibald, Katherine. Wartime Shipyard: A Study in Social Disunity. 1947. Reprint, Urbana: University of Illinois Press, 2006.

"Army of Sharecroppers Trek from Homes; Protest Missouri Landlords' Wage Plans." New York Times, 11 January 1939, http://www.proquest.com.ezp2.harvard.edu/. 29 March 2008.

Arnow, Harriette. The Dollmaker. 1954. Reprint, New York: Avon, 1972.

Attaway, William. *Blood on the Forge.* 1941. Reprint, New York: Collier, 1970.

———. *Calypso Song Book: Authentic Folk Music of the Caribbean.* Literary Licensing, LLC, 2011.

———. *Hear America Singing.* New York: Lion Press, 1967.

———. *Let Me Breathe Thunder.* New York: Doubleday, 1939. Reprinted as *Tough Kid*, Lion Books, 1952.

Babb, Sanora. *Cry of the Tinamou: Stories.* Lincoln: University of Nebraska Press, 1997.

———. *An Owl on Every Post.* New York: New American Library, 1970.

———. *Whose Names Are Unknown.* Norman: University of Oklahoma Press, 2004.

Babb, Sanora, Dorothy Babb, and Douglas Wixson. *On the Dirty Plate Trail: Remembering the Dust Bowl Refugee Camps.* Austin: University of Texas Press, 2007.

"Baptist Preachers Tell of Cotton Slaves in South." *New York Amsterdam News,* 11 February 1939, 6, http://www.proquest.com.ezp2.harvard.edu/. 29 March 2008.

Belfrage, Cedric. "Cotton-Patch Moses." *Harper's Magazine,* November 1948, 94–103.

"The Black Workers." *Chicago Defender,* 29 August 1936, 16.

Blair, Walter. *Native American Humor, 1800–1900.* New York: American Book Co., 1937.

Bonner, Marita. *Frye Street & Environs: The Collected Works of Marita Bonner.* Edited by Joyce Flynn and Joyce Occomy Stricklin. Boston: Beacon, 1987.

Bontemps, Arna W. *Black Thunder.* 1936. Reprint, Boston: Beacon, 1968.

———. "Famous WPA Authors." *Negro Digest,* June 1950, 43–47.

———. *The Old South: "A Summer Tragedy" and Other Stories of the Thirties.* New York: Dodd, Mead, 1973.

———, ed. *Great Slave Narratives.* Boston: Beacon, 1969.

Bontemps, Arna W., and Jack Conroy. *Anyplace but Here.* New York: Hill and Wang, 1966.

———. *They Seek a City.* New York: Doubleday, Doran, 1945.

Botkin, B. A. "The Folk in Literature: An Introduction to the New Regionalism." In *Folk-Say: A Regional Miscellany,* 1:9–20. Norman: University of Oklahoma Press, 1929.

Brooks, Van Wyck. *The Flowering of New England.* New York: Dutton, 1936.

———. *Three Essays on America.* New York: Dutton, 1934.

Browder, Earl. "Communism and Literature." In *American Writers' Congress,* edited by Henry Hart, 66–70. New York: International Publishers, 1935.

Bulosan, Carlos. *America Is in the Heart.* 1946. Reprint, Seattle: University of Washington Press, 1973.

Burke, Kenneth. "Revolutionary Symbolism in America." In *American Writers' Congress,* edited by Henry Hart, 87–93. New York: International Publishers, 1935.

Capra, Frank, dir. *Meet John Doe.* Warner Bros, 1941.

Cayton, Horace R., and George S. Mitchell. *Black Workers and the New Unions.* Chapel Hill: University of North Carolina Press, 1939.

Childress, Alice. *Like One of the Family: Conversations from a Domestic's Life.* New York: Independence Publishers, 1956.

Communist International. "The 1928 Resolution on the Negro Question in the United States." *Daily Worker,* 12 February 1929.

Conrad, Earl. "Blues School of Literature." *Chicago Defender,* 22 December 1945, 11.

———. "I Heard a Black Man Sing." *Negro Story* 1, no. 3 (October–November 1944): 63–64.

Conroy, Jack. *The Disinherited.* 1933. Reprint, New York: Hill and Wang, 1963.

Davis, John P. "'Plan Eleven'—Jim-Crow in Steel." *Crisis,* September 1936, 262–63, 276.

Debs, Eugene V. "The Negro and the Class Struggle." *Internationalist Socialist Review* 4, no. 5 (November 1903): 257–60.

Dorson, Richard. "New England Popular Tales and Legends." Ph.D. diss., Harvard University, 1943.

Dos Passos, John. *U.S.A.* 1937. Reprint, New York: Library of America, 1996.

Drake, St. Claire, and Horace Cayton. *Black Metropolis: A Study of Negro Life in a Northern City*. Vol. 2. New York: Harper, 1945.

Du Bois, W. E. B. "The Negro and Communism." *Crisis*, September 1931, 313–15.

Dunbar, Paul Laurence. *The Sport of the Gods*. 1902. Reprint, New York: Penguin, 1999.

Eastman, Mary Henderson. *Aunt Phillis's Cabin; or, Southern Life As It Is*. 1852. Reprint, New York: Negro Universities, 1968.

Eddy, Simon. "Ballad of a Slightly Addled Culture Worker on the United Front." *New Masses*, 8 June 1937, 19.

Ellison, Ralph. "Camp Lost Colony." *New Masses*, 6 February 1940, 18–19.

———. *Invisible Man*. New York: Vintage International, 1952.

———. *Shadow and Act*. New York: Random House, 1964.

———. "Transition." *Negro Quarterly* 1 (Spring 1942): 87–92.

Galarza, Ernesto. *Barrio Boy*. Notre Dame: University of Notre Dame Press, 1971.

Gold, Mike. "Write For Us!" *New Masses*, July 1928, 2.

Guthrie, Woody. *Bound for Glory*. New York: Dutton, 1943.

———. *Dust Bowl Ballads*. New York: Victor Records, 26 April and 3 May 1940. Reissue, New York: Buddha Records, 2000.

———. "Pretty Boy Floyd." http://www.woodyguthrie.org/Lyrics/Pretty_Boy_Floyd. htm. 3 June 2007.

Guthrie, Woody, and Marjorie Guthrie. *Woody Sez*. New York: Grosset and Dunlap, 1975.

"Harlem Boasts 42,000 Negro Labor Unionists." *Pittsburgh Courier*, 14 August 1937.

Hart, Henry. "Discussion and Proceedings." In *American Writers' Congress*, edited by Henry Hart, 165–92. New York: International Publishers, 1935.

———, ed. *American Writers' Congress*. New York: International Publishers, 1935.

Haslam, Gerald W. *Okies: Selected Stories*. 2nd ed. San Rafael, Calif.: New West Publications, 1974.

Hibbs, Ben. "Footloose Army." *Country Gentleman*, 7–8 February 1940. Reprint, Migrant Labor Collection, Bakersfield Library.

Hill, Frank Ernest. *What Is American?* New York: John Day Co., 1933.

Himes, Chester. "Democracy Is for the Unafraid." *Common Ground* 4 (1944): 53–56.

———. *If He Hollers Let Him Go*. 1945. Reprint, New York: Thunder's Mouth Press, 2002.

———. "Now Is the Time! Here Is the Place!" *Opportunity* 20 (September 1942): 271–73, 284.

———. *The Quality of Hurt: The Autobiography of Chester Himes*. New York: Doubleday, 1972.

———. "Zoot Riots Are Race Riots." *Crisis*, July 1943, 200–201, 222.

Hughes, Langston. *Scottsboro Limited: Four Poems and a Play in Verse*. New York: Golden Stair Press, 1932.

Jones, Claudia. "An End to the Neglect of the Negro Woman!" In *Words of Fire: An Anthology of African-American Feminist Thought*, edited by Beverly Guy-Sheftall, 108–23. New York: New Press, 1995.

Kornbluh, Joyce L. *Rebel Voices, an I.W.W. Anthology*. Ann Arbor: University of Michigan Press, 1968.

Kornhauser, Arthur. *Detroit As the People See It: A Survey of Attitudes in an Industrial City*. Detroit: Wayne State University Press, 1952.

Lange, Dorothea, and Paul Taylor. *American Exodus: A Record of Human Erosion*. 1939. Reprint, Paris: Jean-Michel Place, 1999.

Lee, Ulysses. "On the Road." *Opportunity* 17 (September 1939): 283–84.

Lenin, V. I. *Preliminary Draft of Theses on the National and Colonial Questions: For the Second Congress of the Communist International*. 1920. In *Lenin on Politics and Revolution: Selected Writings*, edited by James E. Connor, 315–19. New York: Pegasus, 1968.

———. "The Three Sources and Three Component Parts of Marxism." *Selected Works*, vol. 11 (1913), 3–8. In *Reader in Marxist Philosophy: From the Writings of Marx, Engels, and Lenin*, edited by Howard Selsam and Harry Martel, 37–41. New York: International Publishers, 1987.

Lewis, Mollie V. "Negro Women in Steel." *Crisis*, February 1948. In *Writing Red: An Anthology of American Women Writers, 1930–1940*, edited by Charlotte Nekola and Paula Rabinowitz, 276–78. New York: Feminist Press at the City University of New York, 1993.

Marcy, Helen. "'Save Us' Negro Boys Write Folks in Chattanooga." *Southern Worker*, 18 April 1931, 12.

Markey, Morris. *This Country of Yours*. Boston: Little, Brown, 1932.

Marsh, Fred T. Untitled review of *Let Me Breathe Thunder* by William Attaway. *New York Herald Tribune Books*, 25 June 1939, 10.

Marx, Karl, and Friedrich Engels. *Manifesto of the Communist Party*. Translated by Samuel Moore. Chicago: Charles H. Kerr & Co., 1906.

McDaniel, Wilma. *The Last Dust Storm*. New York: Hanging Loose Press, 1995.

McWilliams, Carey. *Factories in the Field: The Story of Migratory Farm Labor in California*. 1939. Reprint, Santa Barbara: Peregrine Smith, 1971.

———. *Ill Fares the Land: Migrants and Migratory Labor in the United States*. Boston: Little, Brown, 1942.

———. "Jim Crow Moves West." *Negro Digest*, August 1945, 71–74.

Meltzer, Milton. "William Attaway, Negro Novelist." *Daily Worker*, 26 June 1939, 7.

Milburn, George. *The Hobo's Hornbook: A Repertory for a Gutter Jongleur*. New York: Ives Washburn, 1930.

Morgan, Edmund. "Religion and Family in Seventeenth-Century New England." Ph.D. diss., Harvard University, 1942.

Motley, Willard. "Negro Art in Chicago." *Opportunity* 18 (January 1940): 19–22.

Murray, Pauli. *Song in a Weary Throat : An American Pilgrimage*. 1st ed. New York: Harper and Row, 1987.

———. "Three Thousand Miles on a Dime in Ten Days." In *Negro: An Anthology*, edited by Nancy Cunard, 67–70. New York: Continuum, 1996.

"A New Headache." *Business Week*, 17 October 1942, 46–48.

Nichols, Charles. "A Study of the Slave Narrative." Ph.D. diss., Brown University, 1949.

Odum, Howard W., and Harry Estill Moore. *American Regionalism: A Cultural-Historical Approach to National Integration*. New York: Henry Holt, 1938.

Olsen, Tillie. *Yonnondio: From the Thirties*. New York: Delacorte Press/Seymour Lawrence, 1974.

Page, Evelyn. "Some Americana." *Washington Post*, 13 August 1939, B10.

Park, Robert. "Human Migration and the Marginal Man." *American Journal of Sociology* 33, no. 6 (May 1928): 881–93.

Petry, Ann. *The Street*. 1946. Reprint, Boston: Houghton Mifflin, 1991.

Quinn, Arthur Hobson. *The Soul of America, Yesterday and Today*. Philadelphia: University of Pennsylvania Press, 1932.

Ransdell, Hollace. "Report on the Scottsboro, Ala., Case." Mimeographed report to the American Civil Liberties Union, 27 May 1931. New York Public Library, Humanities and Social Sciences Library, http://law2.umkc.edu/faculty/projects/FTrials/scottsboro/SB_HRrep.html. 9 February 2011.

Reckless, Walter C. "Why Women Become Hoboes." *American Mercury*, February 1934, 175–80.

Reitman, Ben L. *Sister of the Road: An Autobiography of Boxcar Berta*. 1937. Reprint, New York: AMOK Press, 1988.

Ridpath, Ben Morris. "The Case of the Missouri Sharecroppers." *Christian Century*, 1 February 1939, 146–48.

Schuyler, George S. "Firestone Plant Like Heaven Now, Says Akron Worker: Interracial Union Picnic Symbolizes New Labor Deal." *Pittsburgh Courier*, 28 August 1937, 14.

———. "Negro Workers Lead in Great Lakes Steel Drive: Schuyler Makes Startling Revelations of Labor Conditions in Chicago, Gary, and Cleveland—Tells How Companies Used Anti-Negro Propaganda." *Pittsburgh Courier*, 31 July 1937. In *The Black Worker from the Founding of the CIO to the AFL-CIO Merger, 1936–1955*, edited by Philip S. Foner and Ronald L. Lewis, 58–64. Philadelphia: Temple University Press, 1983.

———. "Race Feeling Tense Where C.I.O. Is Flaunted, Schuyler Finds: Schuyler Visits Steel Centers in Ohio and Pennsylvania; Finds Race Workers Loyal to Companies; Making Big Money." *Pittsburgh Courier*, 24 July 1937, 1, 14.

Sears, Paul B. *Who Are These Americans?* New York: Norton, 1939.

Seaver, Edwin. "The Proletarian Novel." In *American Writers' Congress*, edited by Henry Hart, 98–103. New York: International Publishers, 1935.

———. "Sterile Writers and Proletarian Religions." *New Masses*, May 1933, 22–24.

Smith, Henry Nash. "American Emotional and Emotive Attitudes toward the Great Plains and the Rocky Mountains, 1803–1850." Ph.D. diss., Harvard University, 1940.

Springer, Gertrude. "Men Off the Road." *Survey Graphic*, September 1934, 420–23.

Starke, Barbara. *Born in Captivity: The Story of a Girl's Escape*. 1st ed. Indianapolis: Bobbs-Merrill, 1931.

Steinbeck, Elaine, and Robert Wallsten, eds. *Steinbeck: A Life in Letters*. New York: Penguin, 1975.

Steinbeck, John. *The Grapes of Wrath: Text and Criticism*. 1939. Edited by Peter Lisca and Kevin Hearle. Reprint, Viking Critical Library ed. New York: Penguin, 1997.

———. *The Harvest Gypsies: On the Road to the Grapes of Wrath*. Berkeley: Heyday Books, 1988.

———. *Of Mice and Men*. 1937. Reprint, New York: Penguin, 1994.

———. "The Vigilante." In *The Long Valley*, 133–41. New York: Viking, 1938.

Swing, Raymond Gram. *Forerunners of American Fascism*. New York: Julian Messner, 1935.

Taylor, Paul. "Again the Covered Wagon." *Survey Graphic*, July 1935, 348–51.

"To Study Denial of Civil Rights." *Chicago Defender*, 4 February 1939, http://www. proquest.com.ezp2.harvard.edu/. 29 March 2008.

Triplett, Frank. *Life, Times and Treacherous Death of Jesse James*. 1882. Reprint, Stamford, Conn.: Longmeadow Press, 1992.

Untitled review of *Let Me Breathe Thunder* by William Attaway. *Saturday Review*, 1 July 1939, 20

Villareal, José. *Pocho*. Garden City, N.Y.: Doubleday, 1959.

"Virginia and Maryland Negroes Flock to Union." *Pittsburgh Courier*, 7 August 1937.

Vorse, Mary Heaton. "How Scottsboro Happened." *New Republic*, 10 May 1933, 356–58.

W. N. "Boys of Road 'Punchy' Heroes." *Los Angeles Times*, 6 August 1939, C6.

Walker, Margaret. *This Is My Century: New and Collected Poems*. Athens: University of Georgia Press, 1989.

Ware, Caroline. *The Cultural Approach to History*. New York: Columbia University Press, 1940.

Warner, Ralph. "'Blood on the Forge' Is Story of Negro Brothers." *Daily Worker*, 8 November 1941.

"War Posters: American Artists Go All Out for Victory in Big Picture Campaign." *Life*, 21 December 1942, 54–57.

Webb, Walter Prescott. *The Great Plains*. 1931. Reprint, Lincoln: University of Nebraska Press, 1981.

Weiler, A. H. "'Man's Castle.' 'Fiona' to Be Made by Sy Bartlett—Other Matters." *New York Times*, 30 October 1960, X7.

Wellman, William A., dir. *Wild Boys of the Road*. Warner Bros., 1933.

West, Dorothy. *The Living Is Easy*. 1948. Reprint, Old Westbury, N.Y.: Feminist Press, 1982.

White, Max R., Douglas Ensminger, and Cecil L. Gregory. "Rich Land, Poor People." FSA Research Report, Indianapolis, 1938.

White, Walter, and Thurgood Marshall. *What Caused the Detroit Riot?: An Analysis*. New York: National Association for the Advancement of Colored People, 1943.

"Why We Can't Hate 'Reds.'" *Chicago Defender*, 14 January 1933, 14.

Wilkins, Roy. "The Bonuseers Ban Jim Crow." *Crisis*, October 1932, 317.

Wirth, Louis. "Urbanism as a Way of Life." *American Journal of Sociology* 44, no. 1 (July 1938): 1–24.

Wright, Ada. "My Two Sons Face the Electric Chair." *Labor Defender*, September 1931, 172, 182.

Wright, Richard. *Black Boy (American Hunger)*. 1945. Reprint, New York: Harper Collins, 1991.

———. "Blueprint for Negro Writing." In *Within the Circle: An Anthology of African American Literary Criticism from the Harlem Renaissance to the Present*, edited by Angelyn Mitchell, 97–106. Durham, N.C.: Duke University Press, 1994.

———. *Native Son*. New York: Harper Perennial, 1966.

Wright, Richard, and Edwin Rosskam. *12 Million Black Voices*. 1941. Reprint, New York: Thunder's Mouth Press, 1988.

Young, Stanley. "Tough and Tender." *New York Times*, 25 June 1939, BR4.

Secondary Sources

Aaron, Daniel. *Writers on the Left: Episodes in Literary Communism*. New York: Columbia University Press, 1992.

Alvarez, Luis. *The Power of the Zoot: Youth Culture and Resistance during World War II*. Berkeley: University of California Press, 2008.

Arnesen, Eric. "Whiteness and the Historians' Imagination." *International Labor and Working-Class History* 60 (October 2001): 3–32.

Arnesen, Eric, and Alex Lichtenstein. "All Kinds of People." Introduction to *Wartime Shipyard: A Study in Social Disunity*, by Katherine Archibald, ix–lxxiv. Urbana: University of Illinois Press, 2006.

Astro, Richard. *John Steinbeck and Edward F. Ricketts: The Shaping of a Novelist*. Minneapolis: University of Minnesota Press, 1973.

Bakhtin, M. M., and Hélène Iswolsky. *Rabelais and His World*. 1st Midland Book ed. Bloomington: Indiana University Press, 1984.

Baldwin, Davarian L. *Chicago's New Negroes: Modernity, the Great Migration, and Black Urban Life*. Chapel Hill: University of North Carolina Press, 2007.

Baldwin, James. "Everybody's Protest Novel." In *Collected Essays*, edited by Toni Morrison. New York: Library of America, 1998.

Battat, Erin Royston. "Okie Outlaws and Dust Bowl Fugitives." In *The Grapes of Wrath: A Reconsideration*, edited by Michael Meyer, 453–80. Amsterdam: Rodopi, 2009.

Bearden, Romare. "The Negro in 'Little Steel.'" *Opportunity* 15 (December 1937): 362–65, 380. In *Black Workers: A Documentary History from Colonial Times to the Present*, edited by Philip S. Foner and Ronald L. Lewis, 98–102. Philadelphia: Temple University Press, 1989.

Bell, Bernard W. *The Afro-American Novel and Its Tradition*. Amherst: University of Massachusetts Press, 1987.

Benson, Jackson J. "John Steinbeck: Novelist as Scientist." In *John Steinbeck: Modern Critical Views*, edited by Harold Bloom, 103–23. New York: Chelsea House, 1987.

———. *The True Adventures of John Steinbeck, Writer*. New York: Viking, 1984.

Berry, Chad. *Southern Migrants, Northern Exiles*. Champaign: University of Illinois Press, 2000.

Biondi, Martha. *To Stand and Fight: The Struggle for Civil Rights in Postwar New York City*. Cambridge, Mass.: Harvard University Press, 2003.

Bone, Robert. *The Negro Novel in America*. New Haven, Conn.: Yale University Press, 1965.

———. "Richard Wright and the Chicago Renaissance." *Callaloo* 28, Richard Wright: A Special Issue (Summer 1986): 446–68.

Bone, Robert, and Richard A. Courage. *The Muse in Bronzeville: African American Creative Expression in Chicago, 1932–1950.* New Brunswick, N.J.: Rutgers University Press, 2011.

Bordelon, Pamela. "Zora Neale Hurston: A Biographical Essay." In *Go Gator and Muddy the Water: Writings by Zora Neale Hurston from the Federal Writers' Project,* edited by Pamela Bordelon, 1–49. New York: Norton, 1999.

Boris, Eileen. "'Arm and Arm': Racialized Bodies and Colored Lines." *Journal of American Studies* 35 (2001): 1–20.

———. "'You Wouldn't Want One of 'Em Dancing with Your Wife': Racialized Bodies on the Job in World War II." *American Quarterly* 50, no. 1 (March 1998): 77–108.

Boyce Davies, Carole. *Left of Karl Marx: The Political Life of Black Communist Claudia Jones.* Durham, N.C.: Duke University Press, 2008.

Bradley, David. Preface to *12 Million Black Voices,* by Richard Wright and Edwin Rosskam, v–xvii. 1941. Reprint, New York: Thunder's Mouth Press, 1988.

Bramen, Carrie T. *The Uses of Variety: Modern Americanism and the Quest for National Distinctiveness.* Cambridge, Mass.: Harvard University Press, 2000.

Brodhead, Richard H. "The American Literary Field, 1860–1890." In *The Cambridge History of American Literature,* edited by Sacvan Bercovitch, 11–62. Cambridge: Cambridge University Press, 2005.

———. *Cultures of Letters: Scenes of Reading and Writing in Nineteenth-Century America.* Chicago: University of Chicago Press, 1993.

Browder, Laura. *Rousing the Nation: Radical Culture in Depression America.* Amherst: University of Massachusetts Press, 1998.

Brown, Kathleen M. *Good Wives, Nasty Wenches, and Anxious Patriarchs: Gender, Race, and Power in Colonial Virginia.* Chapel Hill: University of North Carolina Press, 1996.

Campbell, Donna. *Resisting Regionalism: Gender and Naturalism in American Fiction, 1885–1915.* Athens: Ohio University Press, 1997.

Cantor, Louis. *A Prologue to the Protest Movement: The Missouri Sharecropper Roadside Demonstration of 1939.* Durham, N.C.: Duke University Press, 1969.

Cappetti, Carla. *Writing Chicago: Modernism, Ethnography, and the Novel.* New York: Columbia University Press, 1993.

Carby, Hazel V. "Ideologies of Black Folk: The Historical Novel of Slavery." In *Slavery and the Literary Imagination,* edited by Deborah E. McDowell and Arnold Rampersad, 125–43. Baltimore: Johns Hopkins University Press, 1985.

Carnes, Mark C. *Secret Ritual and Manhood in Victorian America.* New Haven, Conn.: Yale University Press, 1989.

Casey, Janet Galligani. "Introduction: (Left) Contexts and Considerations." In *The Novel and the American Left: Critical Essays on Depression-Era Fiction,* edited by Janet Galligani Casey, ix–xviii. Iowa City: University of Iowa Press, 2004.

Castro, Joy. "'My Little Illegality': Abortion, Resistance, and Women Writers on the Left." In *The Novel and the American Left: Critical Essays on Depression-Era Fiction,* edited by Janet Galligani Casey, 16–34. Iowa City: University of Iowa Press, 2004.

Castronovo, Russ. "Incidents in the Life of a White Woman: Economies of Race and Gender in the Antebellum Nation." *American Literary History* 10, no. 2 (Summer 1995): 239–65.

Cawelti, John G. *The Six-Gun Mystique*. Bowling Green, Ohio: Bowling Green State University Popular Press, 1978.

Ceplair, Larry. "Albert Maltz, Philip Stevenson, and 'Art Is A Weapon.'" *Minnesota Review*, n.s. 69 (Fall/Winter 2007), http://www.theminnesotareview.org/journal/ns69/ceplair.shtml. 17 April 2012.

Chauncey, George. *Gay New York: Gender, Urban Culture, and the Making of the Gay Male World, 1890–1940*. New York: Basic Books, 1994.

Clark-Lewis, Elizabeth. *Living In, Living Out: African American Domestics in Washington, D.C., 1910–1940*. Washington, D.C.: Smithsonian Books, 1994.

Coats, Lauren, and Nihad M. Farooq. "Regionalism in the Era of the New Deal." In *A Companion to the Regional Literatures of America*, edited by Charles L. Crow, 74–91. Malden, Mass.: Blackwell, 2003.

Cohen, Lizabeth. *Making a New Deal: Industrial Workers in Chicago, 1919–1939*. New York: Cambridge University Press, 1990.

Coiner, Constance. *Better Red: The Writing and Resistance of Tillie Olsen and Meridel Le Sueur*. New York: Oxford University Press, 1995.

Connelly, Frances S., ed. *Modern Art and the Grotesque*. New York: Cambridge University Press, 2003.

Cook, Sylvia J. "Steinbeck, the People, and the Party." In *John Steinbeck's The Grapes of Wrath: Essays in Criticism*, edited by Tetsumaro Hayashi, 19–30. Muncie, Ind.: Steinbeck Research Institute, Ball State University, 1990.

Courtwright, David T. *Violent Land: Single Men and Social Disorder from the Frontier to the Inner City*. Cambridge, Mass.: Harvard University Press, 1996.

Cox, James. "Regionalism: A Diminished Thing." In *Columbia Literary History of the United States*, edited by Emory Elliott, 761–84. New York: Columbia University Press, 1988.

Crockett, H. Kelly. "The Bible and *The Grapes of Wrath*." *College English* 24, no. 3 (December 1962): 193–99.

Cruse, Harold. *The Crisis of the Negro Intellectual: A Historical Analysis of the Failure of Black Leadership*. 1967. Reprint, New York: New York Review of Books, 2005.

Curtis, James. *Mind's Eye, Mind's Truth: F.S.A. Photography Reconsidered*. Philadelphia: Temple University Press, 1989.

Curtis, James C. "Dorothea Lange, Migrant Mother, and the Culture of the Great Depression." *Winterthur Portfolio* 21, no. 1 (Spring 1986): 1–20.

Dagbovie, Sika Alaine. "Mixed-Race Women." In *Black Women in America: An Historical Encyclopedia*, edited by Darlene Clark Hine, 378–82. New York: Oxford University Press, 2005.

Daniel, Cletus E. *Bitter Harvest: A History of California Farmworkers, 1870–1941*. Ithaca, N.Y.: Cornell University Press, 1981.

Dawahare, Anthony. *Nationalism, Marxism, and African American Literature between the Wars: A New Pandora's Box*. Jackson: University Press of Mississippi, 2003.

D'Emilio, John, and Estelle B. Freedman. *Intimate Matters: A History of Sexuality in America*. 1st ed. New York: Harper and Row, 1988.

DeMott, Robert J. *Steinbeck's Reading: A Catalogue of Books Owned and Borrowed*. New York: Garland, 1984.

————, ed. *Working Days: The Journals of the Grapes of Wrath*. New York: Penguin, 1989.

Denning, Michael. *The Cultural Front: The Laboring of American Culture in the Twentieth Century*. New York: Verso, 1997.

————. *Mechanic Accents: Dime Novels and Working-Class Culture in America*. New York: Verso, 1987.

DePastino, Todd. *Citizen Hobo: How a Century of Homelessness Shaped America*. Chicago: University of Chicago Press, 2003.

Deutsch, Tracey. "Great Depression." *The Electronic Encyclopedia of Chicago*. Chicago: Newberry Library, 2005, http://www.encyclopedia.chicagohistory.org/pages/542.html. 12 June 2012.

Dickerson, Dennis C. *Out of the Crucible: Black Steelworkers in Western Pennsylvania, 1875–1980*. Albany: State University of New York Press, 1986.

Dickstein, Morris. *Dancing in the Dark: A Cultural History of the Great Depression*. New York: Norton, 2009.

————. "Depression Culture: The Dream of Mobility." In *Radical Revisions: Rereading 1930s Culture*, edited by Bill Mullen and Sherry Lee Linkon, 225–41. Urbana: University of Illinois Press, 1996.

Dixon, Melvin. "Singing Swords: The Literary Legacy of Slavery." In *The Slave's Narrative*, edited by Charles T. Davis and Henry Louis Gates Jr., 298–317. Oxford: Oxford University Press, 1985.

Dolinar, Brian. *The Black Cultural Front: Black Writers and Artists of the Depression Generation*. Jackson: University Press of Mississippi, 2012.

Dudziak, Mary. *Cold War Civil Rights: Race and the Image of American Democracy*. Princeton, N.J.: Princeton University Press, 2000.

Entin, Joseph. "Monstrous Modernism: Disfigured Bodies and Literary Experimentalism in Yonnondio and Christ in Concrete." In *The Novel and the American Left: Critical Essays on Depression-Era Fiction*, edited by Janet Galligani Casey, 61–80. Iowa City: University of Iowa Press, 2004.

————. *Sensational Modernism: Experimental Fiction and Photography in Thirties America*. Chapel Hill: University of North Carolina Press, 2007.

Feldstein, Ruth. *Motherhood in Black and White: Race and Sex in American Liberalism, 1930–1965*. Ithaca, N.Y.: Cornell University Press, 2000.

Fernandez, Manny. "Study Finds Disparities in Mortgages by Race." *New York Times*, 15 October 2007.

Fetterley, Judith, and Marjorie Pryse. *Writing out of Place: Regionalism, Women, and American Literary Culture*. Urbana: University of Illinois Press, 2003.

Fisher, Philip, ed. *The New American Studies: Essays from Representations*. Berkeley: University of California Press, 1991.

Fleischhauer, Carl, Beverly W. Brannan, Lawrence W. Levine, and Alan Trachtenberg. *Documenting America, 1935–1943*. Berkeley: University of California Press in association with the Library of Congress, 1988.

Fleming, Robert E. "Bontemps, Arna Wendell." In *American National Biography Online*. Oxford University Press, 2000.

Fligstein, Neil. *Going North: Migration of Blacks and Whites from the South, 1900–1950*. New York: Academic Press, 1981.

Foley, Barbara. "Race and Class in Radical African-American Fiction of the Depression Years" *Nature, Society, and Thought* 3, no. 3 (1990): 305–24.

———. *Radical Representations: Politics and Form in U.S. Proletarian Fiction, 1929–1941.* Durham, N.C.: Duke University Press, 1993.

———. *Wrestling with the Left: The Making of Ralph Ellison's* Invisible Man. Durham, N.C.: Duke University Press, 2010.

Foley, Neil. *The White Scourge: Mexicans, Blacks, and Poor Whites in Texas Cotton Culture.* Berkeley: University of California Press, 1997.

Foner, Eric. "Response to Eric Arnesen." *International Labor and Working-Class History* 60 (October 2001): 57–60.

Fontenrose, Joseph Eddy. *John Steinbeck: An Introduction and Interpretation.* New York: Barnes and Noble, 1964.

Franklin, Wayne, and Michael Steiner. *Mapping American Culture.* Iowa City: University of Iowa Press, 1992.

Fraser, Steven, and Gary Gerstle, eds. *The Rise and Fall of the New Deal Order, 1930–1980.* Princeton, N.J.: Princeton University Press, 1989.

Freeman, Joshua B. "Labor during the American Century: Work, Workers, and Unions since 1945." In *A Companion to Post-1945 America,* edited by Jean-Christophe Agnew and Roy Rosenzweig, 192–210. Malden, Mass.: Blackwell, 2002.

Freund, David M. P. "Marketing the Free Market: State Intervention and the Politics of Prosperity in Metropolitan America." In *The New Suburban History,* edited by Kevin M. Kruse and Thomas J. Sugrue, 11–32. Chicago: University of Chicago Press, 2005.

Fullbrook, Kate. "Literature of the African-American Great Migration." In *A Companion to the Literature and Culture of the American South,* edited by Richard Gray and Owen Robinson, 454–71. Malden, Mass.: Blackwell, 2004.

Ganz, Marshall. *Why David Sometimes Wins: Leadership, Organization, and Strategy in the California Farm Worker Movement.* New York: Oxford University Press, 2009.

Garren, Samuel B. "William Attaway." *Dictionary of Literary Biography* 76 (September 1988): 3–7.

Gates, Henry Louis, Jr. *The Signifyin' Monkey: A Theory of African-American Literary Criticism.* New York: Oxford University Press, 1989.

Geary, Daniel. "Carey McWilliams and Antifascism, 1934–1943." *Journal of American History* 90, no. 3 (December 2003): 912–34.

Gerstle, Gary. *American Crucible: Race and Nation in the Twentieth Century.* Princeton, N.J.: Princeton University Press, 2001.

———. "The Protean Character of American Liberalism." *American Historical Review* 99, no. 4 (October 1994): 1043–73.

———. "Working-Class Racism: Broaden the Focus." *International Labor and Working-Class History* 44 (Fall 1993): 33–40.

Gilmore, Alec. "Biblical Wilderness in *The Grapes of Wrath*: Steinbeck's Multi-layered Use of the Biblical Image." In *The Grapes of Wrath: A Reconsideration,* edited by Michael Meyer, 151–74. Amsterdam: Rodopi, 2009.

Gilmore, Glenda Elizabeth. *Defying Dixie: The Radical Roots of Civil Rights, 1919–1950.* 1st ed. New York: Norton, 2008.

Gingras, George E. "Travel." In *Dictionary of Literary Themes and Motifs*, edited by Jean-Charles Seigneuret, 1292–331. New York: Greenwood, 1988.

Glaude, Eddie. *Exodus! Race, Religion, and Nation in Early Nineteenth-Century Black America.* Chicago: University of Chicago Press, 2000.

Gleason, Philip. "American Identity and Americanization." In *Harvard Encyclopedia of American Ethnic Groups*, edited by Stephen Thernstrom, 31–58. Cambridge, Mass.: Belknap Press of Harvard University Press, 1980.

Goldberg, Vicki. *The Power of Photography: How Photographs Changed Our Lives.* New York: Abbeville Press, 1991.

Goldfield, Michael, "Race and the CIO: The Possibilities for Racial Egalitarianism during the 1930s and 1940s." *International Labor and Working-Class History* 44 (Fall 1993): 1–32.

———. "Race and the CIO: Reply to Critics." *International Labor and Working-Class History* 46, ILWCH Roundtable: What Next for Labor and Working-Class History (Fall 1994): 142–60.

Goldhurst, William. "*Of Mice and Men*: John Steinbeck's Parable of the Curse of Cain." In *The Short Novels of John Steinbeck: Critical Essays with a Checklist to Steinbeck Criticism*, edited by Jackson J. Benson, 48–59. Durham, N.C.: Duke University Press, 1990.

Goodman, James E. *Stories of Scottsboro.* New York: Vintage, 1994.

Goodwyn, Lawrence. *The Populist Moment: A Short History of the Agrarian Revolt in America.* Oxford: Oxford University Press, 1978.

Gore, Dayo F. *Radicalism at the Crossroads: African American Women Activists in the Cold War.* New York: New York University Press, 2011.

Gottlieb, Peter. *Making Their Own Way: Southern Blacks' Migration to Pittsburgh, 1916–30.* Urbana: University of Illinois Press, 1997.

Gregory, James N. *American Exodus: The Dust Bowl Migration and Okie Culture in California.* New York: Oxford University Press, 1989.

———. *The Southern Diaspora: How the Great Migrations of Black and White Southerners Transformed America.* Chapel Hill: University of North Carolina Press, 2005.

———. "Southernizing the American Working Class: Post-war Episodes of Regional and Class Transformation." *Labor History* 39, no. 2 (May 1998): 135–54.

Griffin, Farah Jasmine. *"Who Set You Flowin'?": The African-American Migration Narrative.* New York: Oxford University Press, 1995.

Grossman, James R. *Land of Hope: Chicago, Black Southerners, and the Great Migration.* Chicago: University of Chicago Press, 1989.

Guerin-Gonzales, Camille. *Mexican Workers and the American Dream: Immigration, Repatriation, and California Farm Labor, 1900–1939.* New Brunswick, N.J.: Rutgers University Press, 1994.

Hadella, Charlotte. "Steinbeck's *Of Mice and Men* (1937)." In *A New Study Guide to Steinbeck's Major Works, with Critical Explications*, edited by Tetsumaro Hayashi, 139–63. Metuchen, N.J.: Scarecrow Press, 1993.

Hahn, Steven. *A Nation under Our Feet: Black Political Struggles in the Rural South from Slavery to the Great Migration.* Cambridge, Mass.: Belknap Press of Harvard University Press, 2003.

Hall, Jacquelyn Dowd. "The Long Civil Rights Movement and the Political Uses of the Past." *Journal of American History* 91, no. 4 (March 2005): 1233–64.

Halttunen, Karen. "Groundwork: American Studies in Place: Presidential Address to the American Studies Association, November 4, 2005." *American Quarterly* 58, no. 1 (March 2006): 1–15.

Hapke, Laura. *Labor's Text: The Worker in American Fiction*. New Brunswick, N.J.: Rutgers University Press, 2001.

Hariman, Robert, and John Louis Lucaites. *No Caption Needed: Iconic Photographs, Public Culture, and Liberal Democracy*. Chicago: University of Chicago Press, 2007.

Harkins, Anthony. *Hillbilly: A Cultural History of an American Icon*. New York: Oxford University Press, 2004.

Harpham, Geoffrey Galt. *On the Grotesque: Strategies of Contradiction in Art and Literature*. Princeton, N.J.: Princeton University Press, 1982.

Harris, Lashawn. "Running with the Reds: African American Women and the Communist Party during the Great Depression." *Journal of African American History* 94, no. 1 (Winter 2009): 21–43.

Harris, Trudier. *Exorcising Blackness: Historical and Literary Lynching and Burning Rituals*. Bloomington: Indiana University Press, 1984.

Harris-Lacewell, Melissa. "Of the Meaning of Progress: Measuring Black Citizenship." Lecture 1, "Subjects or Citizens: Feeling Black in Post-Katrina America." W. E. B. Du Bois Institute Lecture Series, Harvard University, 31 March 2009.

Harrison, Alferdteen. *Black Exodus: The Great Migration from the American South*. Jackson: University Press of Mississippi, 1991.

Harrison, Beth. "Zora Neale Hurston and Mary Austin: A Case Study in Ethnography, Literary Modernism, and Contemporary Ethnic Fiction." *MELUS* 21, no. 2, Varieties of Ethnic Criticism (Summer 1996): 89–106.

Hartigan, John. *Racial Situations: Class Predicaments of Whiteness in Detroit*. Princeton, N.J.: Princeton University Press, 1999.

Hearle, Kevin. "These Are American People: The Specter of Eugenics in *Their Blood Is Strong* and *The Grapes of Wrath*." In *Beyond Boundaries: Rereading John Steinbeck*, edited by Susan Shillinglaw and Kevin Hearle, 247–54. Tuscaloosa: University of Alabama Press, 2002.

Hegeman, Susan. *Patterns for America: Modernism and the Concept of Culture*. Princeton, N.J.: Princeton University Press, 1999.

Herzog, Melanie Anne. *Elizabeth Catlett: In the Image of the People*. Chicago: Art Institute of Chicago, 2005.

Higashida, Cheryl. *Black Internationalist Feminism: Women Writers of the Black Left, 1945–1995*. Urbana: University of Illinois Press, 2011.

Higginbotham, Evelyn Brooks. *Righteous Discontent: The Women's Movement in the Black Baptist Church, 1880–1920*. Cambridge, Mass.: Harvard University Press, 1993.

Hill, Herbert. "The Importance of Race in American Labor History." *International Journal of Politics, Culture and Society* 9, no. 2 (1995): 317–43.

Hill, Rebecca N. *Men, Mobs, and the Law: Antilynching and Labor Defense in U.S. Radical History*. Durham, N.C.: Duke University Press, 2008.

Hills, Patricia. "Jacob Lawrence's *Migration Series*: Weavings of Pictures and Texts." In *Jacob Lawrence: The Migration Series*, edited by Elizabeth Hutton Turner, 141–53. Washington, D.C.: Rappahannock Press (in association with the Phillips Collection), 1993.

―――. *Painting Harlem Modern: The Art of Jacob Lawrence*. Berkeley: University of California Press, 2009.

Hobsbawm, Eric. *Bandits*. New York: Pantheon, 1981.

Honey, Michael K. *Southern Labor and Black Civil Rights: Organizing Memphis Workers*. Urbana: University of Illinois Press, 1993.

Hsu, Hsuan L. "Literature and Regional Production." *American Literary History* 17, no. 1 (2005): 36–39.

Huddle, Mark Andrew. "Exodus from the South." In *A Companion to African-American History*, edited by Alton Hornsby, 449–62. Malden, Mass.: Blackwell, 2005.

Hunter, J. D. "Steinbeck's Wine of Affirmation in *The Grapes of Wrath*." In *Essays in Modern American Literature*, edited by Richard E. Langford, Guy Owen, and William Taylor, 76–89. DeLand, Fla.: Stetson University Press, 1963.

Hunter, Tera W. *To 'Joy My Freedom: Southern Black Women's Lives and Labors after the Civil War*. Cambridge, Mass.: Harvard University Press, 1997.

Hurll, Estelle M. *The Madonna in Art*. Boston: L. C. Page and Co., 1898.

Ikard, David. "Love Jones: A Black Male Feminist Critique of Chester Himes's *If He Hollers Let Him Go*." *African American Review* 36, no. 2 (Summer 2002): 299–310.

Isserman, Maurice. *Which Side Were You On?: The American Communist Party during the Second World War*. Middletown, Conn: Wesleyan University Press, 1982.

Itagaki, Lynn M. "Transgressing Race and Community in Chester Himes's *If He Hollers Let Him Go*." *African American Review* 37, no. 1 (Spring 2003): 65–80.

Jackson, Kenneth. *Crabgrass Frontier: The Suburbanization of the United States*. New York: Oxford University Press, 1987.

Jackson, Mark Allan. *Prophet Singer: The Voice and Vision of Woody Guthrie*. Jackson: University Press of Mississippi, 2007.

Jacobson, Matthew Frye. *Roots Too: White Ethnic Revival in Post–Civil Rights America*. Cambridge, Mass.: Harvard University Press, 2006.

―――. *Whiteness of a Different Color: European Immigrants and the Alchemy of Race*. Cambridge, Mass.: Harvard University Press, 1999.

Jameson, Elizabeth. "Unconscious Inheritance and Conscious Striving: Laura Ingalls Wilder and the Frontier Narrative." In *Laura Ingalls Wilder and the American Frontier: Five Perspectives*, edited by Dwight M. Miller, 69–93. Lanham, Md.: University Press of America, 2002.

Johnson, Marilynn S. *The Second Gold Rush: Oakland and the East Bay in World War II*. Berkeley: University of California Press, 1996.

Johnson, Susan Lee. *Roaring Camp: The Social World of the California Gold Rush*. New York: Norton, 2000.

Jones, Gavin. *American Hungers: The Problem of Poverty in U.S. Literature, 1840–1945*. Princeton, N.J.: Princeton University Press, 2008.

Jones, Jacqueline. *The Dispossessed: America's Underclass from the Civil War to the Present*. New York: Harper Collins Basic Books, 1992.

―――. *Labor of Love, Labor of Sorrow: Black Women, Work, and the Family from Slavery to the Present*. New York: Basic Books, 2010.

Kaplan, Amy. "Nation, Region, Empire." In *The Columbia History of the American Novel*, edited by Emory Elliott, 240–66. New York: Columbia University Press, 1991.

Karem, Jeff. *The Romance of Authenticity: The Cultural Politics of Regional and Ethnic Literatures.* Charlottesville: University of Virginia Press, 2004.

Kaufman, Will. *Woody Guthrie: American Radical.* Urbana: University of Illinois Press, 2011.

Kayser, Wolfgang. *The Grotesque in Art and Literature.* Translated by Ulrich Weisstein. 1957. Reprint, New York: Columbia University Press, 1968.

Kazin, Michael. *The Populist Persuasion: An American History.* Ithaca, N.Y.: Cornell University Press, 1995.

Kelley, Robin D. G. *Freedom Dreams: The Black Radical Imagination.* Boston: Beacon, 2002.

———. *Hammer and Hoe: Alabama Communists during the Great Depression.* Chapel Hill: University of North Carolina Press, 1990.

Kersten, Andrew E. *Labor's Home Front: The American Federation of Labor during World War II.* New York: New York University Press, 2006.

Killens, John Oliver. Foreword to *Blood on the Forge*, by William Attaway. 1941. Reprint, New York: Monthly Review Press, 1987.

Kimmel, Michael. *Manhood in America: A Cultural History.* New York: Free Press, 1996.

King, Richard H. "American Political Culture since 1945." In *A Companion to Post-1945 America*, edited by Jean-Christophe Agnew and Roy Rosenzweig, 155–74. Malden, Mass.: Blackwell, 2002.

Kinnamon, Keneth, and Michel Fabre, eds. *Conversations with Richard Wright.* Oxford: University Press of Mississippi, 1993.

Kirby, Jack Temple. *Rural Worlds Lost: The American South, 1920–1960.* Baton Rouge: Louisiana State University Press, 1987.

Klein, Joe. *Woody Guthrie: A Life.* New York: Random House, 1999.

Klinkner, Philip A., and Rogers M. Smith. *The Unsteady March: The Rise and Decline of Racial Equality in America.* Chicago: University of Chicago Press, 1999.

Klotman, Phyllis. *Another Man Gone: The Black Runner in Contemporary Afro-American Literature.* Port Washington, N.Y.: Kennikat Press, 1977.

Kolchin, Peter. "Whiteness Studies: The New History of Race in America." *Journal of American History* 89, no. 1 (June 2002): 154–73.

Korstad, Robert Rodgers. *Civil Rights Unionism: Tobacco Workers and the Struggle for Democracy in the Mid-Twentieth-Century South.* Chapel Hill: University of North Carolina Press, 2003.

Korstad, Robert Rodgers, and Nelson Lichtenstein. "Opportunities Found and Lost: Labor, Radicals, and the Early Civil Rights Movement." *Journal of American History* 75, no. 3 (December 1988): 786–811.

Kozol, Wendy. "Madonnas of the Fields: Photography, Gender, and 1930s Farm Relief." *Genders* 2 (Summer 1988): 2–23.

Kristeva, Julia. *Powers of Horror: An Essay on Abjection.* Translated by Leon S. Roudiez. New York: Columbia University Press, 1982.

Kruse, Kevin M., and Thomas J. Sugrue, eds. *The New Suburban History.* Chicago: University of Chicago Press, 2005.

Kurashige, Scott. *The Shifting Grounds of Race: Black and Japanese Americans in the Making of Multiethnic Los Angeles.* Princeton, N.J.: Princeton University Press, 2008.

Lang, Amy Schrage. "Class and the Strategies of Sympathy." In *The Culture of Sentiment*, edited by Shirley Samuels, 128–42. New York: Oxford University Press, 1992.

Lasch, Christopher. *The True and Only Heaven: Progress and Its Critics*. New York: Norton, 1991.

Lefebvre, Henri. *The Production of Space*. Cambridge: Blackwell, 1991.

Lemann, Nicholas. *The Promised Land: The Great Black Migration and How It Changed America*. 1st ed. New York: Knopf, 1991.

Lemke-Santangelo, Gretchen. *Abiding Courage: African American Migrant Women and the East Bay Community*. Chapel Hill: University of North Carolina Press, 1996.

Levine, Lawrence W. *The Unpredictable Past: Explorations in American Cultural History*. New York: Oxford University Press, 1993.

Lichtenstein, Alex, and Eric Arnesen. "Labor and the Problem of Social Unity during World War II: Katherine Archibald's *Wartime Shipyard* in Retrospect." *Labor: Studies in Working-Class History of the Americas*, 3, no. 1 (2006): 113–46.

Lichtenstein, Nelson. "From Corporatism to Collective Bargaining: Organized Labor and the Eclipse of Social Democracy in the Postwar Era." In *The Rise and Fall of the New Deal Order, 1930–1980*, edited by Steve Fraser and Gary Gerstle, 122–52. Princeton, N.J.: Princeton University Press, 1989.

Limerick, Patricia. *The Legacy of Conquest: The Unbroken Past of the American West*. New York: Norton, 1987.

Lipsitz, George. *The Possessive Investment in Whiteness: How White People Profit from Identity Politics*. Philadelphia: Temple University Press, 1998.

———. *Rainbow at Midnight: Labor and Culture in the 1940s*. Urbana: University of Illinois Press, 1994.

Lisca, Peter, and Kevin Hearle, eds. *The Grapes of Wrath: Text and Criticism*. New York: Penguin, 1997.

Loftis, Anne. *Witnesses to the Struggle: Imagining the 1930s California Labor Movement*. Reno: University of Nevada Press, 1998.

Lotchin, Roger W. *The Bad City in the Good War: San Francisco, Los Angeles, Oakland, and San Diego*. Bloomington: Indiana University Press, 2003.

Lubin, Alex. Introduction to *Revising the Blueprint: Ann Petry and the Literary Left*, edited by Alex Lubin, 3–14. Jackson: University Press of Mississippi, 2007.

Lukács, Georg. "Propaganda or Partisanship?" *Partisan Review* 1, no. 2 (April–May 1934): 36–46.

MacLean, Nancy. *Freedom Is Not Enough: The Opening of the American Workplace*. Cambridge, Mass.: Harvard University Press, 2006.

———. Review of *The Politics of Whiteness: Race, Workers, and Culture in the Modern South*, by Michelle Brattain. *American Historical Review* 107, no. 4 (October 2002): 1239.

Margolies, Edward. Introduction to *Blood on the Forge*, by William Attaway. 1941. Reprint, New York: Collier, 1970.

Margolies, Edward, and Michel Fabre. *The Several Lives of Chester Himes*. Jackson: University Press of Mississippi, 1997.

Marks, Carole. *Farewell, We're Good and Gone: The Great Black Migration*. Bloomington: Indiana University Press, 1989.

Maxwell, William J. *New Negro, Old Left: African-American Writing and Communism between the Wars*. New York: Columbia University Press, 1999.

McDuffie, Erik S. *Sojourning for Freedom: Black Women, American Communism, and the Making of Black Left Feminism*. Durham, N.C.: Duke University Press, 2011.

McElvaine, Robert S. *The Depression and New Deal: A History in Documents*. Oxford: Oxford University Press, 2000.

———. *The Great Depression: America, 1929–1941*. Toronto: Fitzhenry and Whiteside, 1984.

McMath, Robert C. *American Populism: A Social History, 1877–1898*. New York: Hill and Wang, 1993.

Meltzer, Milton. *Dorothea Lange: A Photographer's Life*. Syracuse: Syracuse University Press, 2000.

Mickenberg, Julia L. *Learning from the Left: Children's Literature, the Cold War, and Radical Politics in the United States*. Oxford: Oxford University Press, 2006.

Miller, James A. *Remembering Scottsboro: The Legacy of an Infamous Trial*. Princeton, N.J.: Princeton University Press, 2009.

Miller, James A., Susan D. Pennybacker, and Even Rosenhaft. "Mother Ada Wright and the International Campaign to Free the Scottsboro Boys, 1931–1934." *American Historical Review* 106, no. 2 (April 2001): 387–430.

Moon, Michael. "Whose History: The Case of Oklahoma." In *A Queer World: The Center for Lesbian and Gay Studies Reader*, edited by Martin Duberman, 24–34. New York: New York University Press, 1997.

Morgan, Stacy. *Rethinking Social Realism: African American Art and Literature, 1930–1953*. Athens: University of Georgia Press, 2004.

Morrison, Toni. "City Limits, Village Values: Concepts of the Neighborhood in Black Fiction." In *Literature and the Urban Experience: Essays on the City and Literature*, edited by Michael Jaye and Ann Chalmers Watts, 35–43. New Brunswick, N.J.: Rutgers University Press, 1981.

———. "Rootedness: The Ancestor as Foundation." In *Black Women Writers (1950–1980): A Critical Evaluation*, edited by Mari Evans, 339–45. New York: Anchor Books, 1984.

Moscovici, Serge. *The Age of the Crowd: A Historical Treatise on Mass Psychology*. Cambridge: Cambridge University Press, 1985.

Mullen, Bill V. "Breaking the Signifying Chain: A New Blueprint for African American Literary Studies." *Modern Fiction Studies* 47, no. 1 (2001) 145–63.

———. "Object Lessons: Fetishization and Class Consciousness in Ann Petry's *The Street*." In *Revising the Blueprint: Ann Petry and the Literary Left*, edited by Alex Lubin, 35–48. Jackson: University Press of Mississippi, 2007.

———. *Popular Fronts: Chicago and African-American Cultural Politics, 1935–46*. Urbana: University of Illinois Press, 1999.

Muncy, Robyn. *Creating a Female Dominion in American Reform, 1890–1935*. New York: Oxford University Press, 1991.

Murphy, James F. *The Proletarian Moment: The Controversy over Leftism in Literature*. Urbana: University of Illinois Press, 1991.

Nadell, Martha Jane. *Enter the New Negroes: Images of Race in American Culture*. Cambridge, Mass.: Harvard University Press, 2004.

Naison, Mark. *Communists in Harlem during the Depression*. Urbana: University of Illinois Press, 1983.

Natanson, Nicholas. *The Black Image in the New Deal: The Politics of F.S.A. Photography*. Knoxville: University of Tennessee Press, 1992.

Nekola, Charlotte, and Paula Rabinowitz, eds. *Writing Red: An Anthology of American Women Writers, 1930–1940*. New York: Feminist Press at the City University of New York, 1987.

Nelson, Bruce. *Divided We Stand: American Workers and the Struggle for Black Equality*. Princeton, N.J.: Princeton University Press, 2001.

Nelson, Cary. *Repression and Recovery: The Politics of Cultural Memory, 1910–1945*. Madison: University of Wisconsin Press, 1989.

Ngai, Mae M. *Impossible Subjects: Illegal Aliens and the Making of Modern America*. Princeton, N.J.: Princeton University Press, 2004.

———. "'A Nation of Immigrants': The Cold War and the Civil Rights Origins of Illegal Immigration." Institute for Advanced Study School of Social Science Occasional Paper 38 (April 2010), http://www.sss.ias.edu/publications/occasional. 17 August 2012.

———. "A Short History of American Immigration History." Lecture given at Harvard University, 27 April 2011.

Nieland, Justus. "Everybody's Noir Humanism: Chester Himes, *Lonely Crusade*, and the Quality of Hurt." *African American Review* 43, no. 2–3 (Summer/Fall 2009): 277–93.

Obermiller, Phillip J., Thomas E. Wagner, and Edward Bruce Tucker. *Appalachian Odyssey: Historical Perspectives on the Great Migration*. Westport, Conn.: Praeger, 2000.

Owens, Louis. "Deadly Kids, Stinking Dogs, and Heroes: The Best Laid Plans in Steinbeck's *Of Mice and Men*." *Western American Literature* 37, no. 3 (Fall 2002): 319–33.

———. *The Grapes of Wrath: Trouble in the Promised Land*. Boston: Twayne, 1989.

———. "*Of Mice and Men*: The Dream of Commitment." In *John Steinbeck: Modern Critical Views*, edited by Harold Bloom, 145–50. New York: Chelsea House, 1987.

———. "Writing 'in Costume': The Missing Voices of *In Dubious Battle*." In *Steinbeck: The Years of Greatness, 1935–1939*, edited by Tetsumaro Hayashi, 77–94. Tuscaloosa: University of Alabama Press, 1993.

Oxford English Dictionary Online. Oxford University Press, 2007.

Payne, Stanley G. *A History of Fascism, 1914–1945*. Madison: University of Wisconsin Press, 1995.

Peddie, Ian. "Poles Apart? Ethnicity, Race, Class, and Nelson Algren." *Modern Fictional Studies* 47, no. 1 (2001): 124–28.

Pells, Richard. *Radical Visions and American Dreams: Culture and Social Thought in the Depression Years*. New York: Harper and Row, 1973.

"Percentage of High School Dropouts among Persons 16 to 24 Years Old, by Race/ Ethnicity." 2007. *National Center for Education Statistics*, nces.ed.gov/fastfacts/display. asp?id=16. 6 March 2008.

Perkin, J. R. C. "Exodus Imagery in *The Grapes of Wrath*." In *Literature and the Bible*, edited by David Bevan, 79–93. Amsterdam: Rodopi, 1993.

Peterson, Rachel. "Invisible Hands at Work: Domestic Service and Meritocracy in Ann Petry's Novels." In *Revising the Blueprint: Ann Petry and the Literary Left*, edited by Alex Lubin, 72–96. Jackson: University Press of Mississippi, 2007.

Phillips, Kimberley L. *AlabamaNorth: African-American Migrants, Community, and Working-Class Activism in Cleveland, 1915–45*. Urbana: University of Illinois Press, 1999.

Pinckney, Darryl. Introduction to *Blood on the Forge*, by William Attaway. 1941. Reprint, New York: New York Review of Books, 2005.

Postel, Charles. *The Populist Vision*. Oxford: Oxford University Press, 2007.

Powell, Richard J. "Face to Face: Elizabeth Catlett's Graphic Work." In *Elizabeth Catlett: Works on Paper, 1944–1992*, edited by Jeanne Zeidler, 49–53. Hampton, Va.: Hampton University Museum, 1993.

"Prison Statistics." 2006. *U.S. Department of Justice, Bureau of Justice Statistics*, www.ojp. usdoj.gov/bjs/prisons.htm. 6 March 2008.

Quam-Wickham, Nancy. "Who Controls the Hiring Hall?: The Struggle for Job Control in the ILWU during World War II." In *The CIO's Left-Led Unions*, edited by Steve Rosswurm, 47–67. New Brunswick, N.J.: Rutgers University Press, 1992.

Rabinowitz, Paula. *Labor and Desire: Women's Revolutionary Fiction in Depression America*. Chapel Hill: University of North Carolina Press, 1991.

———. "Women and U.S. Literary Radicalism." In *Writing Red: An Anthology of American Women Writers, 1930–1940*, edited by Charlotte Nekola and Paula Rabinowitz, 1–16. New York: Feminist Press at the City University of New York, 1987.

Ramirez, Catherine. *The Woman in the Zoot Suit: Gender, Nationalism, and the Cultural Politics of Memory*. Durham, N.C.: Duke University Press, 2009.

Rampersad, Arnold. *Ralph Ellison: A Life*. New York: Vintage, 2007.

Rauty, Raffaele. Introduction to *On Hoboes and Homelessness*, by Nels Anderson, 1–17. Chicago: University of Chicago Press, 1998.

Reilly, John M. "Richard Wright Preaches the Nation: *12 Million Black Voices*." *Black American Literature Forum* 16, no. 3 (Autumn 1982): 116–19.

"Return Migration to the South." In *In Motion: The African American Migration Experience*. Schomburg Center for Research in Black Culture, www.inmoitinaame.org/print. cfm?migration-11. 10 August 2005.

Rideout, Walter. *The Radical Novel in the United States, 1900–1954*. Cambridge, Mass.: Harvard University Press, 1956.

Rivera, Tomás. *Y no se lo trago la tierra* [And the earth did not swallow him up]. 1971. Reprint, Houston: Arte Publico Press, 1992.

Roche, Claire M. "Reproducing the Working Class: Tillie Olsen, Margaret Sanger, and American Eugenics." In *Evolution and Eugenics in American Literature and Culture, 1880–1940: Essays on Ideological Conflict and Complexity*, edited by Lois A. Cuddy and Claire M. Roche, 259–75. Lewisburg, Pa.: Bucknell University Press, 2003.

Rodgers, Lawrence R. *Canaan Bound: The African American Great Migration Novel*. Chicago: University of Illinois Press, 1997.

———. Foreword to *Whose Names Are Unknown: A Novel*, by Sanora Babb, vii–xii. Norman: University of Oklahoma Press, 2006

Roediger, David. "Guineas, Wiggers, and the Dramas of Racialized Culture." *American Literary History* 7, no. 4 (Winter 1995): 654–68.

———. *The Wages of Whiteness: Race and the Making of the American Working Class*. London: Verso, 1991.

Rombold, Tamara. "Biblical Inversion in *The Grapes of Wrath*." *College Literature* 14, no. 2 (Spring 1987): 145–66.

Rose, Sonya O. "Class Formation and the Quintessential Worker." In *Reworking Class*, edited by John R. Hall, 133–66. Ithaca, N.Y.: Cornell University Press, 1997.

Rosenfelt, Deborah. "From the Thirties: Tillie Olsen and the Radical Tradition." In *The Critical Response to Tillie Olsen*, edited by Kay Hoyle and Nancy Huse, 54–89. Westport, Conn.: Greenwood, 1994.

Rotundo, E. Anthony. *American Manhood: Transformations in Masculinity from the Revolution to the Modern Era*. New York: Basic Books, 1993.

Rowley, Hazel. *Richard Wright: The Life and Times*. 1st ed. New York: Henry Holt, 2001.

Rubin, Rachel Lee. "'My Country Is Kentucky': Leaving Appalachia in Harriet Arnow's *The Dollmaker*." In *Women, America, and Movement: Narratives of Relocation*, edited by Susan L. Roberson, 177–89. Columbia: University of Missouri Press, 1998.

Rubin, Rachel, and James Smethurst. "Ann Petry's 'New Mirror.'" In *Revising the Blueprint: Ann Petry and the Literary Left*, edited by Alex Lubin, 15–34. Jackson: University Press of Mississippi, 2007.

Rushdy, Ashraf H. A. *Neo-Slave Narratives: Studies in the Social Logic of a Literary Form*. New York: Oxford University Press, 1999.

Schrecker, Ellen W. *Many Are the Crimes: McCarthyism in America*. Boston: Little, Brown, 1998.

———. "McCarthyism and the Labor Movement: The Role of the State." In *The CIO's Left-Led Unions*, edited by Steve Rosswurm, 139–57. New Brunswick, N.J.: Rutgers University Press, 1992.

Schreiber, Rebecca M. *Cold War Exiles in Mexico: U.S. Dissidents and the Culture of Critical Resistance*. Minneapolis: University of Minnesota Press, 2008.

"Schuyler Finds Philadelphia Negroes Are Rallying to 'New Deal' Call." *Pittsburgh Courier*, 14 August 1937.

Self, Robert O. *American Babylon: Race and the Struggle for Postwar Oakland*. Princeton, N.J.: Princeton University Press, 2003.

Sernett, Milton C. *Bound for the Promised Land: African American Religion and the Great Migration*. Durham, N.C.: Duke University Press, 1997.

Shillinglaw, Susan. Introduction to *Of Mice and Men*, by John Steinbeck, vi–xxvi. 1937. Reprint, New York: Penguin, 1994.

———. "Steinbeck and Ethnicity." In *After the Grapes of Wrath: Essays on John Steinbeck*, edited by Donald V. Coers, Paul D. Ruffin, and Robert J. DeMott, 40–55. Athens: Ohio University Press, 1995.

Shindo, Charles J. *Dust Bowl Migrants in the American Imagination*. Lawrence: University of Kansas Press, 1997.

Sides, Josh. "Battle on the Home Front: African American Shipyard Workers in World War II Los Angeles." *California History* 75, no. 3, African Americans in California (Fall 1996): 250–63.

———. *L.A. City Limits: African American Los Angeles from the Great Depression to the Present*. Berkeley: University of California Press, 2004.

Singal, Daniel Joseph. "Towards a Definition of American Modernism." *American Quarterly* 39, no. 1, Special Issue: Modernist Culture in America (Spring 1987): 7–26.

Singh, Nikhil Pal. *Black Is a Country: Race and the Unfinished Struggle for Democracy*. Cambridge, Mass.: Harvard University Press, 2004.

―――. "Retracing the Black-Red Thread." *American Literary History* 15, no. 4 (December 2003): 830–42.

Slade, Leonard A., Jr. "The Use of Biblical Allusions in *The Grapes of Wrath*." *College Language Association Journal* 11 (March 1968): 241–47.

Slotkin, Richard. *The Fatal Environment: The Myth of the Frontier in the Age of Industrialization, 1800–1890*. Norman: University of Oklahoma Press, 1985.

―――. *Gunfighter Nation: The Myth of the Frontier in Twentieth-Century America*. New York: Atheneum, 1992.

―――. *Regeneration through Violence: The Mythology of the American Frontier, 1600–1860*. Middletown, Conn.: Wesleyan University Press, 1973.

Smethurst, James Edward. *The New Red Negro: The Literary Left and African American Poetry, 1930–1946*. New York: Oxford University Press, 1999.

Sollors, Werner. "Anthropological and Sociological Tendencies in American Literature of the 1930s and 1940s: Richard Wright, Zora Neale Hurston, and American Culture." In *Looking Inward/Looking Outward: From the 1930s through the 1940s*, edited by Steve Ickringil, 22–66. Amsterdam: Vu University Press, 1990.

―――. *Beyond Ethnicity: Consent and Descent in American Culture*. New York: Oxford University Press, 1986.

―――. "Theories of American Ethnicity." Foreword to *Theories of Ethnicity*, edited by Werner Sollors, x–xliv. New York: New York University Press, 1996.

Solomon, Mark. *The Cry Was Unity: Communists and African Americans, 1917–1936*. Jackson: University Press of Mississippi, 1998.

Sowinska, Suzanne. "Writing across the Color Line: White Women Writers and the 'Negro Question' in the Gastonia Novels." In *Radical Revisions: Rereading 1930s Culture*, edited by Bill Mullen and Sherry Lee Linkon, 120–43. Urbana: University of Illinois Press, 1996.

Stange, Maren. *Symbols of Ideal Life: Social Documentary Photography in America, 1890–1950*. Cambridge: Cambridge University Press, 1989.

Steckmesser, Kent L. "Lawmen and Outlaws." In *A Literary History of the American West*, 119–34. Fort Worth: Texas Christian University Press, 1987.

Stein, Judith. *Running Steel, Running America: Race, Economic Policy, and the Decline of Liberalism*. Chapel Hill: University of North Carolina Press, 1998.

Steiner, Wendy. *The Colors of Rhetoric: Problems in the Relation between Modern Literature and Painting*. Chicago: University of Chicago Press, 1985.

"Steinbeck, John." In *The Richard Wright Encyclopedia*, edited by Jerry W. Ward and Robert J. Butler, 360–61. Westport, Conn.: Greenwood, 2008.

Stepan-Norris, Judith, and Maurice Zeitlin. *Left Out: Reds and America's Industrial Unions*. Cambridge: Cambridge University Press, 2003.

Stewart, Jacqueline Najuma. *Migrating to the Movies: Cinema and Black Urban Modernity*. Berkeley: University of California Press, 2005.

Stott, William. *Documentary Expression and Thirties America*. New York: Oxford University Press, 1973.

Sugrue, Thomas J. *The Origins of the Urban Crisis: Race and Inequality in Postwar Detroit*. Princeton, N.J.: Princeton University Press, 1996.

―――. *Sweet Land of Liberty: The Forgotten Struggle for Civil Rights in the North*. New York: Random House, 2008.

Sundquist, Eric J. "Realism and Regionalism." In *Columbia Literary History of the United States*, edited by Emory Elliott, 501–24. New York: Columbia University Press, 1988.

Susman, Warren. *Culture as History: The Transformation of American Society in the Twentieth Century*. New York: Pantheon, 1984.

Taylor, Quintard. *In Search of the Racial Frontier: African Americans in the American West, 1528–1990*. New York: Norton, 1998.

Thernstrom, Stephen. Introduction to *Harvard Encyclopedia of American Ethnic Groups*, edited by Stephen Thernstrom, v–ix. Cambridge, Mass.: Belknap Press of Harvard University Press, 1980.

Trotter, Joe William, ed. *The Great Migration in Historical Perspective: New Dimensions of Race, Class, and Gender*. Bloomington: Indiana University Press, 1991.

Von Eschen, Penny M. *Race against Empire: Black Americans and Anticolonialism, 1937–1957*. Ithaca, N.Y.: Cornell University Press, 1997.

Wald, Alan M. *Exiles from a Future Time: The Forging of the Mid-Twentieth-Century Literary Left*. Chapel Hill: University of North Carolina Press, 2002.

———. *Trinity of Passion: The Literary Left and the Antifascist Crusade*. Chapel Hill: University of North Carolina Press, 2007.

———. *Writing from the Left: New Essays on Radical Culture and Politics*. New York: Verso, 1994.

Wald, Sarah. "'We Ain't Foreign': Constructing the Joads' White Citizenship." In *The Grapes of Wrath: A Reconsideration*, edited by Michael Meyer, 525–53. Amsterdam: Rodopi, 2009.

Walker, Margaret. *Richard Wright, Daemonic Genius: A Portrait of the Man. A Critical Look at His Work*. New York: Warner Brothers, 1988.

Walzer, Michael. *Exodus and Revolution*. New York: Basic Books, 1985.

Ward, Jerry W., Jr. "Everybody's Protest Novel: The Era of Richard Wright." In *The Cambridge Companion to the African American Novel*, edited by Maryemma Graham, 173–88. Cambridge: Cambridge University Press, 2004.

Warren, Frank. *Liberals and Communism: The 'Red Decade' Revisited*. Bloomington: Indiana University Press, 1966.

Washington, Mary Helen. "Alice Childress, Lorraine Hansberry, and Claudia Jones: Black Women Write the Popular Front." In *Left of the Color Line: Race, Radicalism, and Twentieth-Century Literature of the United States*, edited by Bill V. Mullen and James Smethurst, 183–204. Chapel Hill: University of North Carolina Press, 2003.

Webb, Constance. *Richard Wright: A Biography*. New York: Putnam, 1968.

Weber, Devra. *Dark Sweat, White Gold: California Farm Workers, Cotton, and the New Deal*. Berkeley: University of California Press, 1996.

White, Kevin. *The First Sexual Revolution: The Emergence of Male Heterosexuality in Modern America*. New York: New York University Press, 1993.

Williams, Raymond. *Culture and Society, 1780–1950*. New York: Columbia University Press, 1983.

Wixson, Douglas. "'Black Writers and White!': Jack Conroy, Arna Bontemps, and Interracial Collaboration in the 1930s." *Prospects* 23 (1998): 401–30.

———. "Sanora Babb (1907–2005): A Brief Overview of Her Life." Unpublished manuscript, January 2006.

————. *Worker-Writer in America: Jack Conroy and the Tradition of Midwestern Literary Radicalism, 1898–1990*. Urbana: University of Chicago Press, 1994.

————, ed. *On the Dirty Plate Trail: Remembering the Dust Bowl Refugee Camps*. Austin: University of Texas Press, 2007.

Worster, Donald. *Dust Bowl: The Southern Plains in the 1930s*. New York: Oxford University Press, 1982.

Wray, Matt. *Not Quite White: White Trash and the Boundaries of Whiteness*. Durham, N.C.: Duke University Press, 2006.

"Wright, Richard." In *A John Steinbeck Encyclopedia*, edited by Brian Railsback and Michael J. Meyer, 438. Westport, Conn.: Greenwood, 2006.

Yacovone, Donald. "'Surpassing the Love of Women': Victorian Manhood and the Language of Fraternal Love." In *A Shared Experience: Men, Women, and the History of Gender*, edited by Laura McCall and Donald Yacovone, 195–221. New York: New York University Press, 1998.

Yetman, Norman R. "Ex-Slave Interviews and the Historiography of Slavery." *American Quarterly* 36, no. 2 (Summer 1984): 181–210.

Zieger, Robert H. *The CIO, 1935–1955*. Chapel Hill: University of North Carolina Press, 1995.

INDEX

Bonner, Marita, 2, 56, 107, 109–15, 125

Bontemps, Arna, 72, 73, 129, 133, 141–42, 148, 167, 198 (n. 24); *They Seek a City*, 128, 141–48. *See also* Conroy, Jack

Bonus March, 18

Boxcar Bertha, 20. *See also* Hobo: women as

Brooks, Gwendolyn, 72

Browder, Earl, 141

Browder, Laura, 99, 179 (n. 42)

Brown, Sterling, 33, 82

Bulosan, Carlos, 20, 46, 61–62; *America Is in the Heart*, 20, 61

Burke, Kenneth, 10, 121, 193 (n. 60)

Burroughs, Margaret, 72, 167

Business Week, 159–60

California: Arvin, 48, 62; Hollywood, 121, 147, 150; Imperial Valley, 47, 65; Kern County, 48; Pixley, 42; Richmond, 136; San Francisco, 5, 8, 31, 120, 128, 129, 131; San Joaquin Valley, 57, 62. *See also* Babb, Sanora; Dust bowl migration; Farm Security Administration: migrant camps; Himes, Chester; Los Angeles, Calif.; Strikes: agricultural

California Emergency Relief Administration, 44

Campbell, Grace, 37

Cannery and Agricultural Workers' Industrial Union, 42

Cantwell, Robert, 120–21

Catlett, Elizabeth, 2, 13, 97, 99, 101–7, 109; *Mother and Child*, 101–2; *The Negro Woman*, 103–6

Cayton, Horace R., 89–90, 116

Cerf, Bennett, 49, 121

Challenge, 7, 169, 198 (n. 24)

Chicago, Ill., 4, 7, 17, 31, 71–73, 75, 78, 80, 90, 99, 102–3, 107, 110–15, 116, 142, 166, 178 (n. 11)

Chicago, University of, 92, 140

Chicago Defender, 72, 148, 149, 154

Civil rights: and Communist Party, 1, 5, 15, 145, 163–66; long civil rights movement, 2–3, 104, 126; and black women,
9, 104–5; and unions, 12, 133, 164; liberal, 16, 166; radical, 128, 164; and white backlash, 173–74

Civil Rights Act, 174

Class consciousness, 4, 50, 58–59, 60–61, 65, 80–81, 91–93, 121, 136–38, 146, 166, 187 (n. 111), 189 (n. 30)

Coats, Lauren, 53

Cold War. *See* Anticommunism

Cole, Willis I., 16

Collins, Tom, 47–49

Colonialism, 53, 74, 128, 148–49, 152–54. *See also* Anticolonialism; Double V

Common Ground, 88, 135, 142, 146. *See also* Ethnicity

Communist Party (CP), 5–6, 46, 105, 141; African American support of, 1, 15–16, 36, 148–50; African American critique of, 1–3, 37, 145, 167–68; stance of, on the Negro Question, 33, 84–85, 87; and white migrants, 41, 44; stance of, on the Woman Question, 56–57, 61; and Civil Rights, 145, 164–65; definition of terms regarding, 176 (n. 25). *See also* Anticommunism; Black nation thesis; International Labor Defense; Popular Front; Scottsboro

Congress of Industrial Organizations (CIO), 6, 7, 36, 40, 47, 88, 90, 131, 133, 140, 150, 164–66, 184 (n. 57), 194 (n. 15)

Conrad, Earl, 149–50, 163

Conroy, Jack, 68, 72, 129, 133, 141, 167; *They Seek a City*, 128, 141–48. *See also* Bontemps, Arna

Conversion narrative. *See* Class consciousness

Crisis, 18, 110, 149

Crossman, Richard, 3

Cullen, Countee, 110, 198 (n. 24)

Cunard, Nancy, 19

Dahlberg, Edward, 37

Daily Worker, 7, 21, 26, 31, 32, 45, 72–73, 93, 105

Davis, Benjamin, 165

Davis, Frank Marshall, 72

Dawahare, Anthony, 3, 189 (n. 40)

Debs, Eugene, 120. *See also* Socialism

Defense industries. *See* Archibald, Katherine: *Wartime Shipyard*; Fair Employment Practices Commission; Himes, Chester: *If He Hollers Let Him Go*; World War II: and labor migration

Democracy Functioning, 47

Denning, Michael, 1, 3, 6, 10, 61, 111, 115, 175 (n. 5), 181 (n. 4)

DePastino, Todd, 18

Detroit, Mich.: riot of 1943, 36, 130, 133, 144–45; autoworkers in, 82, 90, 132, 133, 141; in Arnow, *The Dollmaker*, 125–26, 171–72

Didacticism. *See* Proletarian literature: didacticism in

Dixon, Riley, 48

Documentary photography. *See* Photography, documentary

Domestic labor: in Babb, *Whose Names Are Unknown*, 55–61; Communist Party theory on, 57; and African American women, 103–11, 113–15, 131, 144, 191 (n. 21); in Olsen, *Yonnondio*, 123–25

Dos Passos, John, 99

Double V, 94, 145, 149, 150–51, 162

Du Bois, W. E. B., 3, 16, 145, 149, 164, 195 (n. 40)

Dunbar, Paul Lawrence (*Sport of the Gods*), 81

Dust bowl migration, 5, 12, 41–51, 57–58, 62–64, 69, 96, 127–28, 173, 199 (n. 39). *See also* Babb, Sanora; Farm Security Administration; Guthrie, Woody; Lange, Dorothea; Steinbeck, John

Ellison, Ralph: disavowal of, of communism, 3, 37, 167; *Invisible Man*, 37, 68, 169, 170; and Sanora Babb, 45–46; critique of, of Babb, *Whose Names Are Unknown*, 46, 48, 49, 53, 58, 66, 67, 68, 93; critique of, of Attaway, *Blood on the Forge*, 92, 93, 168; and Chester Himes, 155

Entin, Joseph, 41, 58, 115, 117, 124, 193 (n. 52), 194 (n. 75)

Ethnicity, 135; in Babb, *Whose Names Are Unknown*, 61–65; in Attaway, *Blood on the Forge*, 87–89; and FSA photography, 97–99; in Marita Bonner's Frye Street stories, 111–12; nation of immigrants trope, 134–48; in Arnow, *The Dollmaker*, 171–72

Fair Employment Practices Commission, 133, 194 (n. 15)

Farm Security Administration (FSA): photography, 9, 95–100, 108, 115–19; migrant camps, 44, 47–48, 49, 62

Farooq, Nihad M., 53

Farrell, James, 36

Fascism, 25, 38–40, 85, 127, 135, 149, 151. *See also* Popular Front

Father Coughlin, 38

Fauset, Jessie, 110

Federal Emergency Relief Administration, 20

Federal Housing Authority, 129, 144, 173

Federal Writers' Project, 7, 32, 53, 72, 141–42, 149

Filipino workers, 12, 43, 50, 62–63, 65–66

Foley, Barbara, 3, 68, 81, 141, 167, 189 (nn. 30, 40)

Food, Tobacco, Agricultural, and Allied Industries, 164, 165

Ford, James, 35

Freeman, Joseph, 10

Fugitive slave narrative, 142, 163

Geer, Will, 44

Gender consciousness, 50, 60–61

George Washington Carver School, 166

Gerstle, Gary, 36, 134, 140, 147, 196 (n. 61)

Ghetto pastoral, 111–12

Gilley, Orval, 22

Gold, Mike, 68

Goss, Bernard, 71

Graham, Shirley, 164

Great Depression, 1, 4–5, 71

Phillips, Kimberley, 78
Photography, documentary, 4, 9, 12–13, 41, 49, 58, 96–99, 107–8, 115–19, 193 (nn. 52, 54). *See also* Lange, Dorothea; Wright, Richard: *12 Million Black Voices*
Pietà, 118–19
Pitts, Rebecca, 57
Pittsburgh Courier, 79, 80
Plain folk Americanism, 50
Popular Front, 6, 10, 68–69, 91, 115; African American participation in, 72, 102, 104, 107–8, 110, 150–51, 163–64
Populism: and antiracism, 1–3, 10–11, 40, 42, 69, 174; and regionalism, 12, 50–54; producerist ethic of, 28, 34–35, 171
Porter, James, 102
Pregnancy and birth, 50, 54, 57–59, 67, 122–25
Price, Victoria, 21–22, 23
Proletarian literature: and activism, 7, 8, 32, 49, 72, 92, 121, 167, 177 (n. 36); definition of, 7–8, 48, 67–68; in relation to African American literature, 11, 69, 92–93, 189 (n. 30); bottom dogs category of, 37; conventions of, 50, 59; didacticism in, 67–68, 121

Racism: of white working class, 13, 16, 17, 38, 50, 62, 93, 132–33, 138; of employers and unions, 78–79
Rahv, Philip, 67–68
Randolph, A. Philip, 77, 145, 196 (n. 83)
Rape, rape-lynch triangle. *See* Lynching: rape-lynch triangle
Regionalism, 9, 12, 49–50, 52–55, 61, 67, 122, 184 (n. 58)
Reitman, Ben, 17, 178 (nn. 11, 22); and Boxcar Bertha, 20. *See also* Hobo
Reportage, 57. *See also* Photography, documentary
Rideout, Walter, 37
Riots. *See* Detroit, Mich.: riot of 1943; Watts; Zoot suit riot
Robeson, Paul, 3, 163, 164; "Ballad for Americans," 10, 141
Rodgers, Lawrence, 167, 192 (n. 33)
Rogin, Leo, 138
Roosevelt, President Franklin D., 129, 135
Rose, Sonya O., 124
Rosenfelt, Deborah, 121
Rosie the Riveter, 128. *See also* World War II
Rosskam, Edwin, 97, 107, 116, 193 (n. 54). *See also* Photography, documentary
Russia, 46, 84, 120, 150, 166, 168–69, 176 (n. 25). *See also* Hitler-Stalin Non-Aggression Pact

San Francisco News, 43, 95
Saturday Review, 26
Scab. *See* Strikebreaker
Schrecker, Ellen, 166
Schuyler, George S., 79, 80, 90
Scottsboro, 11, 15–17, 20–24, 27, 40, 69, 141, 154, 158, 178 (n. 26)
Seaver, Edwin, 8, 67
Selb, Henry, 48, 68
Sensational modernism, 41, 58, 115, 193 (n. 52)
Singh, Nikhil, 137, 139, 148, 149, 150
Smethurst, James, 3, 177 (n. 44), 188 (n. 118)
Smith Act, 165
Socialism, 50–51, 73, 120
Social Security Act, 104, 144, 181 (n. 8)
Solidarity, 18, 20
Solomon, Mark, 6
Southern Worker, 21
South Side Community Art Center (SSCAC), 72, 102, 166–67
South Side Writers' Group, 72, 142
Soviet Union. *See* Russia
Stalin, 150, 176 (n. 25)
Steel Workers' Organizing Committee, 79–80
Steinbeck, John, 1–2, 43, 49, 53, 182 (n. 12), 183 (n. 45); *The Grapes of Wrath*,

9, 11, 41, 119–20, 121, 163; *Of Mice and Men*, 11–12, 16–17, 24–31, 40, 48; "The Vigilante," 38

Steward, Bettie, 66

Stott, William, 41

Strikebreaker, 12, 73, 77–80, 93

Strikes, 5–6; agricultural, 41, 42–44, 46–47, 183 (n. 49); in Babb, *Whose Names Are Unknown*, 50, 58–68 passim; in Attaway, *Blood on the Forge*, 73, 80, 87, 89; in steel industry, 78–79, 80, 88; in Olsen, *Yonnondio*, 120–21; during World War II, 131, 132–36, 144, 164–65; textile, 194 (n. 76)

Sugrue, Thomas, 165, 175 (n. 8)

Survey Graphic, 43, 44, 95

Susman, Warren, 10

Swing, Raymond Gram, 38

Taft-Hartley Act, 165

Taller de Gráfica Popular, 102, 167

Taylor, Paul, 43–44; *American Exodus*, 4, 9. *See also* Lange, Dorothea

Terry, Sonny, 44

Texas, 4, 34, 62, 142

Third Period, 6, 10, 69, 84–85, 91, 188 (n. 118). *See also* Communist Party

Thompson, Florence, 95–96

Thompson, Louise, 106

Thurmond, Strom, 165

Townshend, Dr., 38

Transient Program, 20

Truman, President Harry S., 166

Truth, Sojourner, 104

Unemployed Councils, 6

Unions. *See* Strikes; *and individual unions*

United Cannery, Agricultural, Packing, and Allied Workers of America (UCAPAWA), 46, 183–84 (n. 49)

United Mine Workers, 79, 188–89 (n. 25)

Urban League, 71, 79, 130

U.S. Camera Annual, 95

U.S. Steel, 80

Vorse, Mary Heaton ("How Scottsboro Happened"), 21–22, 40

Wagner Act, 5, 42, 43, 144

Wald, Alan, 3, 80

Walker, Margaret, 7, 72, 73

Wallace, Henry, 165

Warner, Ralph, 93

Washington, D.C., 102, 110. *See also* March on Washington Movement

Watts, 143–44

Weber, Debra, 43, 50, 182 (n. 10)

Wellman, William A. (*Wild Boys of the Road*), 20, 24, 178 (n. 26)

Wells, Ida B., 158

West, Dorothy, 168–69, 198 (n. 24); *The Living Is Easy*, 168–71

White, Charles, 72, 103

White, Walter, 133, 146, 162

Whiteness, 1, 38, 62–65, 137, 156, 158, 160, 186 (nn. 91, 95), 187 (n. 103), 195 (n. 40)

Wilkins, Roy, 18

Williams, Walter, 133, 194 (n. 15)

Wilson, Edmund, 5

Wixson, Douglas, 52, 181 (n. 5)

Wobblies. *See* Industrial Workers of the World

Woman Question, 56–57, 61. *See also* Communist Party

Woman Worker/Woman Today, 56–57

Working Woman, 46

Works Progress Administration (WPA), 7, 72, 75, 82, 189

World War I, 71, 74, 75, 145, 176 (n. 17), 178 (n. 11)

World War II: and Himes, *If He Hollers Let Him Go*, 13, 151; and labor migration, 43, 127–32, 136; and national unity, 77, 93; and women workers, 128–29, 131, 136, 158–60; and racial tensions, 129–31, 132–34, 136–40, 144–49; and anti-Japanese propaganda, 151–52. *See also* Double V

Wray, Matt, 64, 137, 186–87 (n. 95)

Wright, Ada, 15, 16, 21

Wright, Andy, 21
Wright, Richard, 1–3, 7, 32, 72–73, 93, 167, 168, 169; *Native Son*, 1, 27, 192 (nn. 33, 44); "Blueprint for Negro Writing," 85, 94; *12 Million Black Voices*, 97, 103, 106–7, 116–19, 125

Yoniken, August, 36
Young, Stanley, 26
Young Communist League, 120

Zadkine, Ossip, 101, 102
Zoot suit riot, 130–31, 148–49, 152–53

4-10 - 14